Queneau's fiction

Queneau's fiction

an introductory study

CHRISTOPHER SHORLEY

Lecturer in French
The Queen's University of Belfast

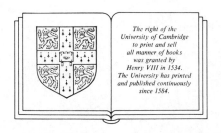

The right of the
University of Cambridge
to print and sell
all manner of books
was granted by
Henry VIII in 1534.
The University has printed
and published continuously
since 1584.

CAMBRIDGE UNIVERSITY PRESS

Cambridge
London   New York   New Rochelle
Melbourne   Sydney

Published by The Press Syndicate of the University of Cambridge
The Pitt Building, Trumpington Street, Cambridge CB2 IRP
32 East 57th Street, New York, NY 10022, USA
10 Stamford Road, Oakleigh, Melbourne 3166, Australia

First published 1985

Printed in Great Britain at
the University Press, Cambridge

Library of Congress catalogue card number: 84-29290

British Library Cataloguing in Publication Data
Shorley, Christopher
Queneau's fiction: an introductory study.
1. Queneau, Raymond – Criticism and interpretation
I. Title
843'.912   PQ2633.U43Z/
ISBN 0 521 30397 4

CE

Contents

v

Preface

Although in France and elsewhere in Europe Queneau's work is now widely respected, it has not, on the whole, enjoyed a comparable degree of appreciation in English-speaking countries. Instead it has tended to remain the preserve of a small band of enthusiastic initiates, thus sustaining an unjustified reputation for esotericism, even inaccessibility. What follows is an attempt to present Queneau to a wider anglophone readership, using established critical perspectives while avoiding, as far as possible, the obscurities of critical jargon. It is hoped thereby to identify particularly useful lines of approach to Queneau's fictional writings, and to suggest the considerable satisfactions and rewards they have to offer.

I take pleasure in recording my thanks to all who have helped in the various stages through which this book has passed, and particularly André Blavier, Jean Queval, Claude Rameil, Malcolm Bowie, Rhiannon Goldthorpe and Peter Hoy. Special thanks, also, to Carina Rourke, for typing the manuscript; and to my wife, for assistance far too extensive to detail here. My gratitude is also due to The Queen's University of Belfast, and to the British Academy, for help in financing research in France and Belgium.

Parts of this book have already appeared, in different form, in *French Studies*, *Temps Mêlés Documents Queneau* and *Les Amis de Valentin Brû*. I gratefully acknowledge permission from the respective editors to use this material.

Abbreviations

An alphabetical list of the principal works by Queneau mentioned in the text, together with dates of the editions used, the series to which they belong, where appropriate, and the abbreviations adopted.

In all cases the place of publication is Paris and, unless otherwise stated, the publisher is Gallimard.

Bâtons, chiffres et lettres (Coll. Idées) 1965 *Bâtons*

Bords: mathématiciens, précurseurs, encyclopédistes Editions Hermann 1966 *Bords*

Chêne et chien (Coll. Poésie) 1969 *Chêne et chien*

Le Chiendent 1968 *Chiendent*

Contes et propos 1981 *Contes*

Les Derniers Jours 1977 *Derniers Jours*

Le Dimanche de la vie 1966 *Dimanche*

Les Enfants du limon 1952 *Limon*

Entretiens avec Georges Charbonnier 1962 *Charbonnier*

Exercices de style (Coll. Soleil) 1964 *Exercices*

Les Fleurs bleues 1965 *Fleurs bleues*

Gueule de pierre 1934 *Gueule de pierre*

Une Histoire modèle 1966 *Histoire modèle*

Loin de Rueil 1966 *Rueil*

Odile 1969 *Odile*

Les Œuvres complètes de Sally Mara 1962 *Sally Mara*

Pierrot mon ami 1957 *Pierrot*

Un Rude Hiver 1968 *Rude Hiver*

Saint Glinglin 1961 *Glinglin*

Les Temps mêlés 1941 *Temps mêlés*

Le Vol d'Icare 1968 *Icare*

Le Voyage en Grèce 1973 *Voyage*

Zazie dans le métro 1961 *Zazie*

Introduction

Il venait d'ouvrir les yeux. *Le Chiendent*, p. 7

Queneau and his reader

'QUAND j'énonce une assertion, je m'aperçois tout de suite que l'assertion contraire est à près aussi intéressante, à un point où cela devient presque superstitieux chez moi', announced Queneau in the course of an interview in 1962 (*Charbonnier*, p. 12), thus formulating in characteristically elusive style what is perhaps his most basic attitude. Like Rabelais's Trouillogan, for whom he had a sneaking admiration (*ibid.*, p. 14), he is notoriously reluctant to commit himself to a fixed opinion about any subject – and particularly about his own work. This does not mean that he refrains from all comment; on the contrary, he offers a wide variety of illuminating reflections on his writings. But there is no guarantee that his views can be taken as definitive, or that a declaration dating from one period will not conflict with some earlier or later statement. Thus the claims he made – mostly in the forties and fifties – to the effect that his books were significant above all for their radical treatment of the French language were flatly contradicted by his admission, in the late sixties, that his advocacy of 'le néo-français' had been unjustified. It would be a fruitless exercise, then, to seek total consistency between Queneau's stated views.

One of Queneau's assertions, however, remains constant throughout his career, and claims a more permanent validity. He repeatedly insisted that it is not his responsibility to have the last word on the works that he writes – and

I

more than once resorted to the same simple image to explain his position:

Je suis un pommier. Je donne des pommes. A vous de choisir si vous les aimez rondes ou oblongues, sphériques ou piriformes, lisses ou ridées, pommelées, ou bien vertes et pas mûres. Vous ne voudriez tout de même pas que je vous fournisse par-dessus le marché la fourchette et le couteau.[1]

Rather than himself determining the way or ways in which his books are to be considered, Queneau prefers to leave the widest possible scope for his reader. Indeed he rejects utterly the notion of the passive reader whose sole function is to absorb a preordained content presented in a readily palatable form. Instead he invites the active participation of a reader who is prepared for a literary text to make demands on his own resources: 'Car toute œuvre demande à être brisée pour être sentie et comprise, toute œuvre présente une résistance au lecteur, toute œuvre est une chose difficile' (*Voyage*, p. 140). The intention is not to threaten the collaboration between author and reader, but simply to give more balance to it, by extending the reader's sphere of activity. The initial access to a work, if difficult, is not impossible, and the reader will – ideally – progress from this point of contact to an increasingly rich and varied response to the work as a whole:

Une œuvre ne doit pas être difficile par simple provocation [...]. L'œuvre doit être susceptible d'une compréhension immédiate, telle que le poète ne soit pas séparé de son public possible [...]. Et cette compréhension immédiate peut être suivie d'appréhensions de plus en plus approfondies.
(*ibid.*)

An essential prerequisite for the collaboration which Queneau seeks is an awareness of the exercise in question. He effectively prevents his reader from ever taking for granted the nature of his activity, namely running his eyes along lines of print and turning the pages which make up the artefact known as the book. Hence Saturnin, in a monologue towards the end of *Le Chiendent*, addresses a whole series of remarks to the reader and informs him that given the number of the page, 'il ne reste plus beaucoup à lire, spa?' (p. 279). Similarly one of the rebels in *On est toujours trop bon avec les femmes* refers back to something a colleague has said 'quelques pages plus haut' (*Sally Mara*, p. 307).

This permanent awareness is a vital part of the act of reading, but the reader must first be involved through his initial encounter with the text – through the 'resistance' with which he is confronted in the first few pages. Most conventional criticism of Queneau has taken little account of experiences of this order, concentrating instead on organising and assessing the experiences that remain when a book has been read in its entirety.[2] However, this first contact – made before critical reflection sets in – can be crucial in determining the reader's response to a work as a whole. In the words of another novelist: 'Starting a novel is opening a door on a misty landscape; you can see very little but you can smell the earth and feel the wind blowing.'[3] And the openings of most of Queneau's novels create precisely this effect: the atmosphere is communicated immediately, while the larger design remains obscure. Further, it is obscured deliberately, so that the reader is completely enveloped in the immediate situation and deprived of all landmarks. In *Le Chiendent* the action of the first few pages is difficult to follow because Queneau intentionally avoids naming his characters, designating them instead by pronouns or by vague terms such as 'la silhouette', 'l'autre' and 'la femme'. At this stage all the outlines are blurred – it is only later that the focus sharpens and characters and events are brought into relief. In the meantime the reader is left to ponder on an anonymous, alien urban setting and thus to experience directly, rather than take for granted, the milieu from which the rest of the novel will develop. *Pierrot mon ami* begins with a still more explicit loss of definition, with Pierrot being instructed to remove his spectacles, so that his surroundings in the Parisian funfair where he works 'se perdaient dans le brouillard' (p. 7). The reader, like Pierrot, is plunged into a world in which he can hear sounds and voices without seeing where they come from. In the opening sequence of *Un Rude Hiver* the visual outlines are clearer, but the sense of bewilderment is much the same:

Les Chinois avançaient précédes par deux sergents de ville [...]. Derrière les deux flics marchaient primo deux Chinois ayant sans doute quelque autorité sur leurs compatriotes, secundo un Chinois porteur d'un parasol jaune, tertio un Chinois porteur d'un objet également jaune formé de deux ellipsoïdes enfilés sur un bâton selon leur plus grand axe.

(pp. 7–8)

Even after this weird situation is explained – it is the feast of the Chinese New Year, being celebrated in Le Havre during the First World War – the reader's initial sense of strangeness still lingers: the normal world has been completely 'de-familiarised'.[4]

In each of these cases, although the reader may not be aware of it at the time, he is sharing the perceptions of one of Queneau's characters. The Chinese parade, it transpires, is being watched by Lehameau, the central figure in *Un Rude Hiver*; the beginning of *Pierrot mon ami*, as has been noted, is presented from Pierrot's standpoint; and it eventually emerges that the first scene of *Le Chiendent* is the product of the observations of Pierre Le Grand. In each case, therefore, the reader in effect participates in the initial act of observation from which the fictional creation springs. The example of Pierre Le Grand is particularly telling in this respect, since Queneau emphasises Pierre's privileged role of observer and even hints that he is of almost equal status to the novelist himself (see *Chiendent*, p. 25).[5] But perhaps the reader's strongest sense of collaboration with one of Queneau's observers comes at the beginning of the Saint Glinglin trilogy. Here, once again, the privileged observer goes under the name of Pierre; and the whole of the opening section, both in the original *Gueule de pierre* and in its reworked form in *Saint Glinglin*, consists of Pierre's abstruse meditations, which are based on his observation of marine life in an aquarium. Only after encountering this bizarre extended monologue does the reader proceed to a broader, more balanced view of events in the subsequent sections of the text.

The feeling of unfamiliarity and 'difficulty' is not limited to the level of actions and events, moreover. The opening line of *Zazie dans le métro* runs: 'Doukipudonktan, se demanda Gabriel excédé' (p. 9). The reader is inevitably disconcerted by the unfamiliar combination of letters, and even when he comes to recognise them as representing the question 'D'où qu'ils puent donc tant?' he is still left with the realisation that the words before his eyes, like the situations they evoke, are in some degree foreign to his normal experience.[6] *Le Diman-che de la vie* opens with the deviation from standard literary syntax, with similar effect (while introducing yet another observer in the process): 'Il ne se doutait pas que chaque fois qu'il passait devant sa boutique, elle le regardait, la commer-çante, le soldat Brû' (p. 11).

The initial experience of strangeness, then, is of the utmost importance: it simultaneously presents the reader with prob-lems – with 'résistance' – and invites him to transcend these by involving himself in the work before him. It constitutes, in one critic's neat phrase, 'un malaise dans lequel il est utile de jeter le lecteur'.[7] But even after this feeling is dispelled and the 'mist' begins to lift over the 'landscape' of the novel, the text still retains some of its difficulty. The sequence of events in most novels requires minute examination if the reader is to make any sense of them, and the task is complicated by the fact that explanations lurk in unexpected parts of the text. In *Les Enfants du limon*, for instance, a mysterious violinist mentioned in the second part of the first book (p. 10) is named only much later (pp. 57, 88); equally it is explained at one point that Agnès is to marry Denis in November (p. 55), but only later is Denis identified with 'le petit Coltet', who has already appeared several times before the news of the wedding is given. One Pierre is belatedly accounted for as Hachamoth's chauffeur (pp. 183, 184). In the words of the original *prière d'insérer* to the novel: 'Le lecteur sera donc amené devant ce problème de la *reconnaissance*, problème que posent également différentes démarches de certains person-nages du roman.'[8] And this process of reconstructing facts and situations on the basis of pieces of evidence dispersed through the text is vital to the reading of most of Queneau's works.[9]

The reader has still other, more important tasks to perform. He frequently has little firm evidence with which to work but rather a profusion of clues which are as likely to mislead him as to help. And as hard facts become scarcer, so the scope for speculation increases. In the early stages of *Zazie dans le métro* there is much uncertainty about what Zazie's uncle, Gabriel, does for a living: is he a night watchman? (p. 38); does he *really* wear lipstick? (p. 39); if he is an artist, what sort of artist can he be? (p. 55). When it eventually emerges that he is a dancer in a night-club for homosexuals, it seems that no more secrets remain – until the last page of the novel, when Marceline, who has hitherto been presented as his wife, is revealed as a man called Marcel. Further, Zazie's mother does not share the reader's surprise; and if Jeanne Lalochère knows that 'Marceline' is not a woman, perhaps other characters know it too. As the reader finally becomes aware of the deception which has been practised on him, he is left to dwell on its implications for the rest of the story. In *Le Chiendent* an impenetrable mystery surrounds the sudden death of the waitress, Ernestine, following her wedding feast. She could have been murdered by interested parties seeking her supposed fortune, such as Mme Cloche or Dominique Belhôtel and his wife, or else poisoned by the two enigmatic waiters lent, for the wedding feast, by the Restaurant des Alliés; and death from natural causes cannot be excluded. The deaths of Agnès and Chambernac, in *Les Enfants du limon*, are never adequately explained. Once again, the reader is free to conjecture – as he is when confronted with the calamitous fire in *Pierrot mon ami*, where several interpretations are possible but none can be proved. The *prière d'insérer* to the first edition of *Pierrot mon ami* recalled the words of Claude Bernard: 'Il y a un certain plaisir à ignorer, parce que l'imagination travaille.'[10]

It becomes increasingly clear that just as Queneau emphasises the reader's responsibility – his obligation to work with the text – so he allows him a large degree of freedom. On the one level the reader is at liberty to apply his imagination to the situation before him, 'filling in the gaps' by his own conjectures. But more crucially still, he has freedom of interpretation – and is urged to use it. The original *prière d'insérer* describing *Gueule de pierre* emphasises the point:

Comme tout mythe, il est susceptible d'interprétations diverses. Au lecteur de les découvrir, car – pourquoi ne demanderait-on pas un certain effort au lecteur? On lui explique toujours tout au lecteur. Il finit par être vexé de se voir si méprisamment traité, le lecteur.[11]

Certainly *Gueule de pierre*, and with it the whole of the Saint Glinglin trilogy, is open to widely divergent readings. If the centre of the work is taken to be the Kougard/Nabonide family, then the events can be interpreted in personal and psychological terms. But if the fortunes of the community as a whole are regarded as the basic interest, the work can be treated as an exercise in social anthropology. Both interpretations are perfectly plausible, but neither can be said to invalidate the other.[12] And the possibility of yet other readings is not excluded.

In Queneau's works it is more than usually futile to talk of predetermined 'meanings', for he positively encourages the reader to make his own judgement. And by extension, the reader is not obliged to embrace the text in its full complexity, or to extract meaning from any given element within it; he is free to concentrate on the elements of his own choice. As Queneau argues, resorting to another favourite image: 'un chef d'œuvre est [...] comparable à un bulbe dont les uns se contentent d'enlever la pelure superficielle tandis que d'autres, moins nombreux, l'épluchent pellicule par pellicule' (*Voyage*, p. 141). It is doubtless no mere coincidence that the onion is a recurrent leitmotif in *Le Chiendent* (pp. 29, 36, 199, 211), or that one of the characters is seen peeling one (p. 19).

Through the various ways in which he exercises the reader, Queneau also brings into question the act of reading itself.[13] More specifically, by allowing the reader so much personal scope in his response to the text, he stresses the essentially individual and subjective aspect of the reading process.[14] It is an obvious – but perhaps too easily forgotten – fact that this process is at the origin of any act of literary criticism. Yet however much articulation and formalisation of the reading experience is involved in criticism, the initial, unmediated experience of the text is in itself decisive. Such is the argument of the critic Françoise van Rossum-Guyon:

La critique en effet est d'abord et avant tout une lecture. Lecture d'une aventure, qui n'est pas seulement celle des personnages, mais aussi celle des objets, des idées et des thèmes, ainsi que celle des descriptions, des images et des mots. Lecture d'une aventure qui n'est autre que celle de l'avènement d'un sens par la médiation des formes.[15]

But clearly, the orientation and emphasis of a particular reading depend on the intellectual predilections of the individual reader. As Jean Starobinski has pointed out:

Les divers types de lecture choisissent et prélèvent des structures *préfér-entielles*. Il n'est pas indifférent que nous interrogions un texte en histori-ens, en sociologues, en psychologues, en styliciens ou en amateurs de beauté pure. Car chacune de ces approches a pour effet de changer la configuration du *tout*, d'appeler un nouveau contexte, de découper d'autres frontières, à l'intérieur desquelles régnera une autre loi de cohér-ence.[16]

With Queneau's fiction Starobinski's idea is perfectly illus-trated, for the response has been exceptionally diverse. Critics have discerned and discussed different layers in the texts and applied to them all manner of criteria. And some have actually acknowledged the basis of their criticism in the active reading role Queneau offers to them.[17]

Critical approaches

Many modern writers receive more attention from critics than has Queneau, but few can have provoked a more varied critical reception. And yet there has been little attempt to compare and combine differing attitudes to his work. This was perfectly understandable in the early years of Queneau's career, when none of his works enjoyed any degree of commercial success and he was more or less unknown outside a small circle of admirers.[18] During this time his potential impact was severely restricted for various external reasons: the linguistic originality of *Le Chiendent* (1933) had been in part foreshadowed by Céline's annexation of popular speech in *Voyage au bout de la nuit*, published in the previous year; *Un Rude Hiver* appeared just before the outbreak of the Second World War; and wartime conditions did not favour a wide circulation for *Les Temps mêlés* (1941), *Pierrot mon ami* (1942) and *Loin de Rueil* (1944). Although the volume of criticism has steadily accumulated since Queneau came to prominence in the post-war period[19] – especially since the first academic thesis, in 1955,[20] and the first full-length book, in 1960[21] – there has been a widespread tendency to apply rigid and exclusive interpretations to his work. For however much Queneau stresses that his work can be viewed on various levels – that the reader can choose between a number of different 'layers of the onion' – his critics have often concentrated on one level and shown a marked reluctance to consider others, or even, sometimes, to acknowledge their existence.

The most blatant examples of exclusive criticism are to be found in the writings of those who refuse to go beyond the most superficial characteristics of Queneau's writings. Not surprisingly, many of these examples date from the early stage of Queneau's career, as in the review of *Les Derniers Jours* where L. de Gérin-Richard sees little further than 'la grossièreté de son langage, et même parfois de sa pensée'.[22] But much later Robert Poulet bases most of his review of *Zazie dans le métro* on the fact that Zazie says 'Mon cul' twenty-one times and the novel contains forty-four examples of the use of 'merde et ses dérivés'.[23] Criticus, in his discussion of the same book, develops a similar condemnation of Queneau's supposed wilful vulgarity, and concludes that *Zazie dans le métro* never rises above 'les galipettes d'un clown qui méprise son public, autant que la langue, la grammaire et toute la littérature'.[24] The significance of these comments lies not so much in their vehement castigation of Queneau as in the narrow point of view from which their judgements are made. For while presenting Queneau purely as a 'fumiste' and an iconoclast they ignore the other vital characteristics of his work. And there are indications that this highly selective image of Queneau persisted; as a reviewer of an entertainment based on Queneau's writings pointed out in 1966: 'Ce spectacle met seulement l'accent sur le Queneau chansonnier, joueur de mots, insolent et burlesque. C'est [...] limiter son œuvre et donner de celle-ci ce que le public en sait déjà.'[25]

Other critics, who are willing to acknowledge that Queneau's work does have substance and depth, sometimes cling to outdated and inaccurate views of it and thereby inhibit more comprehensive approaches. During the period when he regularly expounds his views on 'le néo-français' – a fusion of literary and popular language – Queneau explains how during a journey to Greece he had been so struck by the total separation of these two registers that he attempted to re-unite them by translating the *Discours de la méthode* into the style of contemporary spoken French, and this attempt turned into his first published novel, *Le Chiendent* (see, for instance, *Bâtons*, pp. 17, 42, 59).[26] This explanation established the orthodox view on *Le Chiendent* and Queneau's attitude to language for a number of years. Later, however, in a small article entitled 'Errata' (*Voyage*, pp. 219–22),[27] Queneau gives a revised version of the story, indicating that it was really J. W. Dunne's *An Experiment with Time* that he had undertaken to translate in Greece, and acknowledging that 'le néo-français' has not advanced as he had hoped. This account has, however, gone unnoticed in some quarters. Thus Stanley E. Gray, some time afterwards, refers to *Le Chiendent* as 'a curious formalistic construction modelled on the *Discours de la méthode*'.[28]

When critics do acknowledge the existence of different levels in Queneau's work, it is often merely in order to assert the primacy of one as against others. If there is occasional confrontation of critical attitudes in this matter, there is little dialogue between them. In his survey of Queneau's work, Félicien Marceau states bluntly: 'La forme est sans doute, dans cette œuvre, ce qu'il y a de plus important.'[29] On the other hand, Claude Simonnet, when interviewed about his book *Queneau déchiffré*, declared that he emphasised content far more than form, adding: 'La forme! Elle a empêché beaucoup d'approfondir Queneau.'[30] There is more than an echo of Félicien Marceau in a *Times Literary Supplement* review: 'It is form [...] not content, which reveals the preoccupations of the man in Raymond Queneau's novels.'[31] But this claim, at least, does not go unchallenged, for Richard Cobb counters it, arguing that 'Queneau is not just a writer who indulges in intellectual gymnastics' and stressing that his preoccupations are not revealed by form alone.[32]

The opposition of form and content reveals a basic division in Queneau criticism. But on each side of this division there are two main groups, each of which concentrates on a different 'layer' within Queneau's fiction. And in all four groups of critics clear indications of a certain exclusiveness are to be found.

The criticism which presents form as the essential element in Queneau's fiction can be divided into linguistic approaches and interpretations based on the structure and shape of his works; and to a considerable extent both derive from statements made by Queneau. Critics specialising in Queneau's use of language draw support from his many pronouncements on the subject,[33] while those who emphasise his preoccupation with the construction of literature can adduce a number of his theoretical texts in which this preoccupation predominates.[34] Among the many linguistic studies, those of Pierre Léon,[35] Ernst Kemmner[36] and Régis Boyer[37] are particularly thorough; and it is Boyer who gives the most extreme justification of a purely linguistic critique of Queneau's fiction: 'Son seul soin est d'enrichir, de colorer le langage de toutes les nuances [...] que lui apporte une immense culture [...]. C'est cette attention passionnée, vigilante encore qu'amusée aux mots [...] qui fait la valeur de son œuvre.'[38] But according to the second school of thought, the essence of Queneau's work lies not in its language but in the functioning of its autonomous narrative structures. The most uncompromising statement of this approach comes from Gerald Prince, who sees Queneau above all as a creator of anti-novels which possess 'la qualité d'un poème, c'est-à-dire d'une création autonome, qui se tiendrait d'elle-même par la force et la rigueur de son organisation, sans besoin d'attaches extérieures'.[39] For Prince, Queneau's emphasis on the formal qualities of his texts precludes any possibility of traditional novelistic content; for his 'scepticism' with regard to literature 'ne peut que le forcer à abandonner les grands thèmes psychologiques, sociologiques et métaphysiques qui ont fait la fortune du genre romanesque'.[40]

On the other side of the basic dividing-line, however, are to be found critics who, despite the formal qualities of Queneau's writings and his own emphasis on these, emphasise precisely those areas which, in Prince's view, Queneau is obliged to abandon. Thus Albert-Marie Schmidt declares: 'Raymond Queneau condense une épaisse substance humaine derrière un masque de mots qui le révèle et la dissimule à la fois.'[41] But here, too, there is a further division to be made – this time between those critics who value Queneau's work as the fictional representation of a recognisably human world, and those who approach it as the expression of a particular philosophy or view of life. The first of these groups includes both those who, like Richard Cobb,[42] insist above all on Queneau's qualities as an observer and recorder of social life, and those who concentrate on an imagined world parallel to the real one but independent of it, which they see reflected in his fiction; a notable example is Paul Gayot in his study of the world of the Saint Glinglin trilogy.[43] The second group embraces the studies of, among others, André Blavier,[44] Stuart Johnston[45] and Alexandre Kojève,[46] and the most succinct expression of this line of approach is perhaps that of Jean Blanzat in a review of *Zazie dans le métro*: 'Entre l'histoire racontée et sa signification profonde, il y a, constamment, à travers chaque détail, la place d'une "morale" au sens le plus large du mot, c'est-à-dire une philosophie, une interprétation particulière du monde.'[47] In similar vein, Martin Esslin writes that Queneau is 'of particular importance in that his thought represents a point of intersection between French existentialism on the one hand and Anglo-Saxon linguistic philosophy on the other'.[48]

Each of these four basic approaches, then, reveals a different level in Queneau's fiction, with its own adherents – not all of them as outspoken as those quoted but most, nevertheless, emphasising some element to the exclusion of others. However, if each approach has its own justification, none can legitimately claim exclusive rights; each 'layer of the onion' requires individual consideration. And such is the activity of those readers and critics who take a broad view of Queneau's work – who, in his own phrase, 'l'épluchent pellicule par pellicule'. For almost all of his most perceptive critics show themselves willing to recognise, if not to dwell on, the multiplicity of layers in his writings. And a significant number of them, including Claude Simonnet, Anne Clancier and Paul Gayot,[49] have themselves resorted to the image of the onion in order to describe it. Andrée Bergens, whose basic interpretation is narrowly absurdist,[50] nevertheless discerns three distinct levels – 'L'Univers', 'La Construction Littéraire' and 'L'Expression' – within Queneau's fictional work and treats them individually in her book.

The flexibility necessary to a balanced consideration of the different levels of Queneau's work is also needed in more specialised questions of methodology. The onion can be sliced, as well as peeled, in a number of ways. And here, too, flexibility is often lacking, for there are numerous cases where the use of one method is taken to exclude all possibility of another. Whereas one reviewer claims that 'Queneau [...] is a hermeneutic writer not a hermetic one; all the necessary clues are present in the text and not somewhere outside it',[51] it has been argued with at least equal vehemence that 'in order to establish the intended meaning of *Le Chiendent* and *Les Enfants du limon*, the reader must consult the gnostic texts which have influenced Queneau's creative work'.[52] Similarly, there has been disagreement – if not debate – about the relative merits of synchronic and diachronic treatments of Queneau's fiction.[53] And beyond these obvious oppositions, the diverse techniques of Jungian criticism,[54] of intertextual interpretation,[55] and of post-structuralist narratology,[56] to name but a few, have been brought to bear on the texts.

While no method can be definitive, however, it is obvious that there must be strict limits to flexibility if criticism is to have any real bearing on its chosen subject. Robert Kanters makes the point wittily in an article on *Zazie dans le métro* in which he simply reviews the novel in a succession of critical styles – 'Objectif', 'Ésotérique', 'Orienté', 'Linguistique', 'Freudien' – thus parodying Queneau's technique in *Exercices de style*, where one and the same story is told in ninety-nine different ways.[57] If, as in Kanters's article, no discrimination is made in the application of critical methods, then all are equally arbitrary. In accepting the freedom Queneau offers him, the reader cannot abdicate all responsibility. On the contrary, he is left with the vital task of finding a middle way between the extremes of exclusive and non-discriminating criticism.

In the chapters that follow, Queneau's fictional texts are analysed successively in terms of the four principal layers or levels which have been identified. The first chapter concentrates on the linguistic element; the second deals with the ways in which Queneau constructs his fictional works and the forms he gives to them; the third examines the fictional world which he creates in his writings; and the fourth treats the question of the values and vision which might emerge from his work. The order of the chapters is intended to reflect a progression from the more immediately recognised features to those less readily acknowledged. Within the chapters, moreover, there is a comparable movement: in general, the attempt is made first to take account of the more familiar or accessible territory and thereafter to investigate neighbouring areas which have, for the most part, received less attention. The first chapter moves from Queneau's well-known experiments with linguistic forms to an examination of his uses of other modes of communication – typographical and non-verbal – which have usually been disregarded. The second chapter begins with another well-documented phenomenon, namely the mathematical and geometrical patterning in some of Queneau's narrative, but then turns to more general questions such as his use of narrative techniques and literary genres, and his assimilation of other art-forms. In the third, the emphasis is initially on how Queneau adopts both realistic and non-realistic registers to present his fictional world, and then on the perhaps more marginal subject of the conditions and rules which govern existence within that world. The final chapter deals first with Queneau's much-discussed preoccupation with the values of art and science, but thereafter seeks to set this in a broader context.

The subject under consideration is defined as Queneau's fiction because while the main object is to extend existing discussion of the whole range of his novels (including *Gueule de pierre*, *Les Derniers Jours* and *Les Temps mêlés*, republication of which Queneau opposed), account will also be taken of works closely associated with the novels – notably his short stories. However, his early contributions to Surrealist publications, and the examples of his juvenilia published to date, are considered to fall outside the scope of this study. Queneau's poetry will be considered only insofar as it sheds light on his fiction; for despite the common ground which exists between the two, differences of form, tone and content are such as to make it hard, if not impossible, to envisage a study which could give them a balanced treatment. The task is attempted by Andrée Bergens, who claims that her book, *Raymond Queneau*, makes no distinction between the two areas; but in fact she concentrates far more on fiction than on poetry – which strongly suggests the difficulty of the enterprise. While it is possible to distinguish different areas within Queneau's literary writings, some of his works do defy simple classification, and two of these require individual comment. *Chêne et chien*, an autobiographical novel in verse, has important thematic links with the main body of Queneau's fiction and will be considered. *Exercices de style* is a literary experiment which cannot be assigned to a single genre, since it embraces many different ones. However, since the work contributes significantly to an appreciation of Queneau's attitudes both to language and to literary form, it will be included in the discussion.

But finally – and above all – it is never forgotten that Queneau defies all attempts at watertight classification and definitive interpretation. In the words of one of his most perceptive critics, Maurice Nadeau: 'Pelons l'oignon, et perdons l'espoir de parvenir au bulbe.'[58]

1 Raw material

THROUGHOUT HIS CAREER, Queneau readily acknowledged that the resources of human communication formed the very basis of his activity as a writer. As he once remarked: 'Le langage, c'est mon métier.'[1] Indeed his commitment to language is perhaps the most consistent element in his work. But commitment is not satisfaction, much less blind faith, and Queneau's view of writing depends precisely on the fact that no system of communication is completely adequate. He accepts that all languages are merely arbitrary codes, and that no utterance has to be expressed exactly as it is. 'Pourquoi qu'on dit des choses et pas d'autres?' asks Zazie, and continues: 'On est tout de même pas forcé de dire tout ce qu'on dit, on pourrait dire autre chose' (*Zazie*, p. 116). No one contradicts her. There is always scope for change, for experimentation and improvement, since language is condemned to be an imperfect instrument, and a mere approximation to whatever it might designate. As Queneau himself explained, 'contrairement à la théorie gréco-chrétienne, je ne pense pas que le langage soit un absolu, que la vérité soit dans le langage, c'est-à-dire qu'en décortiquant le langage on trouve la vérité' (*Charbonnier*, p. 14). Vincent Tuquedenne, elaborating his philosophical system in *Les Derniers Jours*, goes further, seeing language as an actual barrier between human beings and the metaphysical universe they inhabit:

20. Le monde métaphysique est en dehors de toute catégorie de temps, d'espace, de causalité, etc., et même de substance.
21. Tout problème que l'on peut se poser au sujet du monde métaphysique est insoluble par là même que le langage est régi par les catégories. Tant que le langage s'interposera entre lui et nous, il nous sera inintelligible. (pp. 52–3)

'Le langage' should here be understood in the widest possible sense, so as to embrace any kind of sign-system, for although Queneau is most often concerned with the modern French language, he is forever conscious that this is only one among an infinity of codes. This emerges, for example, in what Roland Travy says about mathematics in *Odile*: 'Ce langage se révèle encore plus impuissant à décrire les richesses du monde mathématique que la langue française à formuler la multiplicité des choses, puisqu'ils ne se situent pas au même degré d'existence' (p. 28). Moreover, there are times when language fails not only to mediate between man and his metaphysical situation, but also to allow effective contact between individuals. Two characters in *Loin de Rueil* exchange embarrassed banalities ('Vos parents vont bien? —Oh oui très bien. Et les vôtres?') until they realise the utter futility of their conversation; then 'ils se regardent. Ils entrevoient très légèrement la connerie du langage humain' (p. 73).[2]

On the other hand, if language did perform its tasks perfectly, it would seem mechanical, predictable and thus devoid of all artistic interest. It may, for Queneau, be deficient in its operation, but for this very reason it remains an intriguing phenomenon, of inexhaustible interest in its own right, and to be endlessly explored, if never completely mastered. This is what underlies his attitude to the role of the writer: 'Avec lui, l'écrivain, on est sûr qu'il ne réussira jamais à utiliser le langage de la façon la plus satisfaisante possible; je pense que c'est là tout son effort' (*Charbonnier*, p. 25). It also helps to account for the fact that although he occasionally produced studies of a strictly linguistic nature, such as 'L'analyse matricielle du langage'[3] and *De quelques langages animaux imaginaires et notamment du langage chien dans 'Sylvie et Bruno'*,[4] Queneau's most ambitious explorations in language are to be found in his fiction and poetry. He acknowledges that in its most basic form language is purely practical, serving – however imperfectly – the needs of communication, but his principal concern is with what happens to language when, in Roman Jakobson's phrase, it appears 'in its aesthetic function' – when it is removed from the utilitarian sphere and becomes literature:

Le langage de l'homme sert à rédiger les ordres du jour et les articles de lois, serf alors de l'implacable activité de ce bipède. Le langage sert aussi à faire de la littérature, c'est-à-dire une chose mystérieuse qui accompagne l'homme avec fidélité le long du sentier qui mène des cavernes à la bombe atomique.[5]

But whatever heights literature may reach, 'le langage' is its one indispensable and irreducible component. And just as Queneau refuses to let his reader take the act of reading for granted, so he constantly draws attention to the various elements which make up the language of literature: they, too, demand the closest scrutiny.

The broad notion of language embraces, among others, two totally different modes of expression: one written, the other oral, and Queneau is fascinated by the individual and collective importance of these. At one extreme, the written mode appears as the aggregate of 'bâtons, chiffres et lettres' – symbols inscribed or printed on the page – which he recalls having learned as a child (*Chêne et chien*, p. 34) and which give the title to a collection of articles and essays largely devoted to linguistic problems. At the other extreme, however, oral language need be nothing more elaborate than a grunt or a yell. Queneau went so far as to suggest that all language may have originated in cries of pain: 'Les gémiss-ements de la douleur, les plaintes de la souffrance sont à l'origine du langage' (*Histoire modèle*, p. 19). Further, despite all the resources of modern written forms, oral language retains its own unique qualities: 'L'oral comporte des éléments qui ne relèvent pas de la grammaire ou de la linguistique; la modulation, le ton, les bégaiements, les accrocs.'[6] These elements can have a precise meaning, more-over: 'Le langage oral comprend, outre les mots plus ou moins organisés en phrases, un nombre incroyable de gro-gnements, raclements de gorge, grommellements, interjec-tions, qui participent à la communication et qui ont une valeur sémantique' (*Bâtons*, p. 87). But of course, Queneau, as a writer devoted to the cause of literature, cannot be analysed purely in terms of semantics – or grammar, for that matter. The very treatment of 'l'oral' itself goes beyond such categories; in Queneau's words 'c'est ici où le problème du langage devient un problème de style' (*ibid.*, p. 91) – and

thus the question broadens still further. Between the refinements of the printed word and the simplicity of oral communication lies the central area usually denoted by the term
'language': a system of words susceptible of graphical representation and morphological change, and underpinned by
syntactical structures. And it is these elements which serve as
starting-points in Queneau's enterprise.

Language and style

Queneau never allows it to be forgotten that in the
first instance language, and nothing else, is the material from
which all his works are fashioned. At the beginning of one
dialogue, for instance, he confronts his reader with the following: 'Lorsque arrivé à sa hauteur, Bonjour, dit-il, et Narcense le regarda. Il commença par employer exclamativement
la deuxième personne du singulier de l'impératif présent du
verbe tenir, puis énonça les syllabes composant le nom de la
personne reconnue par lui' (*Chiendent*, pp. 86–7). The habitual process – which would permit the reader constantly to
look through the words to their referents – cannot take hold.
Like their creator, the characters repeatedly point to the language that they use. In *Les Fleurs bleues* someone asks
Cidrolin: 'Pourquoi, monsieur, y a-t-il comme ça des mots
qui sortent de l'usage? Moi qui vous parle, en ai vu, de mon
vivant même, disparaître quelques-uns sous mes yeux: ciné-
matographe, taximètre, chef d'îlot, etcétéra' (p. 123). In *Le
Dimanche de la vie*, finding himself in an argument,

Paul Brétouillat envisagea pendant quelques instants d'orienter la con-
troverse vers les questions philologiques. Il n'admettait pas que l'on
employât les mots dans des acceptions inexactes et il lui avait fallu une
grande force de volonté pour se retenir de critiquer l'utilisation constante
que faisait sa belle-soeur du verbe causer au lieu de son cousin parler.

(p. 50)

The verb 'causer' represents the essential activity not only of
Paul's sister-in-law, but of all Queneau's characters; for Laverdure's much-quoted refrain, 'Tu causes, tu causes, c'est
tout ce que tu sais faire' (*Zazie, passim*), is less a piece of
impudence than a telling comment on human behaviour as
such.

The reader is regularly taken by surprise by the unusual linguistic formations which Queneau sets before him. Certainly, surprise is the effect of the formula 'Doukipudonktan', which begins *Zazie dans le métro*, or the opening sentence of *Le Dimanche de la vie*: 'Il ne se doutait pas que chaque fois qu'il passait devant sa boutique, elle le regardait, la commerçante, le soldat Brû.' In both cases, of course, Queneau is introducing into written language elements of popular speech – in the first, by attempting to reproduce current pronunciation, and in the second by adopting a word-order often used by French speakers. Both, therefore, are illustrations of an important linguistic undertaking. Queneau's treatment of spoken language has perhaps been discussed more than any other aspect of his work – and Queneau himself has contributed as much as most to the discussion.

'Le néo-français'. His premise was that in French, the spoken language had been completely divorced from its written counterpart – to the serious detriment of the latter. In an article entitled 'Écrit en 1937', one of several on a similar theme in *Bâtons, chiffres et lettres*, he recalls his early experiences of colloquial French – before the First World War, in the children's comic *L'Épatant* (especially its comic strip 'Les Pieds Nickelés'), in the popular nineteenth-century writers Henri Monnier and Jehan Rictus, and, in the twenties, during his military service, which exposed him to Parisian *argot*. The decisive intellectual influence, he goes on, was his reading of *Le Langage* by Joseph Vendryes, who, earlier than most other linguists, denounced traditional French orthography as unrepresentative of the spoken language, showed how, in speech, plurals were marked by prefixes rather than suffixes (*arbre, z-arbres* etc.), and analysed the widespread tendency in spoken French to divide sentences into sets of grammatical indications, or morphemes, and sets of substantive indications, or semantemes (e.g. 'Elle n'y a encore pas//voyagé, ta cousine, en Afrique'). Vendryes compares this with certain structures in the Red Indian language Chinook – which Queneau draws on, as in the example from the beginning of *Le Dimanche de la vie*. Vendryes's argument is summed up strikingly in the conten-

tion 'Nous écrivons une langue morte' (quoted in *Bâtons*, p. 14).[7] Later in the same article Queneau remembers the journey he made to Greece in 1932, when he found a comparable linguistic split – between the traditional *catharevousa* and modern, demotic Greek:

C'est alors [...] qu'il me devint évident que le français moderne devait enfin se dégager des *conventions* de l'écriture qui l'enserrent encore [...] et qu'il s'envolerait, papillon, laissant derrière lui le cocon de soie filé par les grammairiens du XVIe et les poètes du XVIIe siècle.   (*ibid.*, p. 16)

At the time of this early text he predicted the collapse of conventional French at a point when written and spoken language became totally irreconcilable; and his own declared aim was to promote a new linguistic code which he called, variously, 'le troisième français' and 'le néo-français', and which would, in time, replace the traditional written register. All this was to be achieved through a far-reaching programme of radical change:

Pour passer du français écrit ancien [...] à un français moderne *écrit*, au *troisième* français correspondant à la langue réellement parlée, il faut opérer une triple réforme, ou révolution: l'une concerne le vocabulaire, la seconde la syntaxe, la troisième l'orthographe.   (*ibid.*, p. 19)

Queneau makes few specific recommendations on the first two of these, but devotes considerable space to a new system of notation which would not correct the spelling of conventional French, but rather give an orthography to the new code. Accordingly, he presents a phonetic alphabet in which each symbol corresponds to one sound, and goes on immediately: 'Mézalor, mézalor, késkon nobtyin! Sa dvyin incrouayab, pazordinèr, ranvèrsan, sa vouzaalor indsé drôldaspé dontonrvyin pa' etc. (*ibid.*, p. 22).

But for all the energy and enthusiasm with which it is presented, Queneau's argument already poses problems at the theoretical level, most of all through the *a priori* assumption that because speech precedes script chronologically, it is the superior form (as on p. 25). The case for the parallel development of the codes is dismissed before it is even considered. And in the event of the need for spelling reform being proved, Queneau's notation (which, incidentally, has no basis in Vendryes) suffers from basic weaknesses, as it is

too close to the standard alphabet to allow accurate transcription, while being unnecessarily detailed for the reader.[8]
Further, there are inconsistencies in the sample he gives. He
writes, for instance, *mézifobyindir* (= 'mais il faut bien dire')
and then, five lines later, uses a different notation for the
same vowel in *ifôdra* (= 'il faudra'); on the other hand one
and the same symbol, *e*, is used for three distinct sounds – /ə/,
/Ø/ and /O/ – in *on lrekonê, tan mye* and *tousel*.

The traces of the proposed reform can be easily found in
Queneau's fiction – and in narrative sections as well as in
dialogue, for the reform is, of course, aimed at literary
language as a whole, and not simply at the presentation of
speech. Forms such as *vlà* and *exétéra* (*Zazie*, pp. 11, 44), and
some of the modifications used in *Le Chiendent* ('Monsieur
s'y orthographie toujours meussieu [...] et *i* remplace *il*, sans
apostrophe, ce que je juge de la plus extrême importance, car
l'apostrophe est encore une attache avec le passé' (*Bâtons*,
p. 17)) all attest the phonetic shifts which have taken place
since the standardisation of French orthography – which
Queneau in any case castigated as 'un système de graphies
chaotiques, absurdes et arbitraires, une invention des
premiers imprimeurs pour rendre le métier difficile et se créer
ainsi des privilèges corporatifs' (*ibid.*, pp. 78–9). As to
vocabulary, there are any number of examples of Queneau
using expressions drawn from popular speech, of the type
'Pollop, que je lui ai répondu. Va te faire voir par les crouilles
si ça te chante et m'emmerde plus avec tes vicelardises' (*Zazie*,
p. 46). Finally, Queneau's syntactical innovations include
not merely 'le chinook' (notably in *Pierrot mon ami*: see pp. 9,
28, 90, 112) but also other attempts to capture the rhythms
and structures of spoken French: 'D'abord, un truc marant:
en arrivant au cimetière, on s'est aperçu qu'il y avait quelqu'un qui avait suivi le convoi qu'on s'était pas aperçu qu'il le
suivait, et devinez qui c'était qui? Mon Valentin' (*Dimanche*,
p. 98). Queneau also claimed that new grammatical structures could give rise to fresh patterns of thought (see for
example, *Bâtons*, p. 63), which is why, in *Le Chiendent*, the
philosophical speculations of Ernestine (pp. 205–8), and of
Saturnin (pp. 256–8) are couched in their own homely
idioms.

Queneau's polemics, which – superficially at least – are borne out in his fictional texts, might suggest that he set himself the task of founding a whole new language. However, closer inspection reveals a very different state of affairs, and there is no question of such a target being realised. None of his literary texts reads remotely like the 'phonetic' passage in 'Écrit en 1937', and none of the linguistic reforms he proposed there has been developed to any great extent. The proportion of orthographic reform in his work is relatively small. Over all, he uses it as a sort of linguistic seasoning and little more than that. Further, his 'néo-français' orthography shows scant internal consistency and little connection with his attacks on allegedly moribund features of written French. Pierre Léon's rigorous analysis of the language of *Zazie dans le métro* makes this abundantly clear:

Les notations phonétiques de Queneau ne sont pas plus systématiques que son orthographe réformée. Les exemples de parler populaire sont rares pour certains phénomènes pourtant importants comme la palatalisation. Certaines formes divergentes sont normales, on dira une fois 'voilà' et une fois 'vlà', à quelques secondes d'intervalle, 'il' puis 'i'. Mais on doute que des personnages populaires prononçant 'chsuis' ne disent pas de la même manière 'chte' pour 'je te' [...]. Les E caducs supprimés représentent un total de moins d'une centaine pour un texte de 250 pages, en grande partie de dialogue. Les agglutinations syllabiques sont en tout petit nombre et revêtent des formes divergentes. Pourquoi 'st'année' (p. 175), 'à stage-là' (p. 182), 'staprès-midi' (p. 200)? Pourquoi 'les coudocors' (p. 50), et non 'lécoudocors' ou 'lescoudocors'?[9]

Similarly, the attempt to refurbish French vocabulary is merely sporadic; and the 'modernisation' of French syntax has certainly not gone as far as some of the theoretical writings might suggest. However startling some of his variations on traditional grammar may appear, he in fact depends on the order which this same traditional grammar imposes. As another critic has argued: 'Queneau demeure soumis aux lois de la grammaire française [...]. Les incorrections du parler populaire n'échappent véritablement à la logique de notre syntaxe.'[10]

In any case, by 1969 Queneau came to repudiate many of the claims he had previously made, and declared that the question of 'le néo-français' now seemed less important to him, recognising also that the theories he had advanced twenty or more years earlier had not been supported by subsequent developments. He admitted, for instance, that 'le néo-français' had not made the progress he had anticipated, essentially because of the influence of the mass media, which had consolidated the position of traditional usage and brought together spoken and written language, rather than creating possibilities for a more modern code (see 'Errata', in *Voyage*, pp. 219–22).

Because of Queneau's admission, and because of the strict limitations of 'le néo-français' insofar as Queneau ever practised it, it is clearly futile to consider Queneau's language from a strictly theoretical point of view – as has been recognised: 'Quelques centaines de mots suffisent à créer le "climat sonore" [. . .]. Tout l'art est dans la suggestion. Nous ne demandons pas à Queneau de suivre ses théories linguistiques mais de faire œuvre de poète, de créateur.'[11] Ultimately, Queneau's 'néo-français' emerges not as the systematic application of a linguistic doctrine, but as one device among many by which he experiments with the constituent parts of the French language. This is corroborated by the fact that its distribution varies enormously from novel to novel – as between, for example, *Zazie dans le métro*, where it is probably more widespread than anywhere else, and *Odile* and *Un Rude Hiver*, in which it figures very little. Indeed, the mixture of conventional French and 'néo-français' is never of exactly the same proportions in two different books, as Queneau pointed out – again from the vantage point of the nineteen-sixties:

Quand il y a mélange, l'apparition du langage parlé est, je crois, toujours spontané et involontaire, c'est-à-dire qu'il y a un moment donné où j'ai l'impression qu'il faut que ce soit comme ça, enfin que ce soit noté dans une orthographe plus ou moins phonétique. Je dis 'plus ou moins phonétique' parce que quelquefois elle l'est complètement, d'autres fois moins. Enfin je ne sais pas . . . ce n'est pas du tout systématique.   (*Charbonnier*, p. 89)[12]

With hindsight, it is clear that 'le néo-français' was never an end in itself; rather, it always formed part of a much more general literary undertaking: an attempt to explore the existing resources of French and to propose new ones – in short, to reinvigorate the language and redeem it from staleness. And therein lies its still vital importance. As Queneau once put it: 'Je demande simplement qu'on donne au français vivant les possibilités que l'on accorde bien au breton et au provençal' (*Bâtons*, p. 40) – and his efforts to open up new possibilities need no supporting manifesto.

Once it is accepted that Queneau is not creating a new system, but rather extending choices within the existing one, the entire picture changes, for emphasis shifts to the expressive qualities of the forms chosen. In the words of Stephen Ullmann, 'the pivot of the whole theory of expressiveness is the concept of *choice*. There can be no question of style unless the speaker or writer has the possibility of choosing between alternative forms of expression.'[13] In Queneau's terms, style is what makes language effective on other levels than the strictly utilitarian one of 'les ordres du jour' and 'les articles de lois'. At the same time, there is no neat dividing-line between the province of language and that of style. Queneau himself insists on their inseparability when discussing some of the writers he admires most:

Le style [...] (précisément depuis Flaubert) n'est pas conçu comme une réussite appréciable selon des règles rhétoriques ou grammaticales, mais comme une méthode d'invention. Il n'y a pas de recherches de style chez un Proust [...] la méthode est elle-même invention. Et chez Joyce, ce qu'il est devenu courant d'appeler des 'recherches de langage', n'est-ce pas plutôt son style? [...]. Pour Joyce, comme pour Proust, la langue est le style, et le style la langue même.[14]

The difference between a linguistic analysis and a stylistic one is a matter not of substance, but of attitude. As Ullmann argues: 'Stylistics is not a branch of linguistics; it is a parallel science which examines the same problems from a different point of view.'[15]

Within the three basic linguistic categories – orthography, vocabulary, and morphology and syntax[16] – elements of 'le néo-français' can be seen as features of style coexisting with and complementing other elements which have no necessary or immediate connection with speech.

Orthography.   Queneau's spelling will sometimes produce a closer approximation to the sounds made by a speaker than does the conventional form, as when he replaces *oi* by *oua* in *orlaloua* (*Rueil*, p. 39) and *toua* (*Chiendent*, p. 292), or using *ss* instead of *x* in *s'essprima* (*Glinglin*, p. 151). But it is also possible to find a gratuitously exaggerated liaison which gives a purely comic effect: 'Je ne vois pas pourquoi je n'irai pas moi-z-aussi-z-aux-z-honneurs [...]. Moi-z-aussi je veux-z-être riche et hhonorée' (*Rueil*, p. 17). Queneau also uses spellings which are simply of curiosity value, such as *bounoume* for 'bonhomme' – *Derniers Jours*, p. 18). He even, on occasion, resorts to archaic orthography: 'Y avait des rigolos sur la terre. Et pour aimer tellement que ça le jaune fallayent qu'ils soyent tous un peu cocus' (*Rude Hiver*, p. 9). Expressions derived from other languages generally appear in their original spelling, but sometimes loan-words are gallicised in such a way that the moderately familiar comes to seem positively bizarre. This may be to approximate more closely to French pronunciation, as when a character remembers dancing a *kékouok* (*Pierrot*, p. 95; cf. also *quécoque, Sally Mara*, p. 178); or it may even reveal a hesitation between two possibilities – hence a film of the 'aventures d'un coboua (ou cobouille, on ne savait pas très bien)' (*Rude Hiver*, p. 76). And it can also yield rich Joycean puns, as when an inexperienced drinker is enchanted by his first, exotic experience of a *djinn-fils* (*Chiendent*, p. 123).

Initials offer a further area of orthographical experimentation. Sometimes they are preferred to complete words, notably in *Les Enfants du limon*, with its frequent references to the political party called the 'Nation sans Classes' as the 'N.S.C.', or when the main female character in *Le Vol d'Icare* is designated as 'LN' ('Je suis d'origine cruciverbiste', she explains (p. 30)). But a more frequent procedure is that of connecting up series of initials by inserting appropriate vowels. In this way the United States or États-Unis, turn into *les Éhus* (*Rueil*, p. 223), the C.R.S. become *céhéresses*, and the Sécurité Sociale – or S.S. – is transformed into *la éssésse* (*Fleurs bleues*, pp. 49, 120). A character in *Les Enfants du limon* avoids an embarrassing encounter by hiding in the *doublevécès* (p. 291); Cidrolin, in *Les Fleurs bleues*, speculates on whether his daughters will spend their married lives in an *achélème* (p. 74). By diverting attention from the origin of initials and turning them into words in this way, Queneau bestows on them a whole new identity. One final instance of Queneau's manipulation of orthography is his attempt to capture the speech habits of an individual rather than popular pronunciation as such. This technique can give great emphasis, enhancing, for instance, the pomposity with which a minor car accident is described. Without a good driver at the wheel, 'c'était la catastrophe, lâ câtâstrôpheu. Si je n'avais pas eu tout mon sang-froid, c'était la mort pour nous tous, un accident terrible, tairribleu' (*Chiendent*, pp. 26–7); it also reinforces the brashness of the playboy, Shiboleth, who greets Pierre with the words: 'Le Grand. Pas possibleôôôôôôô. Qu'est-ce que tu fiches ici, mon petit?' (*ibid.*, p. 132).

By such means as these, Queneau amply succeeds in his attempt to produce fresh and original linguistic forms, in, as it were, re-creating existing words. The result, in Roland Barthes's phrase, is to 'faire surgir à la place du mot pompeusement enveloppé dans sa robe orthographique, un mot nouveau, indiscret, naturel, c'est-à-dire barbare'.[17] Moreover, these innovations have an important effect on the reader, forcing him to work out the text rather than passively absorbing it: 'C'est, pour Queneau, une manifestation de la fonction phatique de son langage: il secoue son lecteur en lui proposant périodiquement une sorte de rébus plus ou moins facile ou plus ou moins obscur.'[18]

Vocabulary. In 'Écrit en 1937' Queneau warns against the excessive use of *argot*, but sees in it a fruitful source (*Bâtons*, p. 19), and his fiction faithfully reflects this. Certainly, he often draws on the resources of the popular, spoken language. Not only do most of his novels contain numerous examples of everyday slang – and again, in narrative discourse as well as dialogue – but he also uses expressions peculiar to individual social groups, borrowing from, for instance, the *argot* of the underworld: *lames* (playing-cards), *châsses* (eyes), *thunes* (old twenty-franc pieces) (*Rueil*, pp. 14, 40, 66), *marmite* (mistress of a pimp) (*Pierrot*, p. 17), or the slang of young children: *ducucu* (documentary film – *Rueil*, p. 38), *lolo* (breast – *Sally Mara*, p. 98). He achieves a comic effect by juxtaposing the language of children and adults:

'Dis donc tonton, demande Zazie, quand tu déconnes comme ça, tu le fais esprès ou c'est sans le vouloir?' (*Zazie*, p. 20). More ambitiously, he combines some very different lexical registers. In *Les Fleurs bleues* – a novel which spans the Middle Ages and the 1960s – he puts together the chronological extremes of the linguistic heritage; thus obsolete expressions – *arroi* (p. 10), *inclyte* (p. 13), *nenni* (p. 21), *acort* (p. 22), *ardoir* (p. 31) – coexist with terms which have entered the language since the Second World War – *auto-stop* (p. 17), *mobylette*, (p. 42), *transistor* (*ibid.*), *magnétophone* (p. 43). *Les Fleurs bleues* also sets French vocabulary against that of a jumble of other languages, especially through the various foreigners who pass Cidrolin's barge on their way to their campsite: 'Esquiouze euss, dit le campeur mâle, mà wie sind lost' (p. 15; Cidrolin's response is 'Il cause bien [...] mais parle-t-il l'européen vernaculaire ou le néo-babélien?'). *Le Chiendent* has a similarly macaronic display in the speech of 'Missize Aulini': 'Yo soy la belle saison [...]. Ich bine la tempête [...]. Haillame ...' (p. 293). Théo, in the same novel, parades his knowledge of German (pp. 225–6), while Sally Mara's studies in Irish set up another linguistic contrast (e.g. *Sally Mara*, pp. 22, 32, 33, 36, 42). Purpulan frequently expresses himself in Latin, much to the annoyance of Chambernac, his master (*Limon*, pp. 21, 54, 87, 157 etc.). The lexical stock, in other words, can be extended across national borders as well as social and historical ones.

Queneau also supplements existing resources with a wide range of his own inventions.[19] Some are neat, logical derivations from existing words: *semi-putanat* (for the status of two presumed *demi-mondaines*: *Odile*, p. 15); *mastroquocratie* (bar-owners as a body: *Rude Hiver*, p. 20); *tomater* and *oignonner* (gardening activities: *Chiendent*, p. 36); *huiliproduction* (result of sunbathing: *Limon*, p. 11); *trimelles* (for 'trois jumelles', i.e. triplets: *Fleurs bleues*, p. 124). A similar procedure gives striking results when applied to expressions of foreign origin: an inventor 'rupine à bloc et un jour brraoum il eurêkate ça y est il a trouvé' (*Rueil*, p. 45); 'L'abbé Biroton n'eut pas plutôt itemissaesté que le duc l'entraîna sur le baile' (*Fleurs bleues*, p. 36). As befits an avowed admirer of Lewis Carroll, Queneau seems to take particular delight in the creation of portmanteau words: *craspect* (*Icare*, pp. 13, 146), *concul-puissance* (*Rueil*, p. 42), *phallucinations* (*Sally Mara*, p. 46). He also christens some of the products of his own imagination, as in *Saint Glinglin*, where the elaborately described food traditionally consumed in the ceremony of the 'Printanier' rejoices in the name of *brouchtoucaille*, while the beverage drunk on the same occasion is known as *fifrequet*.

Morphology and syntax. Queneau's explorations and inventions bear significantly on the relationships and structures into which words are organised – and this not only through the device of 'chinook'. In *Les Fleurs bleues* there is a sprinkling of medieval constructions, such as the omission of the subject pronoun: 'Joachim me prénomme' (p. 13). In *Zazie dans le métro* he plays with standard morphology, when Trouscaillon finds himself in grave linguistic difficulties: 'Je me vêts, répéta-t-il douloureusement. C'est français ça: je me vêts? Je m'en vais, oui, mais: je me vêts?' (p. 213), and again:

—M'autorisez-vous donc à de nouveau formuler la proposition interrogative qu'il y a quelques instants j'énonça devant vous?
—J'énonçai, dit l'obscur.
—J'énonçais, dit Trouscaillon.
—J'énonçai sans esse.
—J'énonçai dit enfin Trouscaillon. Ah! la grammaire c'est pas mon fort.

(p. 218)

But although the conventions are finally respected in this case, in others they are deliberately violated: 'Le garçon apporta le mousseux d'un pas guilleret et enleva le bouchon avec de grands airs. Il serva, on trinquit' (*Pierrot*, p. 127). (Queneau claimed to have heard teenagers in a café who were highly amused by this *contrepèterie* but found the greatest difficulty in establishing the corrrect form of the past historic of *servir* (*Bâtons*, p. 72).) In 'Le Caillou', the third section of *Saint Glinglin*, narrated by Jean Nabonide, there is a consistent violation of the past historic: 'j'alla' (p. 99), 'je passa' (p. 101), 'je monta' (p. 102), etc.

Other features of French syntax are brought into question by implicit contrast with some of Queneau's own formulations. His theoretical writings contain several references to the apparently redundant imperfect subjunctive (e.g. *Bâtons*, p. 71), which, in his novels, figures in some comic contrasts: 'Sur le pas de la porte, le patron criait: Mado! – On arrive! répondait-elle avec la force voulue pour que ses paroles fendissent l'air avec la vitesse et l'intensité souhaitées' (*Zazie*, p. 101); 'Du coin de l'œil il admira Yvonne. Quelle belle gosse. Et il n'avait pas l'air de la dégoûter. Quoiqu'il ne fût pas encore très sûr qu'elle ne se foutît point de lui' (*Pierrot*, p. 106). There is also a tense of Queneau's own invention, the 'surjonctif',[20] which is to be found in *Saint Glinglin*: 'il ne cherchait qu'Alice, non d'ailleurs qu'il espérât qu'elle se révélassassât à lui avec des lépidoptères sur des cuisses de soie noire' (p. 177), and in *Zazie dans le métro*, when Mado reminds Gabriel '[vous] n'avez jamais voulu que nous vous admirassassions dans l'exercice de votre art' (p. 197).[21]

There is an exact counterpart to Trouscaillon's struggles with the verb 'énoncer' in the following altercation in *Le Chiendent* – this time on the subject of concord:

—Jusqu'en Syrie et à Constantinople, que je suis été.
—Que j'ai été, corrige Clovis.
—Où ça es-tu allé, mon petit? demande Peter que cette finesse de langage ne semble pas atteindre.
—J'dis j'ai été et pas j'suis été, répond le futur lycéen.   (p. 189)

But such deviations often go unchecked: 'Je suis été au domicile privé de M. Le Maire' (*Temps mêlés*, p. 106); 'Elle savait bien que la N.S.C. avait vécu, et avait mouru' (*Limon*, p. 269).

Some of Queneau's tense sequences are, if anything, still more disconcerting, upsetting as they do the reader's habitual perception of time: 'A la porte on frappe; c'était Catherine. Elle entra en s'excusant de son indiscrétion' (*Chiendent*, p. 136), or:

Pierrot mit quelque temps avant de se décider à se lever; il devient flemmard en vieillissant. Il entendait les chants religieux s'évaporer lentement du couvent. Un voisin mit en marche une radio qui gueula [...]. Le soleil commence à ramper le long du balcon.   (*Pierrot*, p. 209).

Genders can be changed at will – apparently gratuitously as in 'sa belle argent' (*Chiendent*, p. 248) or 'la bonne air du crépuscule' (*Temps mêlés*, p. 107), or with a clear indication of meaning, as with 'quelques serviteurs écossaises', for kilted waiters in a night-club for homosexuals (*Zazie*, p. 201). And unstressed pronouns sometimes replace stressed ones: 'ils et Mme Chambernac partirent pour leur maison' (*Limon*, p. 135); 'puis ils, les Chinois, reformèrent leur cortège' (*Rude Hiver*, p. 10).

There are also variations on standard word-order. A simple deviation from the norm, such as an unusually placed adverb or adjective, can give a sentence a wholly new shape and emphasis: 'Nous venons justement d'acheter un poste, s'empressa-t-il de grossièrement affirmer' (*Limon*, p. 180); 'Suzy [...] se sent attirée par l'anglo-saxonne élégance de Peter' (*Chiendent*, p. 177). A similar effect is also created by the 'telescoping' of normal syntax: 'Le barbu blanc nain' (*ibid.*, p. 268). More striking, perhaps, are Queneau's variations on the standard presentation of dialogue – which are, however, scarcely more arbitrary than the established convention: 'Je, commença l'un, ne connais pas' (*ibid.*, p. 23); 'Mon, continua Chambernac, dixième chapitre' (*Limon*, p. 261); 'Natur, leur dit-il, ellement que je l'ai vu' (*Glinglin*, p. 186).

Foreign languages are also a source for syntactical invention. Again it is English that predominates, as in the following elliptical constructions: 'Mince alors, dit Polo. Tu t'imagines: des places louées. Et c'est des orchestres au moins? C'était' (*Rude Hiver*, p. 47); 'Mme Chamber. ne lisait pas; elle essayait de' (*Limon*, p. 77). But borrowings from German word-order catch the eye, too, particularly the practice of placing verbs at the end of dependent clauses: 'Louis-Philippe des Cigales qui dans un placard fouillait' (*Rueil*, p. 11); 'Il ne sent que les odeurs habituelles et tout particulièrement celles qui de la Cave émanent' (*Zazie*, p. 54).

The language of Queneau's fiction does not constitute a revolution in French usage, or even a systematic reform of it. Yet it performs functions which are no less important on the linguistic level, and a good deal more so when considered from a literary viewpoint, at once underlining the arbitrary nature of conventions by showing that language is far more malleable than is often realised, and creating original and diverting effects through its renewal of the linguistic stock.

Meaning. Although Queneau's own statements on the subject emphasise above all his examination of the component parts of language, his linguistic practice also calls into question the role language plays in conveying sense and meaning. Thus when, in *Le Chiendent*, he writes *meussieu* instead of *monsieur*, he is not merely challenging a given system of orthography, but also raising a semantic issue: the current acceptation of the word, as a general designation of an adult male, is quite different from earlier meanings (e.g. 'Titre donné autrefois aux hommes de condition assez élevée'; 'Titre donné aux princes de la famille royale').[22] And although the shift in pronunciation allows for the change of meaning which has taken place, written convention does not. Accordingly, Queneau repeatedly draws attention to the problem.

Another frequent device is to reverse the accepted relation between *signifiant* and *signifié*; and Queneau does this in two different ways. In some instances words take on a totally unexpected sense which nevertheless derives from their form, and in others they exist remote from any meaning, denoting nothing and having merely the face value they derive from their presence on the printed page. The first case is well illustrated in *Le Vol d'Icare*, where the author Hubert Lubert engages a detective, Morcol, to look for Icare, a missing character, who has escaped from the book he is writing:

HUBERT
Tenez voici dix louis et retrouvez-moi Icare vite.
    MORCOL
Je vous accuse réception des dix louis et note son nom.
Il écrit Nick Harwitt sur son carnet cependant que Lubert lui donne sa carte.
(p. 18)

This initial misunderstanding introduces an entity, 'Nick Harwitt', which does not exist as far as Lubert is concerned, but which holds a meaning for Morcol and plays a decisive role in the subsequent action, as the unfortunate detective searches far and wide for 'mon Nick'. The significance of the very title is modified in the course of the book, for if Queneau refers, predictably enough, to the *myth* of Icarus – adapting it to the circumstances of the age of heavier-than-air machines – the main story is far more concerned with his *flight* from the clutches of his creator, Lubert, and with the possibility that his disappearance is the result of a *theft*. Similarly, the meaning of the myth of Saint Glinglin, Queneau's epic of rain and fine weather, and of the 'chasse-nuage', the charismatic object which seems so necessary to the stable climate of the Ville Natale, derives simply from word-play:

On laissa le corps de Jean se dessécher au soleil. L'ensemble du mât et de la momie fut dénommé nasse-chuages, puis, par contrepetterie, chasse-nuages [...]. Des fêtes furent institutées en l'honneur de Jean que l'on surnomma saint Glinglin (sans doute parce que, lorsqu'il empêche de pleuvoir – ce qu'il fait toujours – il cingle un grain).   (*Glinglin*, p. 267)

The second case – the divorce of word from referent – is a more wide-spread phenomenon and, perhaps, a more important one, as in *Le Dimanche de la vie*, a novel in which labels are readily available but rarely offer a reliable guide to contents, in a puzzling, uncertain Paris. Here, it has been argued, 'le nom importe autant que la chose qu'il désigne'.[23] Thus the ingenuous Valentin Brû, emerging from the Gare d'Austerlitz, supposes that 'un campanile orné d'une vaste horloge' (p. 68) is part of the Gare du Nord, when in fact it can only be the tower of the nearby Gare de Lyon; and later he mistakes the Eglise du Saint-Esprit in the twelfth arrondissement for the basilica of Sacré-Cœur in distant Montmartre (p. 82). Similar confusions abound in *Zazie dans le métro*, where a name and the location it designates are frequently quite unconnected: Gabriel takes first the Gare de Lyon and then the Invalides for the Panthéon (pp. 16–18, 111), and, with the connivance of the tourist-guide, Fédor Balanovitch, persuades a flock of foreign visitors that the Tribunal de Commerce is really the Sainte-Chapelle. The tourists for their part have no way of discriminating: their understanding extends no further than the confusing foreign words uttered by Gabriel, and the words assume a reality of their own. As Tolut puts it in *Les Derniers Jours* – 'On apprend les mots, mais les choses réelles on ne les connaît pas. On sait des noms, mais on ignore complètement de quoi il s'agit' (p. 193). Tolut is a retired geography teacher who knows the world not through direct experience but through

books, but his judgement of himself applies equally to the
tourists in *Zazie dans le métro*. Like the tourists, another
foreigner, the young Sally Mara, sees French words 'from the
outside', and her tenuous grasp of their normal meaning is a
recurrent theme of *Journal intime*. For Sally, even the dictionary does not always provide adequate explanations; 'En
relisant les premières pages de mon journal, je me demande si
j'ai bien employé le mot "vierge". Car dans le dictionnaire, il
y a: "se dit d'une terre qui n'a été ni exploitée, ni cultivée"'
(*Sally Mara*, p. 21).

A word can also acquire a totally arbitrary meaning, as in
Saint Glinglin, where, quite gratuitously, *lansquenet* (= a
German mercenary soldier serving in France in the fifteenth
or sixteenth century) serves to signify a musical instrument:
'On en ferait une chanson avec accompagnement de binious,
vielles, tambourins et lansquenets' (p. 83). That goes unchallenged – within the text anyway – but a dispute in *Les
Fleurs bleues* makes the point clear, when a passer-by tries to
lecture Cidrolin on the subject of fishing:

—Ce sont des maniaques sadiques, les pêcheurs à la ligne [...]. Franchement, ne trouvez-vous pas l'hameçon plus sournois et vicieusement
barbare que l'espadrille?
—L'espadrille?
—Ces trucs qu'ils enfoncent dans le cou du fauve.
—Vous êtes sûr que cela s'appelle comme ça?
—Pour le moment, moi j'appelle ça comme ça, donc ça s'appelle comme ça
et comme c'est avec moi que vous causez en ce moment et avec nul autre,
il vous faut bien prendre des mots à leur valeur faciale.   (pp. 26–7)

Abruptly, and disconcertingly, words are appropriated for
private, idiosyncratic use, and lose their accepted, public
values. The problem is still more extreme in *Le Chiendent*,
where they are sometimes detached from any context, so as
to stand as objects of contemplation in their own right. Early
on Étienne Marcel becomes fascinated with a café signboard
visible from his railway carriage and 's'inquiète un instant de
savoir si FRITES n'est pas un nom de personne: Meussieu
Frites. Cette idée le fait sourire' (p. 26). This apparently
trivial experience is decisive in developing Étienne's
awareness of language, and in a later conversation he draws
the full moral:

—Si je néglige le côté pratique d'un objet fabriqué, dit Étienne.
—Vous faites de l'esthétique, interrompit Pierre. Ou de la magie [...].
—Les mots aussi sont des objets fabriqués. On peut les envisager indépendamment de leur sens.
Étienne venait de découvrir ça, en le disant. Il se le répéta pour lui-même,
et s'approuva. Ça, c'était une idée.
—En dehors de leur sens, ils peuvent dire tout autre chose.
Ainsi le mot 'théière' designe *cet objet*, mais je puis le considérer en dehors
de cette signification, de même que la théière elle-même, je puis la regarder
en dehors de son sens pratique, c'est-à-dire de servir à thé ou même d'être
un simple récipient.   (pp. 125–6)

Through Étienne's experiences, more than anywhere else,
Queneau acknowledges that words can function purely on
the basis of their intrinsic formal qualities, devoid of semantic force. He does not, however, exploit this possibility in his
fictional writings, operating instead at different points along
the semantic spectrum of a given word but stopping short of
meaninglessness.[24] The word with no meaning at all serves
as a logical conclusion, but one which is never reached. As in
other linguistic areas, Queneau's challenge to convention is
issued from within the framework which convention
provides.

A stylistic survey goes a considerable distance towards characterising Queneau's writing, but still leaves unexamined
certain feaures which slip through a net constructed according to linguistic categories:

Disons qu'à partir d'un système d'axiomes, de conventions et d'un vocabulaire, il est possible de composer des propositions, des phrases, des
formules qui ne sont pas démontrables dans ce système [...] et il me
semble que c'est un peu la même chose dans le domaine de la poésie,
c'est-à-dire qu'on a un vocabulaire, on a une syntaxe, et on a des problèmes
d'information et même de communication; et puis, tout d'un coup on sort
de là, et c'est de la poésie.   (*Charbonnier*, pp. 30–1)

However, Queneau remains vague about the exact nature of
this 'poetic' element – both in this general observation and,
during the same interview, with reference to Corneille ('il est
indéniable qu'il y a [...] communication au niveau poétique,
ce qui reste toujours somme toute très mystérieux', *ibid*.,
p. 30). And a number of commentators, conscious of a
quality they cannot define, maintain a similarly evasive tone.

One, while noting the scarcity of autobiographical allusions, insists that Queneau is nevertheless present throughout his work, and declares: 'C'est ça ce que l'on appelle le style.'[25] Another writes: 'Le point commun de tous les livres de Queneau n'est évidemment autre qu'un certain style'[26] – but refrains from committing himself to details.

A full account of Queneau's style is particularly difficult because he ranges so widely among the possibilities open to him that he cannot be securely identified with any particular rhetorical technique, manner or idiom. By the same token, it is hard to isolate 'typical' passages, or to construct successful parodies.[27] The broad distinction established, for example, by Stephen Ullmann, between the expressive qualities of style as such and the 'peculiar form of style which bears the stamp of [the author's] personality',[28] is less than helpful here. In these circumstances a frequent recourse – if not a complete solution to the problem – has been to pick out individual devices which feature regularly in Queneau's work.[29]

Word-play. Given Queneau's propensity for double meanings, it is not surprising to discover a strong emphasis on punning. Most often this is primarily to allow the coexistence of two distinct senses – as when the trappings of des Cigales's room ('hallebardes moyenageuses, crucifikses bretons, acropoles photographiées') are summarised as 'objets aussi faux que loriques' (*Rueil*, pp. 10–11). Characters' names frequently serve the same purpose. This is obvious enough in, say, Miss(ize) Aulini in *Le Chiendent*, or, in *Les Fleurs bleues*, Cidrolin (combining the predictable Norman component of 'cidre' with the exclamation 'Si drôle, hein!') or the silent-screen detective Nick Winter, from *Un Rude Hiver*, whose name links Nick Carter, hero of innumerable early films, with the season which pervades everything in the novel from the title onwards. But sometimes the connotations are less immediately apparent, as with the sleazy tourist-guide Balanovitch (balanite = 'inflammation de la muqueuse du gland' (*Petit Robert*)) or Russule, the woodcutter's daughter, again from *Les Fleurs bleues* (the *russulae* are a genus of fungi, predominantly woodland in habitat and brightly coloured). At the beginning of *Les Fleurs bleues* reference is made to the slow progress of the building of Notre-Dame:

—Si on traîne tellement on finira par bâtir une mahomerie.
—Pourquoi pas un bouddhoir? un confuciussonal? un sanct-lao-tsuaire?

(p. 11)

This is sustained punning in the vein of 'Une traduction en joycien', where Queneau brilliantly rewords the meditation at the aquarium which opens *Gueule de pierre*, so as to bring out at every turn the disturbing metaphysical implications of life and death to be derived from the spectacle. The original begins:

Drôle de vie, la vie de poisson! ... Je n'ai jamais pu comprendre comment on pourrait vivre comme cela. L'existence de la Vie sous cette forme m'inquiète bien au delà de tout autre sujet d'alarme que peut m'imposer le Monde.

– which, 'in translation', becomes:

Doradrôle de vie la vie de poisson. Je n'ai jeunet jamais pu unteldigérer qu'on ment on pouvait vivier comme ce la sol dos rêt. Fishtre, ouïes! Son aiguesistence sucette mortphe m'astruitte et me cotte, mets ta mortphose dans la raie en carnation, euyet-moi ça, l'alarme dont crevette le monde, ô mort faussse, hue mor! Quelle hummer!   (*Bâtons*, pp. 240–1)

On other occasions, however, the effect is less a concentration of meanings than a playful metamorphosis serving to tease the reader and bring out, once again, the gratuitousness of the conventional forms of words. Thus an addition to a letter begins 'Peau s'écrit homme' and a character in a fit of rage 'a eu comme le délire, homme très mince' (*Chiendent*, pp. 152, 157). Similarly, Queneau will occasionally resort to *contrepèterie*: 'un groupe compant et distract', 'un Branleur ou un Pasty, un grand savant quoi' (*Rueil*, pp. 104, 217).

Sound effects.   If the devices just considered depend on a tension between sound and meaning, elsewhere Queneau takes pleasure in sounds more or less for their own sake – in exaggerated alliteration ('Mais les manèges ne tournaient toujours pas, le dancing était désert, et les voyantes ne voyaient rien venir': *Pierrot*, p. 9; 'Il tripotait en tremblant la troubeille de porto': *Dimanche*, p. 106; 'Ah le frocard, le pendard, le flemmard, grogna le duc': *Fleurs bleues*, p. 63); or in onomatopoeia ('Glou glou glou glou, elle est bonne leur bière': *Odile*, p. 31). And sometimes he introduces metric rhythm into dialogue to give particular resonance to what is being said: thus for Gabriel, in an altercation: 'C'était le moment de se forger quelque bouclier verbal. Le premier qu'il trouva fut un alexandrin: – D'abord, je vous permets pas de me tutoyer'; or, at the top of the Eiffel Tower, meditating on his friends and family of whom, 'je ne sais que ceci, alexandrinairement: les voilà presque morts puisqu'ils sont des absents' (*Zazie*, pp. 11, 120). In *Le Vol d'Icare*, whole exchanges are couched in alexandrines – although this time not advertised as such (e.g. p. 21).

Enumeration. The rhythmic accumulation achieved by alexandrines is also a feature of the sustained enumeration which Queneau uses, generally for comic effect. Among a number of striking instances are the recipe for 'brouchtou-caille' (*Glinglin*, pp. 72–3), the bizarre description of the Chinese at the beginning of *Un Rude Hiver* (pp. 7–8) and the extensive lists of guests at tea-parties attended by Sally Mara (*Sally Mara*, pp. 28, 145–6). In *Les Fleurs bleues*, when Labal accuses Cidrolin of putting the graffiti on his own fence, Lalix's verbal attack gains both in strength and in comic force from its cumulative presentation:

Tout ce que vous avez raconté prouve par a plus b que c'est vous le justicier à la con, le judex à la manque, le monte-christo de papa, le zorro de grand-mère, le robin des bois pourris, le rancunier gribouilleur, l'insulteur des murailles, le maniaque du barbouillage, enfin quoi l'emmerdeur patenté anticidrolinique.   (p. 250)

The richest example of all is no doubt the list of horrors imagined by a terrified Mme Cloche lost in the forest at night in *Le Chiendent*:

Elle imagina ce qui pourrait lui arriver: un vagabond qui la violerait, un voleur qui la tuerait, un chien qui la mordrait, un taureau qui l'écraserait; deux vagabonds qui la violeraient, trois voleurs qui la tueraient, quatre chiens qui la mordraient, cinq taureaux qui l'écraseraient; sept vagabonds qui la mordraient, huit voleurs qui l'écraseraient, neuf chiens qui la tueraient, dix taureaux qui la violeraient. Une grosse chenille qui lui tomberait dans le cou; une chauve-souris qui dans l'oreille lui crierait ouh!

ouh!; un oiseau de nuit qui lui crèverait les yeux et les enlèverait des trous.
Un cadavre au milieu du chemin; un fantôme lui prenant la main; un
squelette mangeant un morceau de pain.   (p. 73)

A catalogue of stylistic procedures, however, cannot in itself
define a style, for an account of discrete elements, such as
those just discussed, can never capture the consistency or
texture of a literary work of any length. The best that can be
achieved by this method is some such description as 'a fairly
unified pattern of rhythmic rhetoric, full of puns, coined
words, poly-syllables, alliterations and phonetic ornaments
that cannot be classified under any heading other than that of
"Queneau-ese"'[30] – which in any case assumes a 'unified
pattern' rather than explaining it. But there are other ways of
proceeding towards a definition.

Imagery. Early commentators tended to leave on one side
the question of Queneau's imagery – hence, for instance,
Claude Simonnet's laconic judgement: 'Les images sont rares
mais nettes et audacieuses.'[31] However, it would be a
mistake to suppose that the subject is not worth discussion –
as has been proved by Gérald Antoine.[32] While admitting
that Queneau's images are relatively infrequent, Antoine,
basing himself on Lorca's definition, 'Une image poétique,
c'est toujours un déplacement de sens', shows just how
important they are to an understanding of Queneau's prose.
A large proportion of the images, it is argued, are so
economical as almost to escape notice; but a discreet metaphor which draws little or no attention to itself can nevertheless capture precisely the mood or flavour of a given situation. Thus for the dehumanising urban grind of the early
pages of *Le Chiendent*: 'La silhouette disparut empochée par
le métro'; or again: 'La silhouette avait déjà avalée par
l'ombre disparue' (pp. 7, 9). But, crucially, these self-effacing
images are only part of Queneau's technique: imagery can
assume striking prominence, as in *Les Fleurs bleues*, where the
duc d'Auge, in the thirteenth century, depends on metaphor
to recount his futuristic dream of mechanised road transport,
and the terms of comparison he uses tend to outweigh the
'houatures' themselves: 'Ce sont bestioles vives et couinantes

qui courent en tous sens sur les pattes rondes. Elles ne mangent rien de solide et ne boivent que du pétrole. Leurs yeux s'allument à la nuit tombante' (p. 41). This tendency can go even further – for instance with the similes used to describe Gabriel, locked in a titanic combat at the end of *Zazie dans le métro*: 'Tel le coléoptère attaqué par une colonne myrmidonne, tel le bœuf assailli par un banc hirudinaire, Gabriel se secouait, s'ébrouait, s'ébattait' (p. 240). Here the very position of the 'coléoptère' and the 'bœuf', as well as the presence of two terms of comparison, gives them priority over Gabriel himself. And far from using imagery discreetly, Queneau applies it in an exaggerated way to stress the device rather than the meaning. Another passage, dealing with a railway-compartment discussion early on in *Le Chiendent*, pushes deliberate accumulation and continued anti-climax to the point of parody:

Les 'Meussieu', les 'Meussieu je vous dis', les 'Mais Meussieu', voltigèrent d'un bout à l'autre du compartiment, artillerie brenneuse et polie, boulets miteux et marmiteux [...]. Ces Meussieus introduisaient dans leur 'Meussieu' des abîmes de perfidie, des gouffres de raillerie, des précipices de défi et des potées lorraines de méchanceté.   (p. 13)

While a restrained and unremarkable use of imagery is not excluded, then, Queneau's more characteristic method is to undermine his figures of speech, preventing their full integration into their context, and stressing their artificiality. And this is a clear pointer to a more general suspicion of literary convention, which Queneau sees as being just as arbitrary as the language from which it is built – and just as open to deflation, change, renewal. This involves him in an attack on whatever is stale and hackneyed – which is why he is constantly to be found ridiculing any expression which could be regarded as a cliché. Des Cigales, the poet of Rueil, sets the tone: 'Mais revenons à nos mérinos (je dis mérinos pour éviter le lieu commun des moutons un peu zuzagé depuis Panurge)' (*Rueil*, p. 83); and Queneau proceeds according to this pattern throughout his work. In *Les Fleurs bleues* there is an argument over the proverb 'Il ne faut pas jeter le manche après la cognée', which highlights the absurdity of the expression (pp. 121, 123–4). In *Le Vol d'Icare* outworn aphorisms are signalled by a disdainful introductory formula, then wilfully mutilated: 'Comme il est dit quelque part, le silence est d'argent et la parole d'honneur' (p. 12); 'Comme il est dit quelque part, aux grands mots les grands remèdes' (p. 13). The process assumes another dimension in *Journal intime* with a series of nonsensical inventions:

Il y avait anguille sous roche – je suis très calée sur le chapitre des proverbes; mon prof chéri m'en faisait apprendre des tas par cœur, ou des expressions comme: 'Il en a deux comme le curé de Lisieux'; 'A pine perdue, rien d'impossible'; 'Laisser pisser le mérinos vaut mieux que chier dans la sauce'; 'Bordel pour bordel, j'aime mieux le métro, c'est plus gai et puis c'est plus chaud', etc. Quelle belle langue, tout de même, la française.
(*Sally Mara*, p. 24)

It is in *Le Dimanche de la vie* that Queneau's assault on clichés attains its greatest severity. This is the novel in which the characters 'causent' demonstrably badly, and the hackneyed expressions they employ accord well with their inaccurate use of linguistic forms. When requested to comment on her sister's physical attractions, Chantal can only offer the feeblest of platitudes: 'Ce n'est pas seulement le physique qui compte, dit Chantal, c'est le moral' (p. 14). Asked for his opinion of the apparent misalliance involving Julie's sixty-seven year old mother, 'L'amour est enfant de Bohème, répond sentencieusement le garçon' (p. 90). Elsewhere in the novel the attack is still more explicit:

On dit qu'il est toujours très intéressant de se joindre à des funérailles d'inconnu; on y fait souvent de curieuses rencontres. Valentin savait que ce n'était là qu'une de ces banalités qui s'échangent sans conviction, mais que l'usage rend parfois véritables, comme: 'sucre dans l'eau, fond s'il le faut', mais se sachant un peu désorienté, il résolut d'éprouver la créance qu'on pouvait accorder au proverbe: 'qui suit en terre, monte en train.'
(p. 82)

However, in *Le Dimanche de la vie* Queneau does not stop at singling out stale commonplaces. In symbolic terms he sanctions a continuing assault on clichés in general. It is emphasised that during his military service in Madagascar Valentin Brû was engaged in a campaign against the Hain-Tenys Merinas (see pp. 56, 81); however, the identity of these mysterious adversaries is never established in the course of the novel, and they are not the hostile natives the reader might imagine. The Hain-Tenys Merinas are in fact a part of traditional Malagasy rhetoric: they are stylised discourses performed by tribesmen in the context of a dispute, or else as an exercise in oratory, and based on the use of common proverbs.[33] In his own modest way Valentin Brû stands for the opposition to stereotyped language which is an essential characteristic of all Queneau's fiction.

Valentin also provides a neat reminder of how any literary manner – just as much as any word or phrase – is ultimately gratuitous, performing a function in its given context, but nevertheless completely dispensable. When asked to describe one of the female customers in his shop, he replies, simply:

—Hm très bien.
Valentin se méfiait des descriptions trop lyriques; sinon il aurait dit: une chouette mouquère un peu mûre avec un balcon aux pommes.   (p. 137)

Valentin thus indicates the possibility of choice – not just between synonyms or images, but between different levels of expression. And the choice Valentin makes doubtless reflects Queneau's own mistrust of the predictable and the outworn. Certainly Queneau cites with approval the avoidance of such writing among certain major modern writers, noting that 'les "morceaux de bravoure" (la tempête, le coucher de soleil, la campagne au printemps, la forêt en hiver, la chambre du héros, etc.) sont soigneusement éliminés'.[34] And this finds a precise echo in a mocking passage in Le Chiendent, which lies at the opposite extreme to any flight of lyricism:

Quatre, cinq, six gouttes d'eau. Des gens inquiets pour leur paille lèvent le blair. Description d'un orage à Paris. En été [...]. Quelques coups de tonnerre prétentieux simulent l'orage. Des gens doctes assurent que le temps était orageux et que ça rafraîchira l'atmosphère et que ça fait du bien.
(p. 15)

Essentially, what Queneau is challenging is decorum – the notion, articulated in classical literary theory and implicit in much later thinking, that certain subjects require a specific literary treatment.[35] Queneau's position is the reverse: that the writer is free to write about anything in the manner that he chooses, without any pre-existing constraints. This is the central lesson of Exercices de style, in which a minor altercation on a Paris bus is recounted in ninety-nine different ways – in

'Style noble' ('A l'heure où commencent à se gercer les doigts roses de l'aurore, je montai ...', p. 62) – quickly followed by 'Vulgaire' ('L'était un peu plus dmidi quand j'ai pu monter ...', p. 64), which makes the challenge to decorum quite explicit. There is also a verbal portrait, peasant style, and others just as 'unliterary'. For beyond the straightforward enjoyment to be derived from reading the *Exercices*, and the pleasure Queneau took in writing them,[36] they involve a relentless questioning of all preconceptions on the subject of style.

Most of the novels contain parodies of established stylistic registers. *Le Chiendent* offers mock-Homeric for the arrival of the dilapidated bus bringing the wedding-guests (pp. 173–4), pseudo-documentary for the potted history of the bilboquet (pp. 142–4), and journalese for all the events in the final section of Chapter 4 (pp. 164–8). The opening chapter of *Pierrot mon ami*, evoking the sights and sounds of the funfair at 'Uni-Park', itself combines, in quick succession, the elaborately formal ('Couples et bandes, et, plus rares, des isolés, passaient et repassaient, toujours en état de dissémination, point encore agglomérés en foules', p. 8), an emphatically non-bookish tone ('De tous les jeux [...] le Coney-Island est le plus calé', p. 9), and the precisely technical ('Débarqués de leur escalier par la force des choses, ils se virent en conséquence obligés de glisser sur la face dorsale le long d'un plan incliné soigneusement astiqué', p. 12). And again, the significance of the parodies goes beyond mere playfulness, as Roland Barthes points out in his important discussion of *Zazie dans le métro* – a novel as rich in parody as any other:

Toutes les écritures y passent: l'épique ... l'homérique ... la latine [...] la médiévale [...] la psychologie [...] la narrative [...]. Ces mêmes exemples montrent assez que, chez Queneau, la parodie a une structure bien particulière; elle n'affiche pas une *connaissance* du modèle parodié ... l'expression est ici *légère*, elle désarticule en passant, ce n'est qu'une écaille que l'on fait sauter à la vieille peau littéraire; c'est une parodie minée de l'intérieur, récelant dans sa structure même une incongruité scandaleuse.[37]

Barthes goes on to argue that Queneau, while constantly attacking literary convention, remains, paradoxically, within the bounds of the literary. And it is perhaps through an awareness of this dual stance that Queneau's style can best be understood. Queneau himself strenuously denied all accusations that he wanted to destroy, maintaining instead that his aim was always one of renewal. His own interpretation of the *Exercices de style*, strikingly close to Barthes's comments in its imagery, strikes a fitting balance:

On a voulu voir là une tentative de démolition de la littérature, ce n'était pas du tout dans mes intentions, en tout cas mon intention n'était vraiment que de faire des exercices, le résultat, c'est peut-être de décaper la littérature de ses rouilles diverses, de ses croûtes. Si j'avais pu contribuer un peu à cela, j'en serais bien fier, surtout si je l'ai fait sans ennuyer trop le lecteur.

(*Bâtons*, pp. 43–4).

Typography

If language in its various manifestations is one of the indispensable raw materials of the literary process, then the printed page is another, at least as far as post-medieval literature is concerned. Moreover print embodies immense expressive resources, even if these have generally been underused. In the edition of *Exercices de style* produced by the illustrator, Carelman, and the typographer, Massin, the latter creates typographical equivalents to Queneau's stylistic variations, varying his typefaces to match Queneau's manner. And Michel Butor, for one, clearly grasped the full significance of Massin's achievement, commenting:

A mon avis, il y a dans ce livre une leçon. Les écrivains ignorent trop comment un livre se fabrique [...]. La typographie en effet offre à l'écrivain des possibilités inépuisables, non seulement pour la disposition du texte [...] mais pour l'utilisation, dans une même page, dans une même phrase, de caractères expressifs différents.[38]

In his own writings Queneau shows a keen understanding of typography. He has pointed out, for instance, how the characters of print do not necessarily aid meaning: 'Nées d'images archaïques bien oubliées, il leur arrive donc de s'incarner de nouveau en objets arbitraires. Ou bien, tordues ou distorses, elles s'éloignent de l'aspect commun jusqu'à défier tous efforts de reconnaissance d'une quelconque perception.'[39] His experiments with pictograms show how another set of arbitrary visual symbols can function in much the same way as those used in conventional print (see *Bâtons*, pp. 275–84). At the same time Queneau recognises the rich potentialities which the printed text has to offer, and in 'Délire typographique' (*Bâtons*, pp. 285–91), an article devoted to the nineteenth-century typographer Nicolas Cirier, he notes a whole series of writers who have utilised them, beginning with Laurence Sterne, Charles Nodier and Jean-Paul Richter. 'Le romantisme', he adds, 'puis les écoles subséquentes, ont évidemment trouvé dans le fait même de l'imprimerie une *matière* d'où l'on pouvait tirer et rêveries et suggestions' (*ibid.*, pp. 285–6). Among later examples Queneau mentions the avoidance of capital letters in symbolist poetry, the distinctive use of 'points de suspension' in Céline, and the proliferation of parentheses in Raymond Roussel's *Nouvelles Impressions d'Afrique*. He also identifies two opposed tendencies in the writers he discusses, one embodied in Mallarmé's 'Un coup de dés jamais n'abolira le hasard' – 'où la matière typographique devenait élément poétique' (*ibid.* p. 286), the other typified by Apollinaire's *Calligrammes*, classical in inspiration and representional in manner. (Queneau pays further homage to the *Calligrammes* with his allusion to Apollinaire's 'Lettre-Océan' in *Le Chiendent*: 'Haute de cinq cents mètres, la falaise barrait la mer . . .' (p. 81).) And Cirier himself, the brilliantly inventive author of the calligrammatic *L'Œil typographique* and *L'apprentif Administrateur* (1840) – which uses different coloured inks as well as Greek, Arabic, Hebrew and Chinese characters, and mirror-writing – also finds his way into Queneau's fiction – in *Les Enfants du limon* (p. 250).

The typography of Queneau's own works is characterised not by the recurrent idiosyncrasies of some of his predecessors, but rather by a willingness to exploit a wide range of devices as is shown, for instance, by his use of different sorts of print. This sometimes serves to demarcate different parts of a narrative. In each chapter of *Le Chiendent*, the final section – a sequence of dreams, interior monologue or whatever – is set in italics, which stresses the fact that it is situated '*en dehors* de ce chapitre, dans une autre direction ou dimension' (*Bâtons*, p. 31). Similarly, in 'Apartés' in *Exercices de style*, italics are used to separate the asides – the narrator's personal reflections – from the story proper. In *Les Fleurs bleues*, on the other hand, they convey the clichés of a parodied fairy-tale sequence: 'Aussitôt la porte s'ouvre *comme par enchantement* et une *radieuse apparition* fait son apparition [...]. Le duc a le *souffle coupé*' (p. 102). Italics also give emphasis to a single word of particular – and sometimes obsessive – importance, as with Mme Cloche's nagging fear of her potential rivals for père Taupe's 'treasure': 'Il y a les *Autres* et les *Autres* l'inquiètent' (*Chiendent*, p. 176; see also p. 181). Capitals serve both to stress words ('En même temps, t'entends ça [...] EN MÊME TEMPS': *Zazie*, p. 53) and to restore to them something of their visual impact on fictional characters who themselves encounter them. In *Le Chiendent*, printed matter and telegrams are represented by capitals (see, for example, pp. 104, 152, 168, 266), as is the legend 'FRITES' printed on the signboard which so amuses Étienne Marcel (pp. 26, 33, 93 etc.); similarly the reader of a popular newspaper in *Pierrot mon ami* is confronted by the startling headline 'IL MORDAIT SES LAPINS PAR EXCÈS D'AMOUR' (p. 186).

Queneau also pays attention to the punctuation and disposition of sets of words, realising that this can add significantly to their expressiveness. There can, for instance, be few better ways of underlining the perfunctory and ultimately meaningless nature of the conventional conversational niceties than by running the words together, thus giving the impression of a featureless flow: 'Bonjourmeussieucommentçavacematinpasmaletvousmême' (*Chiendent*, p. 26). Similarly a monotonous voice is effectively conveyed by an abundance of hyphens: 'Est-ce-que-ça-se-man-ge-les-pois-sons-ca-ver-ni-co-les?' (*Glinglin*, p. 53) – or of commas: 'Je, ne, comprends, pas' (*Limon*, p. 268).

Other typographical conventions are put to uncommon use, and with equal effect. In *Loin de Rueil* parentheses introduce a kind of *style indirect libre*, creating an ambiguity between the hero's comments and those of the narrator; in a period of self-abnegation, Jacques l'Aumône 's'applique à se faire estamper par les commerçants (des durs ceux-là)' (p. 159); as for his adored Dominique, 'Ça lui plaisait beaucoup sinon d'être divinisée du moins qu'un amour dont elle était la cause occasionnelle (non moins qu'efficiente et que finale et que matérielle hélas!) fût exalté vers l'empire des idées pures' (p. 169). Parentheses are also used to suggest simultaneity, as in *Zazie dans le métro*: 'Qu'est-ce que (oh qu'il est mignon) t'insinues (il m'a appelée) sur mon compte (une mousmé), dirent, synchrones, Gabriel (et la veuve Mouaque), l'un avec fureur, (l'autre avec ferveur)' (p. 228). This last technique represents, perhaps, a partial solution to the problem of the linearity of language, which Queneau raised elsewhere: 'Le langage est dans le temps, il est linéaire, il est bout à bout; les mots sont les uns après les autres, aussi bien dans l'écriture que dans la parole, et on aurait quelquefois envie de pouvoir les mettre les uns à côté des autres' (*Charbonnier*, p. 13).

There are other equally unusual devices such as the ascending scale of exclamation marks: '—Le métro! beugle Gabriel, le métro!! mais le voilà!!!' (*Zazie*, p. 16), or, even more strikingly: '— Oh¡¡ (¡¡ c'est le point d'indignation)' (*Chiendent*, p. 240). The result, again, is to bring home to the reader the arbitrary nature of print – an effect which Queneau also achieves by replacing conventional punctuation by words: 'La conclusion de tout cela fut, d'un commun accord virgule deux points que les Nabonide étaient responsables des malheurs de la cité' (*Glinglin*, p. 221).

Queneau's most radical experiments, however, are perhaps those concerned with the layout of the printed page. By leaving part of a line blank, for instance, he can complement the sense of the text. This is a section following a character's tortured attempts to write:

Il traça un trait vertical,
et seules subsistèrent les impressions cénesthésiques.   (*Chiendent*, p. 121)

Like parentheses, shortened lines can also render the rhythms of speech, as in this jerky piece of dialogue in *Odile*, with Travy seeking a witness for his wedding:

—Je ne connais personne à Paris en dehors d'un oncle qui refuserait,
    bien que bienveillant.
—Et votre
il hésita
—fiancée

il sourit confus
—ne connaît personne non plus?   (p. 160)

Queneau's manipulation of layout is at its most striking in *Les Enfants du limon*, where it is regularly used to mark different elements of the narrative structure. He employs deep indentation for quotation from the work of the 'fous littéraires' or literary eccentrics whom Chambernac studies (e.g. pp. 124–7), and frequently splits the page into two halves. Queneau often uses the split page for direct quotation – as from the Bible (e.g. pp. 61, 214–16, 218), or from the Larousse dictionary (pp. 204–5), both of which, of course, are printed in columns – likewise the imagined *Who's Who* entry for Jules-Jules Limon (pp. 40–1); but the device may also have a more unusual function. It can serve, for instance, to indicate a debate going on within a character's mind, as in the case of Pouldu, discontented with his holiday at La Ciotat:

> Par-dessus le marché, on le traîne faire des piques niques parce qu'on aime la Nature.
>
> > Le seul contact véritable entre l'homme et la nature, c'est la science [...]. Voilà le contact authentique de l'homme avec la nature, celui de l'action, de la destruction et de la transformation.
>
> Mais croire aux vertus du papier gras étalé en haut d'une colline de faible hauteur au sommet de laquelle on monte par un chemin peint sur des pierres par un syndicat d'initiative – ça non.
>
> (pp. 29–30)

Interestingly, one of the 'fous littéraires' to feature in the text, J.-P. Lucas, himself presented one of his theories in two columns – one for the findings of his contemporary adversaries and the other for his own ideas (pp. 107–8).

Refinements of the same procedure suggest different levels of thought, spoken and unspoken, in a conversation. Here the whimsical Ast encounters a cynical friend, Arnolphe, who asks:

> —Quoi de nouveau donc?
> —Je suis amoureux.

                                        —Tiens, tiens l'amour se
                                        porterait-il cet hiver?

d'une femme que je ne
connais pas.

                                        —Je me disais aussi: c'est
                                        un peu simple.
                                                Que
                        tu as
            rencontrée
Où?
    —Nulle part. Je ne l'ai jamais vue. Je ne sais rien d'elle: seulement son
nom, uniquement son nom. Son adresse et son numéro de téléphone aussi
c'est vrai, mais je ne chercherai ni à la voir ni à lui parler [...]. Je l'aimerai
sans que rien vienne justifier mon amour ni en ternir la pureté.
                                        —Quelle curieuse espèce de
                                        sornettes a-t-il été décrocher
                                        là. Décidément, Ast a bien
                                        baissé ces derniers temps.
                        Dans ce cas-là
            moi
à ta place, j'aurais aimé une femme dont j'aurai même ignoré le nom, le
prénom, l'adresse et le numéro de téléphone.   (p. 43–4)

By dividing the line into sections, Queneau is able to indicate
not only the spoken dialogue, printed on the left, but also
Arnolphe's unspoken thoughts, on the right, and the transition from one to the other, in the lines beginning near the
centre of the page.

   Les Enfants du limon undoubtedly marks the high point
of Queneau's typographical experiments within his fiction –
though they do go further in other areas of his work. In the
first part of *Morale élémentaire*, for example, he expands the
technique of the split page by using three columns in such a
way that the eye is free to travel up and down or across: no
orientation is imposed and a wide variety of readings is
possible. *Morale élémentaire* is perhaps his most complete
realisation of the desire he once expressed to escape from
the constraining linearity of language, as Mallarmé had
sought to do in 'Le Livre' and 'Un coup de dés' (see
Charbonnier, p. 13). But clearly, even within his novels he
goes far enough in this direction to sharpen his reader's
awareness and appreciation of another fundamental of the
literary text.

Non-verbal communication

Queneau's championing of spoken as against written language takes many forms other than 'le néo-français'. Thus, when discussing the literary histories he edited for the *Encyclopédie de la Pléiade*, he stresses the enormous disparity between the few hundred languages which have had a written form and the three or four thousand languages which are known to have existed.[40] And it is not surprising to find that in the novels of the Saint Glinglin trilogy the history and legends of the Ville Natale are preserved by an oral tradition rather than a written one. Further, contemporary written language, for all its range and subtlety, can never completely accommodate the non-verbal qualities of what Queneau rather loosely calls 'le langage oral', and the gap between the two is a critical one:

Il faut établir une différence non seulement entre l'écrit et le parlé, mais aussi entre le parlé et ce qu'on peut appeler l'oral (bien qu'en utilisant d'autres moyens encore que la voix), le langage oral remplaçant les formes syntaxiques de l'écrit et même du parlé par des gestes, des inarticulations, des mimiques, une présence.   (*Bâtons*, pp. 88–9)

These words refer in part to the changes brought about in linguistics by the use of the tape-recorder, but Queneau is well aware of their implications for literature. Indeed he concentrates on these purely literary implications to the extent that he never really comments on non-verbal communication as a system in its own right.[41] Later in the same discussion he quotes from a letter written to him by the Latin-American novelist Alejo Carpentier, who complains that 'peu à peu, depuis les premiers romans réalistes, nous nous sommes habitués à une sorte de mécanisme du réalisme, à une sorte de fixation conventionnelle du parlé qui n'a absolument rien à voir avec le vrai parlé' (*ibid.*, pp. 90–1).

In one of his interviews with Georges Charbonnier, Queneau recalls his long-standing aim of producing a more effective notation of the actions and gestures performed during a conversation, and discusses how, in *Zazie dans le métro*, he went some way towards this by his use of parentheses (*Charbonnier*, pp. 96–7). Hence Gabriel, showing a group of tourists the sights of Paris: 'Oui, oui, dit-il aimablement. La Sainte-Chapelle (silence) (geste) un joyau de l'art gothique (geste) (silence)' (pp. 127–8). On another occasion Gabriel telephones Turandot's café to ask a favour of Charles, but gets the barmaid instead, and in the course of the ensuing dialogue actions speak just as loudly as words:

—Je vais lui demander, dit Mado Ptits-pieds.
  (un temps)
—I dit qu'i veut pas.
—Pourquoi?
—Il est fâché contre vous.
—Le con. Dis-y qu'il s'amène au bout du fil.
—Charles, cria Mado Ptits-pieds (geste).
Charles ne dit rien (geste).
Mado s'impatiente (geste).
—Alors ça vient? demande le téléphone.
—Oui, dit Mado Ptits-pieds (geste).   (p. 181)

In fact Queneau was already using this sort of device twenty or so years earlier, in *Les Enfants du limon*, where the formula *sil* denotes a pause or a silence. But in any case his treatment of 'l'oral' goes far beyond the 'stage directions' to which he specifically draws attention. In the words of Valentin Brû, 'il y a aussi les sons, les bruits, tout ce qui entre par l'oreille' (*Dimanche*, p. 176). He carefully reproduces the formulae with which speakers 'pad out' their utterances, or give them emphasis or rhythm – the 'tenez', 'quand même', 'hein', 'non mais' so common in speech but so generally ignored by novelists – as well as the sort of sentences which finish as soon as the speaker has made himself understood. (For conversations incorporating these and similar traits, see, for instance, *Pierrot mon ami*, pp. 185–7 and *Zazie dans le métro*, pp. 181–3.) He is also sensitive to ways in which speech can tend to incomprehensibility, whether attenuated through distance ('Au revoir tout le monde, qu'elle crie par la portière, et merci pour la bonne ... et merci pour l'ec ... Mais on n'entend pas le reste', *Zazie*, pp. 224–5), or, as in a notable example from *Le Chiendent*, distorted during eating:

—Vdvé houhouh iage? demande Mme Cloche, la bouche pleine.
—Comment?
—Vous d'vez êt' souvent en voyage, que j'dis.   (p. 189)

Characters frequently express themselves as much by their tone of voice and their inarticulate cries of joy, rage or pain as by their words. This tendency reaches its logical conclusion in *Exercices de style*, among which is a version called 'Interjections' which consists solely of non-verbal utterances of this kind (p. 150). And apart from 'tout ce qui entre par l'oreille', Queneau's characters display a wide range of expression which has no real connection with speech. Not only do they laugh and cry: sometimes they do both at once. In *Le Dimanche de la vie* a piece of repartee 'fit pleurire aux larmes' (p. 109). They are also endowed with a remarkable diversity of facial expressions, blushing, smiling, frowning, pouting, turning pale or green or yellow – and sometimes revealing several emotions simultaneously: 'Elle a l'air de triompher, de ricaner, de menacer. Bref, il y a toute sorte de sentiments qui cavalent sur son visage' (*Pierrot*, p. 28). It is clear that Queneau offers considerable refinements on the 'mécanisme du réalisme', the 'fixation' of dialogue of which Alejo Carpentier complained. But it is just as clear that he does not aim for a systematic transcription of sounds and gestures any more than he seeks methodically to reproduce the orthography or the grammar of 'le néo-français'. Essentially, here again, the intention is to extend and enhance his literary resources rather than to confine himself to a system of conventions.

One of the primary aspects of his exploration concerns the various degrees of interdependence between the verbal and the non-verbal, which are concisely demonstrated early in *Zazie dans le métro*, with an anxious discussion of the young heroine:

—C'est bien simple, dit Charles. Elle peut pas dire un mot, cette gosse, sans ajouter mon cul après.
—Et elle joint le geste à la parole? demanda Turandot.
—Pas encore, répondit gravement Charles, mais ça viendra.
—Ah non, gémit Turandot, ah ça non.
Il se prit la tête à deux mains et fit le futile simulacre de se la vouloir arracher.   (pp. 26)

There are words alone (in Zazie's current habit); words plus a non-verbal element (in the conduct which is predicted for her); and the abandonment of words (in Turandot's gestural reaction).[42] A comparable shift from the purely verbal to the verbal-plus-physical to the purely physical occurs in the fairground sequence at the beginning of *Pierrot mon ami*. An argument between two sets of rivals opens with an exchange of spoken – or shouted – insults: 'Les deux malfrats poursuivaient leur chemin en défiant leurs adversaires, et les injures relancées d'un groupe à l'autre croissaient à chaque réplique tant en vigueur qu'en obscénité.' At this moment of increasing tension the first transition occurs: 'Les principales fonctions physiologiques du corps humain furent invoquées par les uns comme par les autres, ainsi que différents organes situés entre le genou et la ceinture. Des gestes redonnaient force aux mots abîmés par un trop fréquent usage' (pp. 16–17). Soon after this the encounter enters its third and final phase when a fist fight breaks out. On other occasions communication – even of a relatively subtle nature – can dispense with the words altogether. In the following scene Turandot, bearing his parrot, calls on Marceline and Gabriel (who is manicuring his fingers and sipping grenadine):

Turandot entre accompagné de Laverdure. Il s'assoit sans qu'on l'en prie et pose la cage sur la table. Laverdure regarde la bouteille avec une convoitise mémorable. Marceline lui en verse un peu dans son buvoir. Turandot refuse l'offre (geste). Gabriel qui a terminé le médius attaque l'index. Avec tout ça on n'a encore rien dit.   (*Zazie*, p. 34)

In a more traditional vein, the heroes of *Odile* and *Un Rude Hiver* both turn away from words at times of personal crisis: in moments of despair the mathematician Roland Travy gives way to tears, as does Bernard Lehameau revisiting the grave of his long-dead wife: 'Il se découvrait se signait croisait les mains, mais il ne priait pas. Il ne priait pas mais ça ne l'empêchait pas de pleurer. Il pleurait le corps immobile, sans hoquets, ni sanglots, comme il en avait l'habitude. Il pleurait ainsi pendant une dizaine de minutes' (*Rude Hiver*, p. 160).

But if in some cases speech is superfluous – or impossible – there is no implication that non-verbal means of communication are necessarily more valid. On occasion they are indecipherable: 'Quant au père Taupe, il se confine dans un silence souriant dont on ne saurait dire s'il mime la dignité ou s'il exprime l'abrutissement' (*Chiendent*, p. 181). Sometimes characters make gestures which are to all intents and purposes meaningless conventions, as in the case of the star of a silent film performing 'un grand geste purement décoratif qui zèbre l'écran de toute la promesse de rares aventures' (*Rueil*, p. 39). Perhaps the best example of ritual of this sort occurs in *Le Dimanche de la vie* when the heroine is visited by her brother-in-law and they exchange the obligatory embrace. The scene is described with mannered ingenuousness:

> Chaque fois qu'ils se voyaient, en bon beau-frère et en bonne belle-sœur qu'ils étaient, ils se déposaient mutuellement sur les deux joues des bécots sonores. Cette opération permettait donc d'entendre par quatre fois le même bruit que celui que font les flèches eurêka que l'on détache des cibles. Une coutume identique précédait la séparation.   (p. 45)

Queneau distinguishes not only between different degrees of significance in non-verbal communication, but also between the different levels of sincerity it can involve. He does so most of all by emphasising the gap between spontaneous, involuntary expression and expression which is deliberately contrived to produce a desired effect. Very often, of course, characters will display their feelings quite naturally by their facial expressions, or their tears, or their laughter, as in *Journal intime* when Sally and her family roll around in helpless mirth for five minutes 'sans pouvoir nous empêcher de rire' (*Sally Mara*, p. 73). But equally, physical manifestations of this sort may be a less than genuine expression of feeling: 'Navrée, Zazie se mit à pleurer. Elle y prit un si vif plaisir qu'elle alla s'asseoir sur un banc pour y larmoyer avec plus de confort' (*Zazie*, p. 58).

Idiosyncratic mannerisms serve as a convenient shorthand means of characterisation. The most familiar of these is doubtless the way in which Marceline, Gabriel's apparently very feminine wife in *Zazie dans le métro*, accomplishes her every act 'doucement' (at least, until her true identity is revealed when, at the end of the novel, 'Marceline' becomes Marcel). But there are many similar cases, such as the timid Charles, who regularly averts his eyes from the person to whom he is talking; or Purpulan, in *Les Enfants du limon*, disposed much more to gesture than to speaking and frequently revealing his embarrassment in blushes. Above all there are the characters in *Le Dimanche de la vie*: Julie, scornful and lascivious, who makes most of her conversation 'en ricanant' and who is generally to be seen sitting 'les jambes écartées'; her sister Chantal, with her interminable habit of flicking her hair back 'fémininement' or 'coquettement'; and the over-hearty sergeant, Bourrelier, who always greets Valentin Brû with a forceful tap on the shoulder.

Almost all Queneau's characters, in fact, have some significant non-verbal element in their make-up. But there is one who seems to exist almost entirely outside the domain of words. This is Jean-sans-Tête, also from *Le Dimanche de la vie*. He could be described as a simpleton – or perhaps as the village idiot of the tightly-knit community living in and around the rue de la Brèche-aux-Loups in the twelfth arrondissement of Paris, where Valentin Brû comes to live and sets up his shop. Jean-sans-Tête is one of a number of vagrants who profit from Valentin's charity; but whereas the others are mere beggars, Jean has wares to peddle – and the nature of these wares is a first indication of the importance Queneau attaches to him. For Jean-sans-Tête is a seller of brooms – a 'porteur de balais de jonc' – and the broom is one of Queneau's most cherished personal emblems.[43] But Jean has a more fundamental importance. On the verbal level he is barely capable of any communication, for he has at his disposal only a tiny stock of words – or snippets of words – which he supplements with his own characteristic mumble: 'Pra, pra, pra, pra, pra'. Yet in broader terms his capacity for self-expression – and understanding – is shown to be exceptionally high. He first appears at a time when Valentin is becoming involved in a profound, quasi-Hegelian meditation on the nature of time and history. And despite his lack of words, Jean – and he alone – whether by intuition or by empathy, is able to follow Valentin's thoughts, nodding his head 'compréhensivement' and making himself clearly understood by dumb-show, so that Valentin, not surprisingly, is 'touché par cet intermède qui témoignait de l'intêret profond que son interlocuteur prenait pour ses tentatives temporelles' (p. 176). The two sequences in which Valentin

and Jean converse together make a telling contrast with the
affected gestures, hypocritical exchanges and empty 'bécots
sonores' to be found in the rest of *Le Dimanche de la vie*; and
Jean-sans-Tête stands as perhaps Queneau's most memorable symbol of the real virtues of non-verbal communication.

Despite its potentially serious implications, however,
Queneau's non-verbal communication is, finally, characterised by a sense of fun, of the sheer pleasure of conveying
something – even the unlikeliest message by the unlikeliest of
means. And this is never truer than in *Pierrot mon ami*, during
a delightful fantasy sequence in which the hero, with two
agreeable and sympathetic companions, sets off to drive a
lorry-load of circus animals down to the south of France.
After several hours (and several pages) they stop at an inn
and Pierrot orders lunch:

> Pour moi des tripes, pour monsieur (il désigna Mésange) un gigot
> flageolets – Ça te va? lui demanda-t-il, (Mésange donna quelques petits
> coups de poing sur la table en signe d'évidente approbation) – et pour lui
> (Pierrot désigna Pistolet), une bonne soupe avec des croûtons et des
> navets, double portion: il est végétarien. Pas vrai, vieux frère, demanda-t-
> il à Pistolet qui ne répondit pas, indifférent sans doute à ce genre de
> qualification.   (p. 162)

It is only at this point that the reader is given to understand
that Mésange and Pistolet are themselves animals (the
former a monkey, the latter a boar). However, this presents
no obstacle to the trio's enjoyment of their travels – or of
each other's company – and Queneau's delight in the possibilities of the situation reaches its peak that evening at dinner
when Pierrot has to make an important explanation: 'Il fit
alors à Mésange une série de signes, de l'œil et de la main.
L'autre comprit admirablement (mais que ne peut-on expliquer par gestes? quel luxe superfétatoire que l'emploi des
cordes vocales! – à de telles hauteurs s'éleva lors la pensée de
Pierrot)' (pp. 172–3).

Queneau's achievement in developing the potentialities of
literary communication is an immense one; and just as he
indicates his spiritual ancestry, from Monnier and Rictus
and Joyce, to Cirier and Mallarmé, to the oral traditions, so he
leaves his own legacy, as can be seen in the work of inheritors

adapting spoken French in their own way, such as Alphonse Boudard or Christiane Rochefort, or, say, breaking out of the restrictions of conventional typography, like Jacques Derrida in *Glas*. All the time, moreover, the same salutary lesson is being reaffirmed: 'L'œuvre a un sens universel, mais elle dépend d'un élément particulier précis sans lequel elle ne saurait avoir, bien évidemment, aucune existence' (*Voyage*, p. 182). Any reading of Queneau reinforces the axiom that language is the indispensable raw material of literature: that literature exists only as a function of language. One critic of *Zazie dans le métro* conveys the experience particularly aptly:

Le livre lu, on pense 'c'est la réalité même'. Et, simultanément, 'le monde ici représenté est purement verbal'. Les deux sentiments sont justes. Il s'agit bien d'un monde réel. Mais ce monde ne tire sa réalité que de l'emploi d'un certain langage [. . .]. Le monde n'y a d'existence que dans le verbe des hommes.[44]

Extreme cases, such as the individual pieces of word-play to which Queneau gives the title 'Foutaises',[45] which have more or less total autonomy and constitute, as it were, minimal works of literature, or his work in 'Oulipo' – the Ouvroir de la Littérature Potentielle[46] – such as lipograms (passages written so as to avoid a particular letter of the alphabet), can function as an elaboration of language devoid of serious outside reference. But this is never true of Queneau's other works, where the information content is immeasurably higher, and language and content are interlocked at all points, so that a modification of the one, however minute, would inevitably involve a modification of the other. These works inevitably amount to more than mere verbal texture, and it is clear that Queneau's linguistic dexterity relies on the context of the words he uses. Even in *Exercices de style*, where language obviously takes precedence over content, information – albeit of the most banal kind – is being communicated.[47] The importance of language is both primary and crucial, yet it does not exclude other considerations; 'Ce n'est certes là qu'un aspect de l'existence littéraire, un sens partiel – il y en a d'autres' (*Voyage*, p. 182).

2 Form

Theory, practice and beyond

THE INDISPENSABLE RAW MATERIAL for Queneau's novels is language – the complex body of sounds and symbols which makes up the major vehicle of human communication. But, for Queneau, a mere accumulation of words could never qualify as literature in the fullest sense of the word: the raw material has to be ordered, shaped, processed. Another of his constant refrains is that the mature literary work cannot exist without careful attention to its formal construction: 'J'ai toujours pensé qu'une œuvre littéraire devait avoir une structure et une forme' (*Charbonnier*, p. 47). Moreover here, as with his views on language, he can be observed taking up his position in reaction to circumstances prevailing at the beginning of his writing career. In his early occasional writings after his break with Surrealism, he frequently attacks the Surrealists' attempts to capture the workings of the subconscious – to which he scornfully refers as 'inspiration', and which he finds both unacceptably haphazard and, often, extremely banal (see 'Lyrisme et poésie', 'Le plus et le moins' and 'Les horizons perdus', in *Le Voyage en Grèce*, pp. 112–21, 122–9, 144–50). He also deprecates the tendency of a writer such as Julien Green in his *Journal*, to publish as literature mere fragments and jottings (see 'Drôles de goûts', *ibid.*, pp. 137–42). More to the point, Queneau is dissatisfied with the shapelessness of the traditional novel, as he makes clear in the article 'Technique du roman':

Alors que la poésie a été la terre bénie des rhétoriqueurs et des faiseurs de règles, le roman, depuis qu'il existe, a échappé à toute loi. N'importe qui

peut pousser devant lui comme un troupeau d'oies un nombre indéterminé de personnages apparemment réels à travers une lande longue d'un
nombre indéterminé de pages ou de chapitres. Le résultat, quel qu'il soit,
sera toujours un roman.   (*Bâtons*, p. 27)

In contrast, he praises Proust's rigorous construction in *A la recherche du temps perdu* (*ibid.*, pp. 223–8), and the way in which Joyce organises every detail of his later texts according to a predetermined strategy (*Voyage*, p. 133). For Queneau there is no question of leaving the composition of his novels to chance; rather, it is the author's responsibility to invent structures which have their own internal coherence and necessity. He seeks to create novels much as medieval bards wrote their *rondeaux* and Renaissance poets their sonnets – that is, by the application of fixed shapes or patterns. This explains one of his best-known remarks, 'Je n'ai jamais vu de différences essentielles entre le roman, tel que j'ai envie d'en écrire, et la poésie' (*Bâtons*, p. 43) – which allows Claude Simonnet to argue plausibly that Queneau's first literary priority is an aesthetic one, deriving from 'un sens artisanal de l'œuvre bien faite qui donne à celle-ci consistance et objectivité'.[1]

Queneau's aim, of course, is not to dictate terms to other novelists, but merely to satisfy his own compelling need for form. While recognising that, in the 1930s anyway, most others were far more casual in their approach, he declared himself unable to 'm'incliner devant un pareil laisser-aller' (*ibid*, p. 28). 'Technique du roman' is a detailed account of how, in his first three novels, he set about avoiding this laxity, while at the same time acknowledging his debt to English-language novelists such as Joyce, from whom he had learned the possibility of technical rigour. The article also serves as a useful point of access to Queneau's technique in his later works. As regards *Le Chiendent*, *Gueule de pierre* and *Les Derniers Jours*, he isolates particular ways in which he imposes pattern and order; notably circularity, number, and the organisation of characters.

Circular patterns.   Since the three novels are, for Queneau, variants on a common theme,[2] they share a similar structure:

Dans le premier, le cercle se referme et rejoint exactement son point de départ: ce qui est suggéré, peut-être grossièrement, par le fait que la dernière phrase est identique à la première. Dans le second, le mouvement circulaire ne retrouve pas son point de départ, mais un point homologue, et forme un arc d'hélice: le signe final du Zodiaque, les Poissons, ne se situe pas sur le même plan que les poissons-bêtes. Dans le troisième enfin, le cycle n'est plus que saisonnier, en attendant que les saisons disparaissent: le cercle se brise dans une catastrophe: ce que le personnage central dit explicitement dans le dernier chapitre.   (*Bâtons*, pp. 28–9)

The last-mentioned, *Les Derniers Jours*, follows the cycles of the seasons over the three academic years of Vincent Tuquedenne's student career in Paris to a *dénouement* in which all the major characters have disappeared, through death or departure, leaving only Alfred, the immobile centre of a turning world, to comment on their passing (pp. 229–33). *Gueule de pierre* rotates from the aquarium fish studied by Pierre at the beginning to a sequence of passages linking events of the novel with the signs of the zodiac – and ending with Pisces. *Le Chiendent*, however, is doubtless the most striking as well as the most explicit example, beginning and ending as it does in the same say: 'La silhouette d'un homme se profila; simultanément des milliers, il y en avait bien des milliers.' Within the body of the novel there are hints of a return to the point of departure and a consequent abolition of the intervening time; 'Qu'ils soient brûlés et qu'ils renaissent de leur cendre' writes Saturnin of the potential readers of his book (p. 279); the modest happiness of the *brocanteur*, père Taupe, who wants to live as far withdrawn as possible from the outside world is an 'idéal de fœtus' (p. 93). And the final section, with its *dramatis personae*, Madame Cloche, Saturnin and Étienne, the survivors of an apocalyptic war, hinges on the notion of return and renewal through the attempt to 'éponger le temps et r'mettre ça' (p. 295). Indeed the final sentences send the reader back not simply to the beginning of the text but to the *prière d'insérer* which precedes it: 'Comment tout cela peut-il finir? C'est bien simple, cela ne finit pas et tout recommence, aussi lugubre et dérisoire qu'à la première page, à peu de chose près.' Which not only negates the impetus of the text as the reader has read it, but also severely compromises the possibility of any new beginnings. The whole notion of irrevers-

ible events, and of the possibility of permanent change –
generally seen as essential to narrative[3] – are thrown into
doubt, while it is simultaneously made clear that, in
Queneau's fiction anyway, the author's control extends over
the entire narrative structure.

'Technique du roman', written in 1937, could cover only
the earliest texts, but Queneau's use of circularity continues
in his later work. The whole of *Saint Glinglin*, not simply
Gueule de pierre, sustains the pattern, through the
movement from the endless fine weather which the con-
servative Ville Natale enjoys initially, thence to the endless
rain, which coincides with and parallels the incursion of
foreign influences, and finally back to its lost paradise of 'le
temps, le beau temps, le beau temps fixe'. And other novels
have their own variations on the theme: *Pierrot mon ami*
takes its unassuming hero through a puzzling adventure,
but leaves him at the end as bereft as before the story began,
save for the conviction that a cycle has been completed:
'C'était un des épisodes de sa vie les plus ronds, les plus
complets, les plus autonomes' (p. 210); *Le Dimanche de la vie*
ends, as it starts, with Julie discovering a Valentin Brû
entirely unaware of her presence; in *Zazie dans le métro* the
first and last scenes are set on the same platform of the Gare
d'Austerlitz. However, significantly, in the final words of this
novel the young heroine announces that as a result of her
weekend in Paris she has grown older. In other words,
circularity does not necessarily negate linear progress as
unequivocally as in *Le Chiendent*: the very presence of
pattern, rather than its possible meaning, is sometimes what
counts most.

Numbers. Whereas the use of the circle serves to impose
order on the shape of the narrative as a whole, number is in
the first instance a means of patterning the formal divisions
of texts; as Queneau explains, 'il m'a été insupportable de
laisser au hasard le soin de fixer le nombre des chapitres de
ces romans'. Instead he bases his construction on numbers
chosen quite arbitrarily or because they have some special
significance for him. His explanation reveals the full extent
of his numerical predilections:

Le Chiendent se compose de 91 (7 × 13) sections, 91 étant la somme des treize premiers nombres et sa 'somme' étant 1, c'est donc, à la fois le nombre de la mort des êtres et celui de leur retour à l'existence, retour que je ne concevais alors que comme la perpétuité irrésoluble du malheur sans espoir. En ce temps-là, je voyais dans 13 un numéro bénéfique parce qu'il niait le bonheur; quant à 7, je le prenais, et puis le prends encore comme image numérique de moi-même, puisque mon nom et mes deux prénoms se composent chacun de sept lettres et que je suis né un 21 (3 × 7).

(Bâtons, p. 29)

Numerical organisation, too, features widely in the rest of Queneau's work – and generally with the same numbers that are privileged in *Le Chiendent*. *Saint Glinglin* consists of seven parts; *Les Fleurs bleues* of twenty-one chapters.[4] Each of the 'books' making up *Les Enfants du limon* has twenty-one chapters, too, and here the artificiality of this structure is the more evident for, say, the complete narrative continuity between Chapters XXVIII and XXIX, and for the brevity of Chapter CXXV, which consists simply of the words 'Chambernac fuyait.' Furthermore, this patterning extends to the smaller units of narrative. It has been demonstrated, for example, that the individual chapters of *Le Chiendent* tend to have a ternary rhythm such that each can be divided into three groups of four sections (given that, as already seen, the final section remains separate and is demarcated from the rest typographically).[5] In the first chapter, the first four sections deal with the 'silhouette' and the 'observer', the next four with the entry of Narcense and the final four with Mme Cloche; chapter two comprises a first group concerned with the burial of Narcense's grandmother, a second leading up to the hanging incident at Les Mygales, and a third actually describing it.

Number can govern the very events and characters, as well as the formal organisation of the text – hence the presence of seven Irish rebels in the Eden Quay post office in *On est toujours trop bon avec les femmes*, which corroborates Queneau's claim that 'mon goût pour les chiffres' also underlay texts which were ostensibly without formal rigour (cf. *Bâtons*, p. 42). In *Les Fleurs bleues*, which has a time-scheme of precisely seven centuries, spanning as it does the years 1264, 1439, 1614, 1789 and 1964 in a series of 175-year leaps, Cidrolin's barge bears the number twenty-one and thus recalls the chapters of the novel. Many characters in *Pierrot mon ami* have names beginning in 'm' – the thirteenth letter of the alphabet – and of these, Mounnezergues and the brothers Mouilleminche have names of thirteen letters – the same number as the title of the novel. Here again, though, *Le Chiendent* shows Queneau's technique at its most fully developed. The first chapter is particularly rich in examples.[6] The period covered by the action is exactly seven days (Monday to Sunday inclusive), and during this time seven principal characters are introduced – to be reviewed in the final section: Étienne, Alberte, Théo, Pierre, Mme Cloche, Narcense and Belhôtel.[7] Seven unforeseen encounters take place: between Pierre and his brother, Narcense and Potice, Pierre and Narcense, then Pierre and Étienne; Étienne also meets Mme Cloche, then the Belhôtel couple, and Théo chances upon Narcense. The number even governs the disposition of anonymous minor figures, so that, for instance, Pierre Le Grand finds himself as one of seven customers in the café where he waits for Étienne:

Ce jour-là, son voisin de droite, étouffant sans arrêt, buvait une potion jaunâtre à même une petite bouteille; le meussieu de gauche se grattait distraitement les parties génitales en lisant le résultat des courses. Au sud-ouest, un couple se couplait devant un raphaël-citron. Au sud-sud-ouest, une dame seule; au sud-sud-est, une autre dame seule. Au sud-est, une table exceptionnellement vide.   (pp. 10–11)[8]

Organization of characters. 'Pas plus que le reste, la répartition des personnages ne doit être laissée au hasard, car toute une partie de leur sens dépend d'elle' (*Bâtons*, p. 32). Queneau offers no explanation of how this is put into practice in *Le Chiendent*, apparently for fear of giving an illusion of excessive rigidity; however it has been clearly pointed out that the most of the *dramatis personae* can be resolved into pairs of various sorts: Étienne links with Pierre Le Grand, by virtue of their simultaneous appearance and development at the beginning of the novel, and through their alliance aiming at possession of père Taupe's door; equally, however, Étienne forms a pair with Saturnin at the end of the novel, when they are opposed to a Mme Cloche metamorphosed into the 'reine des Étrusques'. Even the most insignificant of characters are explicitly deployed in this way, so that of the four girls being driven by Shiboleth to his nightclub, 'deux d'entre elles devraient y faire un numéro de danse, les deux autres n'avaient pour mérite que de coucher avec lui' (p. 132).[9] In *Gueule de pierre*, on the other hand 'tous s'ordonnent selon les lignes de force créées par ces deux pôles: la triplicité des fils (Paul, Pierre et Jean) et la triplicité des règnes' (*Bâtons*, p. 32) – i.e. the animal, vegetable and mineral realms, with which the characters are variously identified. Equally, three merchants in the Ville Natale – Machut, Carqueux and Mandace – correspond to the three counsellors – Nostril, Saint-Pair and Choumaque – who appear in parallel sections in the second part of the novel: and the actions of the young Vincent Tuquedenne and of the ageing Tolut mirror each other in Chapters XXIII and XXV of *Les Derniers Jours*, where, similarly, Rohel parallels another of the older figures, Brabbant, and all the other characters – apart from the pivotal Alfred – also form pairs. Essentially, 'deux personnages ou deux groupes, distincts mais cependant autonomes, peuvent exprimer une même réalité, une même tendance, un même type' (*ibid.*, p. 33). In this regard, too, *Odile* belies its apparent lack of formal rigour. There are two major groups of characters – the artists of the Anglarès circle and the small-time criminals; and the central character, Travy, is linked to each by an acquaintance from his army days – respectively G... and S.... Travy and Odile, whose love affair the novel describes, form a pair in the first place because they are alone among the major characters in not being completely identified with one or other of the main groups. Perhaps the most notable pairing is that of the duc d'Auge and Cidrolin in *Les Fleurs bleues* – the one moving through history with his retinue and his talking horses, the other generally immobile on his barge moored on the Seine. They have the same names: Joachim, Olinde, Anastase, Crépinien, Honorat, Irénée, Médéric; each has three daughters who are triplets; the duke's château is near le pont de l'Arche, while Cidrolin's barge is called 'L'Arche'. The duke tries his hand at painting murals and Cidrolin emerges, eventually, as the author of the graffiti scrawled on his fence. Both men drink 'l'essence de fenouil', both have voracious appetites, and both, when denied the chance of satisfying their hunger, habitually use the expression 'encore un de foutu'. For much of the novel, it seems that one of the two may be merely the creation of the other's dreams, since the action switches between them, but towards the end the duke meets Cidrolin; their identities, if complementary, remain to some degree separate.[10] In any case here, as much as anywhere else, Queneau creates the impression of a formalised dance, with his characters as dancers, moving not according to their own instincts, but in conformity with some predetermined pattern. And he is no less rigorous in arranging their movements – their entrances and exits – during the course of the novel: 'A mon sens, il ne saurait pas [...] être question de laisser se démener les personnages d'un roman comme des homunculi échappés de leurs bocaux brisés' (*Bâtons*, p. 32). He notes with approval the tight construction of Faulkner's *Sanctuary*, and in particular the strict alternation which governs the appearances of its characters (*Charbonnier*, p. 50). He uses a similar procedure himself in *Le Chiendent*, where, for example, Étienne Marcel appears and disappears – very literally – in the first and last chapters, while Bébé Toutout, a secondary figure, appears first in the second chapter, and reappears, as the symmetry requires, in the penultimate chapter. In some of his other novels, where characters' movements are less precisely measured, Queneau still makes a point of re-assembling the major figures at or near, the end: in *Le Dimanche de la vie*, the four principals, Julia, her sister Chantal, brother-in-law Paul and husband Valentin are, as it were, convened in the unlikely location of Toulouse station; the final major scene of *Zazie dans le métro* at the brasserie 'Aux Nyctalopes' brings together the main figures of that novel; in *Loin de Rueil* a similar effect is achieved through the device of the film which Jacques l'Aumône's family sees at the very end of the narrative and which shows Jacques himself reliving his past life.

As well as being limited to the small group of works Queneau had published before 1937, 'Technique du roman' gives only a sample of the devices whereby Queneau avoids shapelessness in narrative. Elsewhere, in interviews, he expands significantly on the identification of novel and poem, declaring: 'On peut faire rimer des situations ou des personnages comme on fait rimer des mots, on peut même se contenter d'allitérations' (*Bâtons*, p. 42), or again: 'S'il y a des répétitions, c'est volontaire [...]. Certains mots, certaines phrases doivent se répéter dans le courant du livre.'[11] And indeed, most novels have their rhymes and repetitions. The very structure of *Loin de Rueil* depends on these, rhyming as it does the scene at the end with the young Michou watching his father, Jacques l'Aumône, in a cowboy film ('Poursuites, coups de revolver, jeunes filles blondes et bottées enlevées par des traîtres bruns et bottés', pp. 228–9), and Jacques' own childhood visit to the cinema early in the book, with its seemingly identical western (pp. 38–43). On a smaller scale, in *Les Derniers Jours*, a seemingly casual reference to a mock blinding carried out as a student prank (pp. 49–50) is echoed by a real blinding described during an account of a street fight (p. 78) and then amplified in an incident in which one of the characters blinds another (p. 88). The process also extends to particular words and phrases, running through sequences, chapters, and whole texts. These may be simple personal refrains, like those of Zazie and Laverdure; but often they prove far more pervasive, particularly in the last novels. In *Les Fleurs bleues* for instance, there are three versions of Cidrolin's warnings to visitors attempting to board his barge from the slippery bank (pp. 141, 181, 227–8), and whole sequences of a conversation can recur, as when Cidrolin and his family discuss the merits of television (pp. 58–9, p. 61). Cidrolin actually draws attention to this, commenting 'Il me semble que ça recommence, que j'ai déjà entendu tout ça autre part.' However lest it should be thought that repetition is by definition a failing, Queneau adds a sequence soon afterwards in which Auge is accused of unconsciously repeating himself, and he replies, unanswer- ably that 'la répétition est l'une des plus odoriférantes fleurs de la rhétorique' (p. 65). Indeed, *Les Fleurs bleues* as a whole reads as an intricate tissue of echoes and cross-references, and yet another proof of the author's conscious control of his creation.[12] A further application of the rhymes and repe- titions is to be seen in Queneau's use of leitmotive, whereby his texts are pervaded by objects which, again, serve to

indicate the deliberate organisation underlying the surface of
the narrative. Queneau's private mythology of symbols,
beginning with the 'chêne' and the 'chien' which he saw as
the two possible Norman derivations of his own name, have
been studied in detail.[13] The frequent references to these
(few novels, if any, are without a canine element, if only a
'chien de faïence' in *Un Rude Hiver*, p. 42), to 'fleurs bleues'
(not only in the novel of this title, but also in others from *Le
Chiendent*, p. 178 to *Zazie dans le métro*, p. 172), or to the
'poissons' of Queneau's birth-sign (*Les Derniers Jours*, p. 8;
Odile, p. 34) or the 'sardines' (almost everywhere, and
especially *Loin de Rueil*, pp. 38, 57, 105, 228) can give rise to
ulterior meanings, but in the first instance their very existence, as indications of the author's presence, like the private
symbols which figure in artists' paintings, is its own justification.

There are also reasons for believing that other personal
signatures are deliberately hidden within the texts.[14] Given
the play of appearance and reality underlying *Le Chiendent*
from the very beginning ('cette oscillation n'était qu'une
apparence; en *réalité*, le plus court chemin d'un labeur à un
sommeil . . .', p. 7; my italics), it is certainly possible to read
into an ostensibly casual observation – 'même un mégot
cache sa vérité' (p. 148) – a hidden 'ego' who is none other
than the author, and the hypothesis is strengthened by the
recurrence of the 'mégot' (e.g. pp. 11, 15, 269). Similarly if
the world of the novel is like a 'jeu de cache-cache' (p. 148),
could it not bear the mark of the 'je' who created it? Moreover, an author who takes pleasure in dispensing the
elements of his name in an overt fashion, as in the poem 'Don
Evané Marquy'[15] may well be hiding in Saturnin's mocking
letter to Pierre Le Grand and Étienne ('Vous voilà quinauds
(vivent les quinauds! vivent les quinauds!)') (p. 250) or in
the frequent instances when shoes are called, not 'chaussures', 'souliers' or 'godasses', but 'croquenots' (e.g. pp. 178,
208, 222, 281).

It is however at points such as these – where Queneau's
devices are not, to say the least, readily apparent – that their
scope is easiest to define. For serving, as they do, as a personal
guide to the author in the process of construction, they are

not, in the first instance, intended for the audience. Certainly
there is no indication that his early readers were fully aware
of them; Queneau sometimes went as far as expressing the
hope that they should remain invisible: 'J'espère que ça ne se
voit pas. Ce serait affreux si ça se voyait',[16] and at least one
later critic would seem to have sustained this hope as late as
the 1960s, by complaining of 'his total disregard of the
structure of his novels'.[17] However Queneau also recognised
that for a modern readership the construction of Le Chiendent, for example, might well be apparent. In any case,
although patterns of number and rhyme play an important
role in Queneau's fiction, it is important to add that they are
by no means a constant feature of it. If early novels, such as Le
Chiendent and Gueule de pierre, or the more recent Les Fleurs
bleues contain numerous examples of circular structures,
numerical patterning and rhymes, other works show little or
no trace of them. In short, like most of Queneau's technical
preoccupations, they are subject to a good deal of fluc-
tuation. As regards his constructions based on number, he
admitted: 'Mes premiers livres étaient conditionnés par des
soucis d'ordre, je ne dirai pas mathématisant, mais arith-
momaniaque, et aussi par un souci de structure [...].
Ensuite, je pense que je me suis dégagé de cette arithmo-
manie' (Charbonnier, p. 56). Similarly, he indicated that he
gradually came to relax his grip on his characters, to allow
them more 'autonomy' in their development (ibid., p. 54).

If the fixed patterns – overt or not – are essentially guides
for Queneau, imposing an internal necessity on the shape of
narrative, another aspect of his technique stands out precisely because it draws the reader's attention to itself and thus
emphasises its own artificiality. Queneau may disguise his
name in various ways in Le Chiendent, but he is far more
obvious elsewhere, as in Loin de Rueil, where the film La Peau
des rêves, which recapitulates the life-story of the novel's hero,
is a production of 'la Ramon Curnough Company' (p. 228).
In Les Enfants du limon he even makes a 'personal appearance', when Chambernac, having failed to find a publisher
for the manuscript of his Encyclopédie des sciences inexactes, has
a chance meeting with a bespectacled individual in his
thirties who introduces himself as 'Queneau' (p. 315). Zazie

dans le métro has a much-quoted passage which stresses the artificial nature of the narrative by both its content and its manner. It comes during Gabriel's oration at the foot of the Eiffel Tower:

Paris n'est qu'un songe, Gabriel n'est qu'un rêve (charmant), Zazie le songe d'un rêve (ou d'un cauchemar) et toute cette histoire le songe d'un songe, le rêve d'un rêve, à peine plus qu'un délire tapé à la machine par un romancier idiot (oh! pardon).   (p. 120)

And interventions of this sort are a frequent feature even of *Le Chiendent*, when the narrator, affecting concern about the accuracy of his enumeration, interposes 'voyons-voir si je n'oublie rien' (p. 22), or when, in a description of the suburbs, he abruptly undermines his own flight of fantasy: 'Chez "Sam Suffi", un chien marmiteux aboie d'une voix indigente; à "Mon-Repos", un canard hurle parce qu'il vient de se casser la patte en faisant du trapèze volant (c'est pas vrai)' (p. 119).

This deliberate flaunting of artifice is also to be seen in the organisation of events, for beyond the covert patterns already discussed, Queneau seeks other ways of emphasising his control. Thus Pierrot, driving south from Paris with his consignment of animals, is forever meeting people who know Uni-Park, where he used to work, and he finally draws the obvious conclusion: 'Décidément, se dit Pierrot, on a fait exprès d'en semer la route, des gens qui ont vécu dans ce coinstot' (pp. 170–1). Chance, in other words, is manifestly the result of the author's wishes – as is even more explicit in the case of Mme Cloche, witnessing two road accidents near the Gare du Nord: 'Par une série de hasards soigneusement préparés, elle se trouva assise, vers la même heure, en face du même endroit, à la terrasse d'un café qu'une bienheureuse coïncidence avait justement placé là' (*Chiendent*, p. 28).

The whole reflexive tendency in Queneau's fiction is summed up in his use of the Gidian technique of *mise en abyme*. In *Loin de Rueil* this takes the form of the film *La Peau des rêves*, described at the very end of the novel and resuming the events of Jacques l'Aumône's life, with which the rest of the book has been concerned. In *Le Chiendent* the ninety-one sections into which the text is divided are mirrored both by a seemingly gratuitous reference to Mme Cloche's address 'au

quatre-vingtonze d'la rue Paradis', (p. 249) and by the
ninety-one positions in which Narcense and Saturnin try to
place the door they have stolen from père Taupe (p. 259).
The importance of this becomes clear when Saturnin,
seeing no further use for the door, smashes it into pieces,
thus symbolically negating the central plot of the novel,
which has consisted precisely in a frenzied and elaborate
treasure-hunt involving most of the characters, and with the
door as its object. The epigraph to *Zazie dans le métro* is a
quotation from Aristotle: 'Ho plasas ēphanisen', meaning
'he who fabricated it destroyed it'[18] – which, as has been
pointed out,[19] would apply equally well to *Le Chiendent*,
Pierrot mon ami or indeed other novels which carry the same
reflexive emphasis.

Gerald Prince seizes on the allusion to Aristotle to
support his sweeping claim that 'l'œuvre romanesque de
Queneau, du *Chiendent* jusqu'aux *Fleurs bleues*, est placée
sous le signe de l'anti-roman'.[20] Prince accumulates other
evidence of the tendency to 'stand on their heads' the traditional components of the novel, like the playful disclaimer
at the beginning of *Le Dimanche de la vie*: 'Les personnages
de ce roman étant réels, toute ressemblance avec des individus imaginaires serait fortuite.' However, his argument is
flawed on the one hand by over-generalisation, and on the
other by the unduly selective approach which leads Prince
to exclude from consideration a large number of texts
(*Odile*, *Un Rude Hiver*, *Chêne et Chien*, the Sally Mara
books) which resist the 'anti-novel' stereotype. In other
words, while it is obviously useful to set Queneau's work
against traditional procedures, there can be little virtue in
obscuring the variety of his output, or denying its more
conventional aspects. Roland Barthes, in his essay on *Zazie
dans le métro*, strikes a more convincing balance. He duly
notes that Queneau zealously subverts many conventions,
but first he makes the preliminary – and too easily over-
looked – point that *Zazie* is by any standards a 'well-made'
novel:

On y trouve toutes les 'qualités' que la critique aime à recenser et à louer:
la construction, de type classique, puisqu'il s'agit d'un épisode temporel
limité (une grève); la durée, de type épique, puisqu'il s'agit d'un itinér-

aire, d'une suite de stations; l'objectivité (l'histoire est racontée du point de
vue de Queneau); la distribution des personnages (en héros, personnages
secondaires et comparses); l'unité du milieu social et du décor (Paris); la
variété et l'équilibre des procédés de narration (récit et dialogue). Il y a là
toute la technique du roman français, de Stendhal à Zola.[21]

In the light of this judgement, which, moreover, concerns
what Prince would take as one of Queneau's most exemplary
anti-novels, it is surely safer to avoid over-simple classification, and to recognise instead that Queneau, regarding
novelistic technique as being arbitrary, is as likely to adopt
existing conventions as to bring them into question. Thus
the troubling anonymity of the early pages of *Le Chiendent* is
an obvious challenge to characterisation; and some characters behave in unpredictable, contradictory, even inexpli-
cable ways, whence, say, the deathbed philosophising of the
unsophisticated young waitress, Ernestine, in *Le Chiendent*,
or Gabriel's altogether unexpected metaphysical speculations in *Zazie dans le métro*. Equally, the problem of
fictional character is a constant theme in *Le Vol d'Icare*, from
the apparent act of freedom whereby Icare 'escapes' from his
author's pages at the beginning, to the end, where authorial
control is reasserted:

> HUBERT
> (refermant son manuscrit sur Icare)
> Tout se passa comme prévu; mon roman est terminé.   (p. 253)

Yet, at the same time, *Un Rude Hiver* can be read as a
psychological study of a readily characterisable Bernard
Lehameau in his passage from despair to hope, and Roland
Travy's emotional development is clearly the central focus of
Odile; and one critic, at least, starts from the basis that,
almost alone among his generation, Queneau has succeeded
in creating a series of characters that are immediately identifiable as being his.[22] By the same token, while the traditional
notion of plot as a meaningful sequence of events would
appear to be undermined – and superseded – by Queneau's
arbitrary organisation of narrative and his flaunting of artificiality, there are novels which read as linear progressions,
apparently free of the extremes of formal constraint. It has
also been noted that, outside *Le Chiendent* and *Les Fleurs*

bleues, Queneau makes meagre use of the free handling of time associated with other innovators of the modern novel, and that he generally relies instead on simple chronological order; indeed he allows himself little more than an occasional break in continuity – as in *Le Dimanche de la vie*, where the fourth chapter ends before Valentin has even met Julia, while at the beginning of the fifth the couple have been married for three months, and where the events of the Second World War are passed over between chapters twenty and twenty-one. The sequences of events in most of Queneau's novels resist simple schematisation – as is proved by Jacques Bens, who, despairing of producing the plot summary required for his study of Queneau in the Bibliothèque Idéale series, fell back on the device of reproducing the *prières d'insérer* (mostly written by Queneau) in order to capture the general flavour. But Queneau remains stubbornly outside the critical pigeonholes of 'traditional novelist' and 'anti-novelist' – or, better, he embraces them both.

The same balance is to be seen in his use of narrators, and of narrative modes. If the third-person narrator of, say, *Le Chiendent* or *Zazie dans le métro*, detached from the action but obtrusive in the text, appears most frequently, he gives place, in *Un Rude Hiver*, to a more self-effacing narrator who sees for the most part through the eyes of Lehameau, the central character. And he is supplanted by a first-person voice for the whole of *Odile*, where much emphasis is placed on Travy's role as teller of a story of which he is himself the centre: 'L'intérêt de tout ceci n'est que médiocre; mais enfin, le prologue de ce récit; et puis, je sais ce que je fais. Je ne raconte pas des histoires à tort et à travers' (p. 9). This identification with individuals is particularly effective in creating a solipsistic world in which personal obsessions predominate. It serves to reinforce Travy's single-minded rejection of a social life in favour of his mathematical research; and in *Saint Glinglin* the recourse to monomaniac narrators in certain sections (Pierre in 'Les Poissons', Jean in 'Le Caillou', Paul in 'Les Ruraux', Hélène in 'Les Étrangers') gives a striking effect of juxtaposition, for here the reader is obliged to respond to the novel as a series of separate narrative voices, rather than relying on a single, consistent narrator. In 'Technique du roman' Queneau makes specific reference to his varied use of narrative modes, explaining that each section of *Le Chiendent* was conceived as a unity not only of time, place and action, but also in the manner of its narration:

> Récit purement narratif, récit coupé de paroles rapportées, conversation pure (qui tend à l'expression théâtrale), monologue intérieur en 'je', monologue rapporté (comme si l'auteur pénétrait les moindres pensées de ses personnages) ou monologue exprimé (autre mode également théâtral), lettres (dont furent composés entièrement des romans fameux), journaux (non intimes, mais carnets de comptes ou coupures de quotidiens) ou récits de rêves (qu'il faut utiliser avec réserve tant ce genre se galvaude).
>
> (*Bâtons*, pp. 30–1)[23]

The range is just as wide in Queneau's other books, and the effects achieved are well judged. In *Le Dimanche de la vie*, for instance, a shift from dialogue into interior monologue is an ideal device for revealing the full discomfiture of one of the speakers. Paul B— claims that Valentin is a heavy drinker, but Julia denies it – and is soon to move into a counter-attack:

> — Pas vrai: il boit pas.
> — Ils disent tous ça. Mais en cachette, ils se rattrapent.
> — Et en cachette, qu'est-ce que tu fais, toi?
> — Il ne s'agit pas de moi.
> — Tu n'as peut-être pas une bouteille de cognac dans un tiroir de ton bureau?
> La vache. Une cliente qui avait dû lui raconter ça. La femme de Pradalier, probablement. Il lui mettrait une drôle de note à celui-là, avant de partir. Et à ses autres subordonnés, itou. Tandis qu'il préparait ses plans de vengeance, il ne pouvait naturellement répondre.   (p. 50)

In *Odile* there is a comparable shift – equally abrupt and equally effective. Travy, at a crucial point of the story, is considering his political future, while at the same time worrying about the girl whom he loves. The political question can be adequately conveyed in conventional narrative, but the emotional problem, being more intimate and therefore difficult for the unexpansive Travy to articulate in his usual laconic way, requires the immediacy which stream-of-consciousness conveys particularly effectively. The change of tense and of rhythm tells all:

> Je me demandais si j'allais adhérer au parti communiste; et dans quelle mesure je pouvais passer pour communiste; et dans quelle mesure les autres pouvaient passer pour communistes: et quel intérêt pouvait présenter la

constitution d'une société sécrète. Et Odile où est-elle? Que fait-elle? Sale egoïste tu ne penses qu'à toi. Ils l'ont peut-être emprisonnée? Mais pourquoi l'auraient-ils emprisonnée? C'est absurde. Elle doit être à l'hôpital. Tesson est peut-être mort. Si l'autre a bien visé. Tesson doit être mort maintenant.

 Odile?   (p. 97)

 It is noteworthy that Queneau's later novels are marked by a move away from narrative and towards dialogue, as in *Zazie dans le métro* and *Les Fleurs bleues*, where the voices of the characters tend to outweigh that of the narrator. However, experiments with the presentation of dialogue go back to *Le Chiendent*, as when Alberte announces her decision to Théo, whose side of the conversation is left to the reader to reconstruct:

— Je m'en irai, moi.
— ...
— Ici, j'ai peur.
— ...
— Je vais habiter Paris. Chez Mme Pigeonnier. Je l'ai vue hier. Elle m'a proposé une chambre dans son nouvel appartement. Oui, j'irai là. Et toi, tu resteras ici, avec l'animal.
— ...
— Non, ce n'est pas absurde. C'est comme ça. Je le veux.   (p. 277)

Similarly, with Valentin Brû talking to a customer in the picture-frame shop:

Bonjour, meussieu. Pour la miniature ou la photo? La photo. Des parents? des sœurs? de la fiancée? Si, ça me regarde, mais certainement, meussieu, ça me regarde, je ne vais pas vous vendre n'importe quoi. Vous êtres jeune. Vous avez dix-neuf ans. Vingt ans, pardon. Du 14 avril dernier. Mais ... est-ce que vous n'êtes pas le neveu de meussieu Houssette? C'est bien ce qui me semblait. Il y a un air de famille. Votre mère est la sœur de meussieu Houssette? Ah! elle a épousé son frère. Alors vous vous appelez Houssette.

                (*Dimanche*, p. 130)

 There are doubtless many other aspects of Queneau's technique which merit further consideration. The more the evidence of technical control accumulates, however, the greater becomes the implication that his texts are dry and lifeless repositories of narrative devices. And nothing could be further from the truth. In his preface to Faulkner's novel *Mosquitoes*, Queneau writes of how once the basic decisions

have been taken, a writer works with increasing spontaneity
and freedom; and the observation seems particularly applic-
able to his own writing:

Lorsque le 'travail' est bien en train, lorsque l'auteur est plongé dans son
œuvre, alors tout vient s'y jeter, tout devient bon, tout semble s'organiser
pour apporter sa contribution, grain de sel ou de calcium, algue ou petit
poisson, les coïncidences se multiplient et les intuitions, les éclairs, les
brusques dévoilements, fournissent au 'plan' conscient les épaisseurs, les
densités voulues.   (*Bâtons*, p. 126)

Certainly, for the reader of Queneau's novels, the impression
of liberty by far outweighs any sense of constraint or restric-
tion in the writing: despite the premeditated designs,
Queneau can always respond to immediate inspiration, and
develop his novel accordingly. As one critic puts it, writing of
Le Dimanche de la vie: 'Comme un mot lui en suggère un
autre, une idée lui en impose une autre et, sans se préoccuper
de leur lien entre elles, il se lance dans la description d'une
nouvelle aventure.'[24] It is an obvious point, but one made
too rarely, that for the uninitiated reader, Queneau's novels
are as remarkable for the sheer readability of their stories as
for their other qualities.[25] And this fact serves to underline
the ultimate futility of identifying Queneau too exclusively
with this or that widely advertised technique. More important still, Queneau explicitly denied that, even at its height,
his concern for the formal features of narrative ever gives
them an independent and absolute value. On the contrary, it
was always an accessory: 'Il me semble que pour moi c'est
limité au rôle d'échafaudage' (*Charbonnier*, p. 53). It is
appropriate, then, to see in Queneau's technique not the
assertion of the primacy of individual elements, but rather a
continual quest for harmony and balance – between con-
tingency and necessity; between production and subversion
of the text; between traditional and experimental methods.

Other genres

Queneau's preoccupation with structure and form
represents an effective challenge to what he saw as the
traditional dichotomy of novel and poetry, and it goes some
way towards bearing out his contention that he had never

seen any essential differences between the two. It has been
noted, moreover, that the word 'roman' is omitted under the
title of *Les Derniers Jours*, as if Queneau was taking extra care
to avoid restrictive classification.[26] Further, he frequently
mixes and amalgamates genres which usually remain separate
entities. Most obviously there is his autobiographical novel
Chêne et chien, which is written entirely in verse, with regular
metres and rhyme schemes for the 'rational' account of
Queneau's childhood in the first part, but moving, in part
two, into a metrical disorder appropriate to the mental chaos
that accompanied his psychoanalysis.[27] But several other
novels have sections in verse – notably *Les Enfants du limon*,
where octosyllabic doggerel conveys a scandalous incident
from Chambernac's past (pp. 14–15) or the scabrous life-
story of Bébé Toutout (pp. 33–5). In this regard the significance of the composition of *Les Temps mêlés*, with its section
of verse monologues, is clearly seen by Maurice Blanchot,
who talks of the book's 'forme originale, qui non seulement
le sépare des ouvrages connus sous le nom de romans, mais
qui met en cause d'une manière profonde le genre auquel il
appartient'.[28]

The combination of prose and verse is but one part of
Queneau's wide-ranging, if little-discussed, attempts to
annex and adapt different types of literature. For if the
principal domain of his work is the extended fictional narrative usually known as the novel, or *roman*, there is also a
sizeable minority of fictional works of very different composition, which adjoin the main territory. Interestingly, when
discussing Gertrude Stein's avoidance of traditional description, Queneau displays a precise territorial sense, listing
Stein's devices, such as simple enumeration and prose poem,
adding that, 'ici on sort du roman'.[29] *Exercices de style*, which
in this sense 'borders' on the novels, is not only Queneau's
most varied compendium of literary registers – and a testing-
ground for narrative viewpoints (as in 'Le côté subjectif',
'Récit', 'Moi je' etc.) – but also an effective, if light-hearted
demonstration of how one story can be recounted in a variety
of genres (e.g. 'Sonnet', 'Ode', 'Comédie'). If closer to
conventional expectations, *Un Rude Hiver*, with its simple
and relatively brief narrative, its tight unity of place (the

action never moves away from Le Havre), and its restricted
cast of characters, is perhaps less a novel than a *novella*, lying
between the longer novels and the small group of short
stories such as 'Dino', 'Panique', 'Une Trouille verte', and 'Le
Cheval troyen' which have generally escaped critical attention.[30] If the novels tend in many cases to be diffuse and
resistant to summarising, these stories are, on the contrary,
highly concentrated, dealing in detail with one small event,
and thus correspond to the classic definitions of the form.
'Dino' is a whimsical reminiscence of a holiday in Portugal in
the company of an imaginary dog; 'Panique' and another
conte, 'Une Trouille verte', recount minor embarrassments in
hotels; and 'Le Cheval troyen' is the story of a fantasy encounter in a bar between a young couple and a talking horse. Each
work, although without elaboration or depth, maintains a
unity of time, place and action and a completely consistent
atmosphere. Each bears the same relation to a novel as does a
cameo or a vignette to a full-scale painting.

Another story, 'A la limite de la forêt', while it has much in
common with the others – it concerns a traveller spending
the night in a country inn, and it, too, has a dog called Dino –
is more substantial and more complex.[31] It comprises a series
of dialogues between the traveller and the various occupants
of the inn, and is divided into two sections – evening and
morning. A noteworthy feature of the story is its close
resemblance to the form of the German *Novelle*, which
traditionally contains fixed elements such as a 'frame' device
surrounding a central narrative, and the motif of the *Doppelgänger*, as well as, often, an atmosphere of mystery or
magic.[32] In 'A la limite de la forêt' there is such a central
narrative, in the shape of the innkeeper's story, which is
'framed' by the circumstances of the traveller's visit to the
inn, while the traveller himself, a deputy, is *Doppelgänger*,
unlikely though it may seem, to a monkey whose return the
innkeeper awaits : 'Vous-même, monsier le député, vous tout
particulièrement, vous entre autres, n'êtes-vous pas une
figure de celui qui doit revenir ici?' (*Contes*, p. 73). While 'A
la limite de la forêt' does not correspond in every respect to
the *Novelle* form, the points of comparison are such as to
suggest that here, once again, Queneau is experimenting

with a specialised fictional genre in order to extend his literary range.

Journal intime, attributed to a young Irish girl, is Queneau's only excursion into the fictionalised diary. The form imposes not only a consistent point of view rare in the rest of his fiction, but also a time-perspective not to be found elsewhere, and Sally alludes explicitly to the implications of this, as when recording the impenetrable stammerings of an embarrassed interlocutor: 'Pendant tout ce temps, je ne pensais qu'à une chose: en aurais-je un souvenir assez exact pour pouvoir scrupuleusement noter cette conversation dans mon journal intime. Et je le fais pourtant huit jours après' (*Sally Mara*, p. 29). Within the terms of this individual text, the diary form plays its usual role of keeping actual events at a distance, while highlighting the heroine's response to them; and in the wider context of Queneau's fiction, *Journal intime* represents one more extension, albeit a small one, of the boundary-lines.

Les Fleurs bleues, while unambiguously a novel, perhaps sums up as adequately as any other text Queneau's view of the territory. For one thing it invokes the historical evolution of the novel form, by exemplifying its forerunners, the epic and the romance (with which, of course, it retains an etymological link, in French if not in English).[33] Louis IX's projected eighth crusade, even if the duc d'Auge refuses to join it, evokes the medieval *chanson de geste*, commemorating knightly deeds of heroism, while Auge's later encounter in the forest with Russule, the woodcutter's daughter, draws explicitly on the conventions of romance, where the uncompromising ethos of warfare is replaced by the more refined atmosphere of sexual dalliance.

Les Fleurs bleues also serves to illustrate how Queneau's radical approach to fictional genres embraces subject-matter as well as strictly formal considerations. His attempt to broaden the scope of literary language, as has been seen, represents an attack on the stratification of language, which prevents the interpenetration of different codes. In much the same way he challenges the assumptions which separate 'serious' and 'popular' fiction according to their respective central preoccupations, and he does so by incorporating in his works features often associated exclusively with the 'popular' novel.

It has been suggested, for instance, that his work contains occasional elements of science fiction, as in a speculative passage in *Saint Glinglin* where Pierre imagines the situation on earth after some imagined catastrophe (see pp. 18–19).[34] And in his occasional writings Queneau has certainly shown great interest in science fiction and its literary potential: 'La S.F. met l'homme en face de toutes les possibilités (toutes – disons du maximum), elle l'affranchit de ses craintes, elle le remet à sa place; bref, elle le libère.'[35] But if Queneau's enthusiasm for science fiction is given relatively little expression in his own fictional writings, theoretical interest and fictional practice come closer in another area of popular literature – that of the detective novel and the thriller. In one article in particular Queneau notes the formal perfection achieved by the 'Anglo-Saxon' detective novel in the nineteen-thirties and quotes with apparent satisfaction some of the rules for the writing of detective fiction enunciated by S. S. Van Dine (*Bâtons*, pp. 202–3). Among Queneau's own works, *Pierrot mon ami* was clearly written with the genre in mind. The *prière d'insérer* reads:

En écrivant *Pierrot mon ami*, l'auteur a pensé qu'évidemment le roman-détective idéal (le lecteur devenant trop malin) serait celui où non seulement on ne connaîtrait pas le criminel, mais encore où l'on ignorerait même s'il y a eu crime, et quel est le détective.[36]

While the novel contains much besides, the element of mystery is certainly prominent, through both the speculation surrounding the fire which destroys Uni-Park – was it an accident or was one of the prime suspects, such as Crouïa-Bey, responsible? – and the investigation which Léonie initiates in order to clarify the hazy past of Jojo Mouille-minche, her first love. As the *prière d'insérer* implies, the mystery of the fire is never resolved; and this is why at the end of the novel Pierrot – and with him the reader – remains utterly confused:

Il voyait le roman que cela aurait pu faire, un roman policier avec un crime, un coupable et un détective, et les engrènements voulus entre les différen-tes aspérités de la démonstration, et il voyait le roman que cela avait fait, un

roman si dépouillé d'artifice qu'il n'était point possible de savoir s'il y avait
une énigme à résoudre ou s'il n'y en avait pas, un roman où tout aurait pu
s'enchaîner suivant des plans de police, et, en fait, parfaitement dégarni de
tous les plaisirs que provoque le spectacle d'une activité de cet ordre.

(pp. 210–11)

However, as this final uncertainty is the opposite of the
typical *dénouement* – Van Dine's rules include one obliging
the author to provide the reader with the means of discovering the truth – perhaps *Pierrot mon ami* is strictly speaking an
anti-detective novel.[37] By contrast, if the element of mystery
in *Les Fleurs bleues* is much slighter – it concerns nothing
more than the authorship of the graffiti on the fence near
Cidrolin's barge – then at least it is resolved at the end, when
Cidrolin himself is found to be the culprit, and for this novel
too, the *prière d'insérer* is borne out: 'Tout comme dans un
vrai roman policier, on découvrira qui est cet inconnu.' But
regardless of how far Queneau observes – or fails to observe
– the 'rules', he is once again exploiting a given genre, both
for its intrinsic resources – in this case by engaging the
reader's curiosity and 'putting him to work' throughout the
narrative – and so as further to broaden the scope of his work
by rejecting the generally accepted compartmentalisation of
fiction.

Queneau traces a different strand in American crime
fiction, beginning with Dashiell Hammett in the 1920s and
characterised by a shift away from intellectualism:

La brutalité et l'érotisme ont remplacé les savantes déductions. Le détective
ne ramasse plus de cendres de cigarette, mais écrase le nez des témoins à
coups de talon. Les bandits sont parfaitement immondes, sadiques et
lâches, et toutes les femmes ont des jambes splendides; elles sont perfides et
traîtresses et non moins cruelles que les messieurs.   (*Bâtons*, p. 203)

He also draws particular attention to the wartime success of
No Orchids for Miss Blandish, while deprecating the sadism
which it exemplifies (*ibid.*, pp. 168–70). But whatever his
attitude to James Hadley Chase's novel, it is clear that
Queneau appropriates the violence of the commercial thriller
in *On est toujours trop bon avec les femmes*. He appends to his
account of the plot of *No Orchids for Miss Blandish* the
observation that: 'Tout ceci s'accompagne d'au moins huit
meurtres, une exhumation de cadavre, plusieurs scènes de

charcuterie, etc., etc.' (*ibid.*, pp. 168–9); by the same token, *On est toujours trop bon avec les femmes* could be described as a story of the abortive occupation of a Dublin post office during the 1916 rising which features at least six violent deaths accompanied by much luridly described bloodshed and an act of necrophilia. The tenor of the book can be gauged from the description, on the opening page, of the killing of the post office's commissionaire:

— Dieu sauve le roi! murmura-t-il pour la troisième fois. Il ne fit que murmurer, cette fois-ci, car il avait fait tant et si bien, avec ses manifestations de loyalisme, que Corny Kelleher, pressé, lui avait injecté une balle dans le citron. L'huissier, mort, vomit sa cervelle par un huitième trou de la tête et s'étala, tout plat, sur le plancher.   (*Sally Mara*, p. 193)

It would be hard to find a better illustration of the characteristics of the 'style américain' which Denis de Rougemont identified in French writers of the 1940s; a striking, anecdotal opening, including the use of a catch-phrase, the tendency to concrete expressions and, of course, an emphasis on brutality.[38] It quickly becomes clear, moreover, that this is no mere *exercice de style*, briefly pastiching the style of the *série noire* school, for the attempt to exploit the preoccupations of the thriller genre is sustained throughout the novel. And as with James Hadley Chase, the brutality is complemented by eroticism: *On est toujours trop bon avec les femmes* contains a number of graphically described sexual encounters between the alluring captive, Gertie Girdle, and various members of the rebel force. (And it might be added that the erotic stream of the American thriller is given full expression in the various encounters – straightforwardly heterosexual, masochistic, lesbian and other – which Sally Mara witnesses or participates in.) Queneau further explains that books in the Hammett tradition are a long way from offering a picture of American life, particularly those of Peter Cheyney and Hadley Chase, English writers whose settings are purely imaginary. And like the America of Boris Vian's Vernon Sullivan novels,[39] which admittedly remain closer to the 'Anglo-Saxon' models, the Dublin of Sally Mara is little more than street names and monuments. As with the 'spaghetti westerns' of the 1960s and 70s, an established genre, transferred to foreign hands, is pared of most of its accessories and reduced to the barest of essentials.

The Sally Mara books, clearly, represent another very different aspect of Queneau's fictional output – so different, in fact, and so restricted to a specific part of Queneau's output (the first appearing in 1947, the second in 1950), that critical opinion has often regarded them as strictly marginal works, or else ignored them entirely.[40] Yet a considerable degree of their significance lies precisely in the qualities which make them marginal – which stretch the limits which apply to the majority of Queneau's fiction. Initially, it is true, the use of the pseudonym 'Sally Mara' supported the idea that the books were not to be grouped with Queneau's other works, but the pseudonym was abandoned when the *Œuvres complètes de Sally Mara* were published and Queneau acknowledged his authorship of the work in question. With hindsight, it seems far more plausible to see here a parodic aspect of Queneau than a separate authorial identity. Individual works such as these may extend the variety and scope of Queneau's fictional output as a whole, and they may, too, have less artistic interest, but they still remain integral parts of that whole.

Other art-forms

Queneau is noted for his sustained interest and involvement in a wide range of artistic forms.[41] At one time or another – and among other things – he painted, wrote on the visual arts, collected the work of Miró and Dubuffet, performed on the radio, composed songs (for Juliette Greco), acted in films (as in Chabrol's *Landru*), and served on the jury at the Cannes Film Festival. He was also constantly sensitive to the expressive resources of different arts and, especially, of their links – actual or potential – with literature. He once stated that immediately after his break with Surrealism, 'la seule chose que j'ai trouvée à faire, c'était les pictogrammes, c'est-à-dire, au-delà ou en deçà de l'écriture et de la littérature'.[42] And what is striking here is not so much that he turned his hand to such an esoteric activity (for which his inspiration apparently came from the pictorial narratives of the Red Indians), but rather that he seems instinctively to define the pictograms in terms of their relationship to the art of literature – more precisely, by 'situating' them territorially, just as he saw certain aspects of Gertrude Stein's technique as falling 'outside' the novel proper. The basic distinction between pictograms and literary language is, of course, that the former consist mainly of signs which resemble what they signify, rather than the conventional and arbitrary signs which make up the latter.[43] But Queneau is concerned more with affinities than differences – hence his jocular classification of individual pictograms of his as being 'en prose' (e.g. 'Récit d'un voyage en automobile de Paris à Cerbère') or 'poème' (e.g. 'Montagnes Pyrénées').[44] Hence also, perhaps, his wholehearted approval of Miró, the Spanish painter, whose work is strongly pictographic in character. In an article entitled 'Miró ou le poète préhistorique', Queneau quotes him as saying: 'Je ne fais aucune différence entre peinture et poésie' – a declaration with obvious enough echoes in Queneau's own theories – and argues that the spectator must learn to 'read' Miró's 'poems' (*Bâtons*, pp. 315–16).

With Queneau's literary texts there is frequently evidence of the translating and adapting, and of the inspiration of other art-forms. Even music, with which he generally had little sympathy, has its influence – as in *Exercices de style*. Michel Leiris, who once accompanied Queneau to a concert performance of *The Art of the Fugue*, notes:

Je me rappelle que nous avions suivi cela très passionnément et que nous nous sommes dit, en sortant, qu'il serait bien intéressant de faire quelque chose de ce genre sur le plan littéraire (en considérant l'œuvre de Bach, non pas sous l'angle contrepoint et fugue, mais édification d'une œuvre au moyen de variations proliférant presque à l'infini autour d'un thème assez mince). A mon avis, Queneau y est parvenu avec les *Exercices de style*.[45]

On some occasions, an individual novel may be pervaded by a particular artistic influence. It has been argued that in *Les Derniers Jours* Cubism is not simply a recurrent theme (as in the controversy of the 'cubist poem' in the second chapter, or the references to Apollinaire and Max Jacob (p. 98) and Braque and Picasso (p. 104)), but a 'concealed model' for the whole text, given, for instance, the collage effect of the unconnected parodies, the shifting points of view and the

sense of incompleteness and indeterminacy which characterise it.[46] More explicit, if less extensive, is the atmosphere
of the popular cartoon in *Les Fleurs bleues*. Queneau acknowledged the importance of, for instance, the Pieds Nickelés, in
the comic *L'Épatant*, during his childhood, and remarked on
the reciprocal influence of words and images in the comic-
book version of *Zazie dans le métro*.[47] The succession of short
scenes or sketches which forms the narrative rhythm of *Les
Fleurs bleues* can readily be compared with the series of
framed images which make up a comic-strip; the larger-than-
life character of the duc d'Auge, ebullient and impulsive,
would no doubt be as much at home in this latter medium as
in the pages of a novel; and some of the acts of violence, in
their defiance of the laws of physics, irresistibly recall the
hyperbolic visual effects of a cartoon – either of the comic-
book variety or else the animated film. It would be hard, in
the following sequence, not to think of Astérix, or Tom and
Jerry; losing patience with his page,

le duc fit pivoter Pouscaillou et, d'un bon coup de pied, l'envoya droit au
but. Après avoir décrit un gracieux arc de parabole, Pouscaillou, tenant
toujours son baluchon à la main, atterrissait devant la porte des écuries.

(p. 173)[48]

Queneau published only one work intended for theatrical
performance – the slight 'En passant', which he subtitled 'un
plus un acte pour précéder un drame' and in which two sets
of characters are caught in a web of repeated words and
actions in a metro passageway. But he frequently showed his
awareness of the areas of contact between drama and novel,
even to the point of noting how certain sections of *Le
Chiendent* – those of pure conversation or of monologue –
tended towards 'l'expression théâtrale' (*Bâtons*, p. 30). He
also observed, in his essay on modern novelists, that Henry
James and Ivy Compton-Burnett based whole novels on
'theatrical' dialogue.[49] Within his own novels, the third part
of *Les Temps mêlés* consists of five sections, each cast in
dramatic form, with dialogue and conventional stage directions, affording an authorial remoteness which enhances, by
contrast, the prominence of the manic narrative voices of
Pierre, Paul and the rest. *Le Vol d'Icare*, destined – by virtue
of its total dependence on a printed text – for a reader, not a

theatre audience, is nevertheless close to drama in many ways. Apart from a few passages of narrative, it is composed entirely of dialogues (with occasional monologues and asides), forming sequences with unity of time and place – in other words, 'scenes' in a theatrical sense. Its structure has been likened to that of a three-act play, and the plot, developing from the hero's 'escape' from Hubert Lubert, to the search, to a climactic reunion of character and 'creator', and ending in the *dénouement* of Icare's fall, follows a familiar dramatic trajectory. The central problem – that of the status, identity or 'reality' of invented characters – is itself used to highlight the overlapping of genres, when Morcol, the detective, announces that in the course of his investigations he has interrogated not only novelists, but also epic poets and dramatists, as he refuses to see a categorical distinction: 'Je ne vois pas pourquoi un personnage de roman ne peut devenir un personnnage de théâtre' (p. 85).[50]

Cinema, however, is without doubt the form with which Queneau is most closely identified, and it is from the cinema that he borrows most frequently and effectively.[51] He described himself in 1945 as one of those 'qui [...] sont nés à peu près avec le cinéma et fréquentent assidûment les salles obscures au moins trois fois par semaine depuis plus de trente-cinq ans' (*Bâtons*, p. 185). More importantly, cinema represents for him a living, modern form in an essentially popular and non-intellectual idiom which is, nevertheless, fit to perform the same lofty tasks as the more established arts:

Tout ce développement (du 'cinquième' art) s'est fait d'une façon auto-nome, indépendamment de celui des autres arts. On ne peut qu'admirer ceux qui, loin des 'élites' ont travaillé avec enthousiasme et désinvolture, avec conviction et fantaisie, à l'élaboration de tout simplement: un nouveau mode d'expression de l'humanité.   (*ibid.*, pp. 185–6)

This championing of a relatively new form, moreover, goes with a recognition that the printed book has no inherent or permanent advantage over other media: 'On servira une mauvaise cause si l'on croit à sa supériorité essentielle et si l'on repousse toute alliance avec d'autres moyens d'expression fournis par la technique moderne' (*ibid.*, p. 160). As this was written in 1944, Queneau was perhaps among the first novelists to suggest that the traditional direction of influence and inspiration – from novel to film – could usefully be reversed.[52]

At the simplest level of adaptation, *Loin de Rueil* (which also dates from 1944) brilliantly captures the experiences of two small boys watching a cowboy film, accompanied by the inevitable thunderous piano, in the days of the silent cinema:

Se profila sur l'écran un cheval énorme et blanc, et les bottes de son cavalier. On ne savait pas encore à quoi tout cela mènerait, le mère Béchut tapait à cœur fendre sur sa grelottante casserole, Jacques et Lucas tenaient leur siège à deux mains comme si ç'avait été cette monture qu'ils voyaient là devant eux immense et planimétrique. On montre donc la crinière du solipède et la culotte du botté et l'on montre ensuite les pistolets dans la ceinture du culotté et l'on montre après le thorax puissamment circulaire du porteur d'armes à feu et l'on montre enfin la gueule du type, un gaillard à trois poils, un mastard pour qui la vie des autres compte pas plus que celle d'un pou.   (pp. 38–9)

Not only does the passage translate a general visual impression, but the slow rhythm of the sentences, particularly the long one consisting of parallel clauses beginning '[l]'on montre' conveys precisely the effect of the series of protracted close-ups typical of silent cinema. A subsequent sequence points up the visual trickery of early films: 'On les voit qui déboulent des pentes, à pic parce qu'on a mis l'objectif de travers, sans le dire' (p. 40).

Film theory has been much concerned with differentiating between *mise en scène*, meaning, broadly, the modifications of plastic space, and montage, the modification of plastic time – the first embracing, among other effects, those of particular camera shots and the second, the editing or cutting of sequences of film.[53] And Queneau's assimilation of cinematic technique can be classified in much the same way. The first category includes both the registering of a simple action ('Il fait un geste, un grand geste purement décoratif qui zèbre l'écran de toute la promesse de rares aventures', *ibid*, p. 39), and the representation of specialised visual effects, as, memorably, in the 'zoom' shot in *Pierrot mon ami*. This occurs when Pradonet and Crouïa-Bey, from their vantage-point on a neighbouring block of flats, are surveying the Uni-Park funfair through a telescope, and following Pierrot as he strolls past the various attractions:

— Ah! le revoilà. Devant le Grand Serpent Vert. Non, ça ne l'intéresse pas.
Le voilà qui se dirige maintenant du côté du dancing, mais il n'a sûrement
pas l'intention d'entrer. C'est bien ce que je pensais, il continue son
chemin. Le voilà maintenant devant une loterie, on pourrait croire qu'il va
jouer, mais non il se contente de regarder tourner la roue. Il en a assez. Il
s'en va.   (p. 50)[54]

A noticeable feature of Queneau's use of montage is the
abrupt, unannounced switch from one image or situation to
another without transition. One occurs at the end of the
'zoom' sequence in *Pierrot mon ami*, when there is a sudden
shift from the observers – Pradonet and Crouïa-Bey – to the
observed – Pierrot himself, as he accosts Pradonet's daughter. Initially, Pradonet is still commenting on what he sees
through the telescope:

Je sais où il va mon gaillard. Naturellement. Je l'avais bien dit. Le revoilà
qui lui fait du plat. Il est culotté alors. Et qu'est-ce qu'il peut bien lui
raconter?
— Ça ne vous ennuie pas que je vienne un peu bavarder avec vous?
demanda Pierrot à Yvonne.   (p. 51)

There are other examples of the cinematic cut in this text,
notably when Pierrot is bodily ejected from Uni-Park and
the reader is immediately returned to Pradonet, still watching through his telescope (p. 53). The device is of crucial
structural importance in *Odile*, which is alone among
Queneau's novels in having no formal divisions into parts or
chapters, apart from a self-proclaimed 'prologue' (pp. 7–14).
Throughout, the rhythm of the narrative is determined by
cinematic cuts. Thus, at an embarrassing point in a conversation,

G... changea de sujet:
— Tu ne veux pas venir avec nous ce soir au meeting du Vel' d'hiv?
— Doriot parlera, dit l'autre.
En effect, Doriot parla. Ce fut magnifique, à coup sûr.
L'autre chantait avec enthousiasme; moi je ne savais pas les paroles.
J'écoutais et regardais.   (p. 24)

This can also yield a comic effect through the suppression of
an expected connecting link in a series of actions, as with this
altercation in a café:

— Vous ne pourriez pas faire un peu moins de bruit, dit le garçon.
— Dites donc, on ne vous demande rien, dit Saxel.

— On n'entend que vous ici, dit le garçon.
— Vous ne pourriez pas être moins insolent, dit Saxel.
— On vous demande de faire moins de bruit, dit le garçon.
— Je ferai le bruit que je voudrai, dit Saxel.
Un autre garçon arriva, puis un autre, puis le gérant, puis un autre garçon encore. Lorsque nous fûmes dehors, nous nous mîmes à marcher dans la nuit.
— Quelle sale boîte, dit Saxel, quelle poubelle.   (p. 33)

There are variations on the technique, as in *Le Chiendent*, where it is used not to pass over a break in time, but to effect a change of speakers, in the argument between Hippolyte and Yves le Toltec:

— Sûr que j'en sais plus qu'un amiral suisse.
— C'est moi que je suis un amiral suisse?
— T'es même pas amiral.
— Répète-le que j'suis un amiral suisse?
— Je l'répéterai si ça m'plaît.
— Fais attention que ça n'te plaise pas.
— Oh mais ils vont se battre, s'écria Alberte.
— Pensez-vous, dit Pierre, les paroles leur suffisent.   (p. 95)

Cinematic cutting also offers other models of transition. In *Le Dimanche de la vie*, the dissolve, or *fondu enchaîné* – i.e. the superimposition of an image fading in over another fading out – serves to link two chapters, one ending with Nanette at the cash-register in Julia's shop and the next beginning with a close-up of Nanette's face, now in repose, in death (pp. 102–3). And in *Loin de Rueil* two actions run in parallel in a way which would be conveyed in a film by a series of alternating camera shots but is mimicked, in the text, by paragraphing. The reminiscences of the Indien Borgeiro are set against the progress of yet another brawl – this time between Jacques l'Aumône and a sexual rival:

— Dis donc tordu, lui prononce-t-il en anglais, if you take one more peak at my doll I break your neck.
Mais Rubiadzan [...] continue à reluquer Lulu Doumer.
— Comment ça vous est venu ce talent, demandait Stahl à l'Indien Borgeiro.
Alors Rubiadzan reçoit
— Déjà quand j'étais garçon de café, répond l'Indien Borgeiro, j'épatais les clients
en pleine pêche
— en croquant des pattes de homard, des coquilles d'escargots et même de marennes. Les portugaises, j'ai jamais pu.

un formidable
— Même qu'un jeune homme bien instruit qui venait souvent déjeuner là
me comparait à vé-hache, vous savez: le poète.
marron.   (pp. 198–9)

Cinematic technique figures in an appreciable number of
Queneau's books, but in *Loin de Rueil* it is the main inspiration, from the silent westerns of Jacques l'Aumône's childhood through to the very end. The final sequence of the
novel is doubly cinematic, since it not only describes a film –
La Peau des rêves – but also bears the same relation to the rest
of the novel as exists between a reel run through at top speed
at the end of a showing, and the film as initially projected.
This novel is, in effect, a sustained act of homage to the
cinema, and as such has been singled out for special consideration in a major study of the relationship of literature and
cinema:

Non seulement le récit est écrit comme on décrit un film, à travers une suite
d'images plates et discontinues, mais aussi le cinéma y joue un rôle
déterminant, fondé sur la fréquentation assidue que font des spectacles
cinématographiques les principaux personnages de l'histoire: le monde de
l'écran et celui de la salle échangent peu à peu leurs héros, et, à la fin du
roman, tout le récit s'avère n'avoir été qu'un film, qui à la fois répète, et
modifie, le film initialement projeté devant un enfant spectateur – ce
dernier devenant le grand acteur adulte du film après avoir engendré un
autre enfant spectateur. Ce mécanisme semblable à celui du rêve est
favorisé par l'absence d'épaisseur d'un style, où l'imitation parodique de
l'image à deux dimensions permet tous les glissements et tous les
emprunts: c'est une sorte de montage, au sens technique du terme,
qu'opère alors Queneau, qui multiplie sans avertissement les fondus
enchaînés ou les flash-backs, et suscite toutes les confusions entre des
temps et des modes différents; et c'est au monde du western, dont les héros
ressuscitent sans cesse pour de nouvelles métamorphoses, qu'il emprunte à
la fois sa composition à répétitions, ses ellipses sans vraisemblance et ses
'effets spéciaux': une philosophie du réel considéré comme illusoire puise
ainsi aux sources d'un art fondé sur l'illusion de réalité.[55]

But if *Loin de Rueil* stands as the most complex assimilation of another art-form, it still remains unequivocally with
Queneau's other novels, rather than belonging in a category
of its own. Whereas his fiction serves to challenge or even
undermine accepted conventions and demarcation lines
within the confines of literature, it does not threaten the
divisions between literature and other art-forms, despite the
borrowings which Queneau makes. His own work remains

strictly within the bounds of the written word; hence, perhaps, his comment on the dialogues in his novels: 'Ce sont des dialogues de romans. Les personnes qui m'ont conseillé de faire du théâtre se trompent.'[56] Those who have tried to adapt his writings into other media also testify to the fact that they are solidly rooted in literature.[57] Beyond which, while Queneau consistently showed polite interest in adaptations of his work, he accepted no responsibility for them, declaring that he was always happy to leave, say, the film-makers and the musicians a completely free hand.[58] Similarly, about the strip-cartoon version of *Zazie dans le métro* he wrote: 'En retrouvant ainsi présentée une œuvre dont je suis, me semble-t-il, l'auteur, j'abandonne toute idée de paternité.'[59] In as much as he attempts to enlarge the scope of his fiction, then, it is by introducing various techniques into an essentially literary framework: by making new imports on an existing territory rather than by redefining its borders.

Other texts

In pointing out the 'classicism' of his attitude to writing, Queneau lays a predictable stress on the formal rigour of his early works: 'Je me considère comme très classique, très classique déjà comme idées [...] comme idée de l'activité littéraire [...] j'ai utilisé alors des ultra-structures, des ultra-constructions.'[60] However, emphasis on construction is only a part of what classicism means for Queneau; the term has another vital significance:

Le classique véritable n'a pas besoin d'être néo pour être classique. Son sens même est d'être une nouveauté continuelle: renouvellement constant, de générations en générations, des œuvres anciennes; originalité réelle des œuvres nouvelles [...]. Imiter, c'est le seul moyen de faire du nouveau et d'être à la fois à hauteur des anciens et de son époque.   (*Voyage*, p. 134)

In a sense, this is apparent even in his use of an inherited language, consecrated expressions, established styles. Clearly, too, his techniques of construction owe much to earlier literature – hence his refusal to claim any originality in this area (*Bâtons*, p. 28); equally, his experiments with genre and form are based on the works of the past. But the second

of the statements makes it plain that Queneau's 'classicism'
also includes an acute awareness that every literary text
derives in some way from those that precede it; and this
manifests itself abundantly in the attention he pays to individual texts from the literary canon, and his constant practice
of imitating them and integrating them – on various levels –
into his own works.

Queneau's fiction is forever invoking the Western literary
heritage. In *Le Chiendent*, Théo's reading-matter includes
Plato's *Apology*, *Les Misérables* and *Les Trois Mousquetaires*,
while his friend Sensitif tackles *La Chanson de Roland*; *Les
Derniers Jours* has references to *Les Caves du Vatican* and *Lord
Jim*, to Defoe, Robert Louis Stevenson and Jack London; in
Journal intime Sally Mara mentions Maurice O'Sullivan's
autobiography *Twenty Years a-growing* (which, as is recalled
in a footnote, Queneau translated into French), the *Odyssey*,
Oedipus Rex and, again, *La Chanson de Roland*; the names of
Pirandello, Jules Lemaître and Anatole France, among
others, figure in *Le Vol d'Icare*. Allusions such as these draw
attention to literary tradition and as a result it becomes a
frequent term of reference existing outside Queneau's own
texts.

However, allusion in itself does nothing more than recall
to the reader the existence of the literary system to which
Queneau's work belongs, whereas for Queneau the creations
of the past are to be actually imitated and thereby absorbed
into the works of the present. In his fiction, moreover, the
process of integration takes a number of distinct forms, and
these should be clearly differentiated from mere stylistic
procedures. They are quite separate from, for example,
pastiche, as Queneau practises it in *Exercices de style* and in the
stylistic exercises which abound in his novels. In these cases he
is dealing with a general stylistic register rather than with a
specific work or author; further, even if his intentions are not
frivolous, since he is trying, among other things, to point out
the arbitrariness and the limitations of the language, the
general effect is never particularly serious. The process of
integration is of a different order. Here Queneau uses discrete elements in the literary tradition to fulfil an important
creative, or re-creative function. Thus one critic prefers to

identify Queneau with parody rather than pastiche, adding: 'Chez Queneau la récréation est re-création, alors que le pastiche ne crée ni ne recrée rien. Elle ne signifie pas non plus dérision: Queneau n'entend pas scier la branche à laquelle il est accroché.'[61]

Even parody is not a completely satisfactory term to describe Queneau's treatment of the literature of the past, because it, too, implies a certain 'second-hand' quality and obscures the extent of originality involved. As Simonnet has stressed:

On ne peut [...] s'empêcher d'éprouver une certaine gêne à employer ce mot de parodie. Sans doute parce qu'il [...] suppose une certaine dépendance à l'égard du parodié, en fait un reflet sans autonomie véritable. Il y a là quelque chose d'absolument contraire au mouvement de la création romanesque chez Queneau, qui vise à la construction d'une œuvre rigoureusement objective et autonome [...]. Pour lui la paraphrase n'est que l'occasion d'une mise en œuvre de sa virtuosité [...]. Queneau n'est jamais plus personnnel que lorsqu'il semble paraphraser.[62]

Paraphrase, then, might appear to be a preferable description; yet it is hardly adequate to specify the nature of the process which Queneau adopts, and even suggests a remoteness from original models which he rarely maintains. Another critic, Bruno Vercier, has proposed a term which has no such inappropriate implications. Drawing attention to Queneau's extensive and varied use of quotation and allusion, Vercier argues: 'Comme son maître Joyce, et d'une façon plus aimable que les tenants actuels de l'"intertextualité", Queneau réactive la culture du passé au même titre qu'il fait entrer dans le domaine littéraire la culture du présent.'[63] 'Intertextualité', which has been defined as 'dialogue d'un texte avec tous les textes, avec l'histoire elle-même considérée comme un texte',[64] represents more satisfactorily than the other terms discussed the complex process whereby Queneau incorporates the literary heritage into his own writings.[65]

Queneau has aptly been called 'une caisse de résonance de toute la littérature française'[66] and at the simplest level the integration involves extensive borrowing in the form of allusion, or paraphrase, or both, serving to give vitality to a new text by mobilising an older one. In *Le Chiendent*, there is

the blood-curdling description of the fight between Hippolyte Azur and Yves le Toltec:

— Ils se cognent la tête.
— Ils se tordent les bras.
— Ils se mordent les yeux.
— Ils se déchaussent les dents.
— Ils se frottent les oreilles.
— Ils s'écrasent les doigts de pied.
— Ils se saignent le nez.
— Ils se heurtent les tibias.
[.....]
— Ils se mutilent.
— Ils s'émiettent.   (pp. 95–6)

– which is a simple reworking of Rabelais' account of the
attack on the abbey of Seuillé in *Gargantua*.[67] *Saint Glinglin* has a deliberate and obvious echo of Villon: 'Où, où,
où mais où pourraient vivre les poissons, les poissons d'autrefois' (p. 164), while the reference to Burns in *Zazie dans
le métro* is no less clear: 'Il médita quelques instants ainsi sur
la fragilité des choses humaines et sur les projets des souris
qui n'aboutissent pas plus que ceux des anthropoïdes'
(p. 216). Less obviously, perhaps, 'Pandore ou les deux
gendarmes', a song by Gustave Nadaud (1820–93) in
Pierrot mon ami (p. 44) is part of a network of veiled references to nineteenth-century entertainment.[68] But if, in
these cases, Queneau's borrowings may seem to be fairly
gratuitous, doing no more than linking his texts in the most
general way with the cultural background, more often they
have a more precise relevance to the contexts in which they
appear. Gabriel, in *Zazie dans le métro*, harks back to
Macbeth: 'Paris n'est qu'un songe [...] et toute cette histoire
le songe d'un songe, le rêve d'un rêve, à peine plus qu'un
délire tapé à la machine par un romancier idiot' (p. 120);
but in so doing he touches on the problem of reality and
illusion – a central preoccupation of a novel in which
nothing is quite what it seems to be, and where much stress
is laid on the artifice of the text as a whole. Similarly, in *Les
Fleurs bleues* Sthène calls to mind a poem by Du Bellay: 'Je
me demande quand je reverrai mon écurie natale qui m'est
une province et beaucoup davantage' (p. 185)[69] and
thereby Queneau not only evokes a common, deeply-felt

homesickness, but also designates, in Du Bellay, a forerunner in linguistic reform.

Queneau gives certain works additional prominence by the frequency of his references. There are echoes of a scene from *Le Misanthrope* in both *Saint Glinglin* – 'Ce beau temps ne fait rien à la chose' (p. 222) – and *Les Fleurs bleues* – 'C'est à vous que ce discours s'adresse' (p. 72).[70] The persistent echo of 'Je regrette l'Europe, aux anciens parapets' from 'Le Bateau ivre' resounds in *Zazie dans le métro*, 'Gibraltar aux anciens parapets' (pp. 131, 159, 222), and is also to be heard, slightly modified in *Les Fleurs bleues*: 'Je quitte la France aux nouveaux parapets' (p. 210). Thus repetition serves a different, newer form of rhetoric as well as the more conventional kind, reinforcing the notion of a fund of familiar literature constantly present to the writer – and the reader. Queneau further intensifies this pattern of allusion by his references to his own writings – and this, particularly, in his last novels. The tourist-guide's refrain from *Zazie dans le métro* is recalled in *Les Fleurs bleues*: 'La Sainte-Chapelle, ce joyau de l'art gothique' (p. 23). *Le Vol d'Icare* contains echoes of Queneau's poetry; Morcol's 'J'ai beau battre la campagne, je suis à caquia' (p. 35) is an open reference to *Battre la campagne*, the collection of poems which appeared in the same year as *Le Vol d'Icare*, while his question 'Oh oh? qui cause? qui ose?' (p. 36) is a reminder of 'Qui cause? qui dose? qui ose?', a poem from an earlier collection, *Le Chien à la mandoline*. Queneau's treatment of his own works, then, simply forms another part of the process of intertextuality, and of the insistence that the individual work belongs to, and derives from, a larger context.

Some patterns of allusion clearly have implications beyond these nods in the direction of literary tradition and beyond simple convergence of words, or ideas, in different texts. This is well illustrated in Queneau's approach to the work of Hugo. The number of references is in itself striking, notably those to line 80 of 'Booz endormi': 'C'était l'heure tranquille où les lions vont boire', which is variously transmuted as 'A l'heure où les lions vont boire' (*Exercices*, p. 138), 'Avant l'heure où les gardiens de musée vont boire' (*Zazie*, p. 131) and 'C'était l'heure où les houatures vont boire' (*Fleurs bleues*,

p. 27). While the version in *Exercices de style*, or *Zazie*, may be seen as a gratuitous indication of the tradition, the reference to a poem in which the hero dreams of a mighty oak-tree could well have a strong appeal for Queneau, given his fascination with the etymology of his own name. And when these are taken up in *Les Fleurs bleues* it seems probable that Queneau is both annexing Hugo's line and referring back to his own previous work. In *Loin de Rueil* there is a fuller pattern, reworking another Hugo poem, 'Oceano nox', and especially the couplet 'On demande – Où sont-ils? sont-ils rois dans quelque île? / Nous ont-ils délaissés pour un bord plus fertile?' (lines 25–6), which functions as a leitmotif for Jacques L'Aumône's evolution, occurring first at an early stage in his acting career (p. 157) and then again when his family speculate on a Jacques they assume to be dead (pp. 218–19, 221). But here the recognition of the literary heritage and the thematic overlaps are not the only points at issue, for the cumulative effect of the allusions is to draw attention to Hugo the writer – 'vé-hache, vous savez: le poète' (p. 199). In Queneau's view Hugo, 'V. H., ce poète monumental' (*Voyage*, p. 206), perhaps better than any other major writer, exemplifies the successful assimilation of the works of the past: 'Les néo-classiques copient: ils sont sourds et aveugles; les néo-romantiques ont la suffisance de croire innover et de trouver en eux des monts et merveilles: ils sont ignorants et bouchés. Victor Hugo est un classique parce qu'il a beaucoup imité; et parce qu'il a donc beaucoup innové' (*Voyage*, p. 134). Queneau's fullest statement on Hugo occurs in a preface he wrote for *Notre-Dame de Paris* (*Bâtons*, pp. 135–42). Here he argues that it was crucial for Hugo to establish his artistic roots – 'Comme tous les révolution-naires, il se cherche des ancêtres' (*ibid*, p. 140) – and, more specifically, that he needed the example of his literary fore-fathers in order to write his own works. Queneau's argument culminates in the claim that *Notre-Dame de Paris* was inspired not only by the model of classical literature in general, but by the qualities of one particular work – the *Iliad*:

Il ne s'agit là, à travers le pittoresque *historique* des personnages, que du développement des mêmes thèmes, ou caractères, ou comportements humains. Ce n'est pas jeu ou paradoxe de dire que la Esmeralda c'est

Hélène, Phoebus Pâris, non plus que Quasimodo Thersite, Notre-Dame la ville de Troie et la Cour des Miracles la collectivité hellénique. C'est simplement reconnaître l'éclosion de germes semés trois mille (environ) ans auparavant [...]. En désignant Homère de son index intuitif, Hugo avait, comme Antée, touché terre et donné un passé à la France romantique.

(*ibid.*, p. 142)[71]

It remains doubtful how far *Notre-Dame de Paris* is consciously modelled on the *Iliad* and how far the parallels between the two works reflect Hugo's spontaneous artistic impulses; it is clear, however, that Queneau's fiction is designed deliberately to introduce and develop situations and themes drawn from existing literature. Thus it has been suggested that a minute analysis of each of Queneau's novels would reveal 'les livres qui sont derrière ces romans et que ces romans vivifient', that in each case 'le livre est livre d'un livre et "doit restituer aux antérieurs leur transparence, leur actualité perdue"'.[72] Certainly, Queneau integrates the literature of the past into his own fiction on levels far deeper than that of mere verbal parallelism.

He has indicated that at the time when he was writing *Le Chiendent* he was considerably influenced by William Faulkner's novel *Sanctuary* (see *Charbonnier*, p. 50), and possible analogies such as the presence of an observer in each case and, respectively of a 'depthless' man and an 'être plat' have been suggested between the openings of the two books.[73] There are a number of comparable instances involving other texts. In *Le Dimanche de la vie*, for example, Valentin's 'voyage de noces à un', during which the ingenuous hero has to cope with the vagaries of the railway system, the complexities of a large city and the advances of an insistent prostitute, is reminiscent of Amédée Fleurissoire's journey to Rome in *Les Caves du Vatican*;[74] equally, the discussion as to the propriety of seeing a comic film immediately after the burial of Julia's mother (*Dimanche*, p. 126) seems to recall one of Meursault's early transgressions in *L'Étranger*.

More conclusively, Queneau himself acknowledges some of the texts he used in the writing of his own works. His early plan of rewriting the *Discours de la méthode* in modern French (see, for instance, *Bâtons*, pp. 17, 42, 59) was in fact abandoned (though there is a verbal allusion to Descartes in the text, p. 65), and the opening of the *Discours* is playfully paraphrased in *Le Vol d'Icare*, p. 185); but he did start to translate J. W. Dunne's *An Experiment with Time* (1927): 'Je dus en faire une vingtaine de pages. C'est cette traduction-là abandonnée qui se transforma en les premières pages du *Chiendent*' (*Voyage*, pp. 220–1). And indeed Dunne's study of premonitory dreams, with its insistence on the role of an 'observer', clearly resounds through the final version of Queneau's text. In *Les Enfants du limon*, Queneau makes extensive use of Huysmans's *Là-bas*.[75] Here, however, he does not borrow from one particular passage or section, but rather reproduces some of its personal relationships and social structures. Thus the relationship between Durtal and Des Hermies in *Là-bas* is in many ways paralleled by that between Chambernac and Purpulan. Queneau also assimilates occupations and characteristics of known fictional characters into his own works. Chambernac preparing his book on the 'fous littéraires' resembles Durtal writing his history of satanism. And in *Zazie dans le métro* the polyglot tourist-guide Fédor Balanovitch, who consistently misrepresents Paris to his charges, gives a clear echo of the Baron d'Ormesan in Apollinaire's story 'L'Amphion faux-messie', who takes delight in passing off the Napolitain as the Académie Française and the Crédit Lyonnais as the Élysée Palace.

Clearly, Queneau ranges widely among different national literatures and different periods, but he returns time and again to a small groups of works and authors – of whom Apollinaire is one, hence, for example, in *Les Derniers Jours*, the direct reference to him (p. 14), and the echoes of his verse in Vincent Tuquedenne's writings (e.g. 'Novembre 1920', p. 24).[76] Further, his profound concern with this group is reflected in more, even, than coincidences of sense, situation and structure. In short, intertextuality in Queneau is no mere surface feature but has a decisive importance for his literary output as a whole, as is apparent from his use of three sources in particular: *Hamlet*, *Bouvard et Pécuchet* and other writings by Flaubert, and the works of James Joyce.

When Queneau writes a poem entitled 'Être ou ne pas être Tobie',[77] or when Sally Mara off-handedly quotes from *Hamlet* – 'Il y a plus de choses dans le ciel et sur la terre que n'en rêve la philosophie' (*Sally Mara*, p. 122) – there may be nothing more serious involved than playful allusion. But when Gabriel ruminates on the transience of things – 'L'être ou le néant, voilà le problème. Monter, descendre, aller, venir, tant fait l'homme qu'à la fin il disparaît' (*Zazie*, pp. 119–20) – his apparently light-hearted paraphrase is not purely casual. And with Queneau's repeated use of graveyards and burial scenes, the adaptation of *Hamlet* assumes a more serious function still. It has even been argued that 'le thème précis de *Hamlet* s'articule sur un thème tellement plus profond que l'on finit par perdre de vue le motif proprement shakespearien'.[78] The *Hamlet*-theme takes on this greater seriousness in *Les Derniers Jours*, both with a graveside conversation between Tolut and a café-proprietor (pp. 190–1) and with Tolut's subsequent reflections on ghosts (p. 197), in which Tolut comes to identify his own grief with that of Hamlet. *Un Rude Hiver* continues this strain with its own version of the gravediggers' scene (pp. 159–62) and its background of storm and seascape. The hero of the novel, Bernard Lehameau, whose very name is of course a punning allusion, spends the novel trying to come to terms with his personal grief and guilt, and the Shakespearian parallel is thereby reinforced. Clearly, intertextuality of this sort operates on too deep a thematic level to be dismissed as mere playfulness.

As well as the first appearance of the *Hamlet*-theme in Queneau's fiction, *Les Derniers Jours* also marks his first assimilation of *Bouvard et Pécuchet*.[79] The openings of the two novels are strikingly similar, both containing detailed meteorological observations and topographical notations which serve as the background to the first encounter between two strangers who quickly engage in animated conversation. In *Les Enfants du limon*, Chambernac and Purpulan – at one point they are called 'les deux encyclopédistes' (p. 157) – bear a strong resemblance to Flaubert's clerks through the common quest for knowledge. The resemblance is reinforced by the parallelism of notations of the type 'Six mois plus tard ils étaient devenus des archéologues'[80] and 'Lorsque vinrent les grandes vacances, on en était toujours aux sciences' (*Limon*, p. 132), conveying as they do the same sense of single-minded, if somewhat comical devotion to science. Moreover, in *Les Enfants du limon* the acquisition of knowledge is not the preserve of Chambernac and Purpulan alone. The childish chemical experiments of the young Daniel and Agnès (pp. 137–8) recall the scientific explorations of the third chapter of *Bouvard et Pécuchet*. Similarly, the learning-process which Flaubert described is resumed, as it were, in miniature, in the self-education of the ambitious Robert Bossu, alias Toto-la-Pâleur-vivre:

> Il s'y connaissait fameusement en mécanique et en éléctricité; il expliquait pourquoi les avions sont plus lourds que l'air et volent tout de même, pourquoi la radio n'a pas besoin de fils et pourquoi les haut-parleurs font tant de bruit. Il [...] connaissait sa géographie et savait de quelle façon vivent les gens riches. (p. 175)

Elsewhere in Queneau's work, the 'Foutaises', with their echoes of the 'Dictionnaire des idées reçues', reveal a further link with Flaubert. Here again Queneau's uses of his literary model go far beyond simple allusion: here again he absorbs the spirit, as well as the letter, of the original text.

Bouvard et Pécuchet also has considerable interest as an example of intertextuality in its own right, containing as it does numerous echoes of literature of all kinds, and, in Queneau's view, revealing, like *Notre-Dame de Paris*, its debt to Homer, 'père de toute littérature et [...] arrière-arrière-arrière-arrière ... arrière-grand-père de *Bouvard et Pécuchet*' (*Bâtons*, p. 124).[81] But *Bouvard et Pécuchet* looks forward as well as back – and to *Ulysses* as much as to anything else: *Ulysses* 'où l'on reconnaît [...] l'influence directe de *Bouvard et Pécuchet*' (*ibid.*, p. 117), *Ulysses* which also has its own specific allusions to *Hamlet*.[82]

References to the works of Joyce, which of course themselves abound in intertextuality, outnumber references to any other writer. It has been argued that certain passages in *Le Chiendent* echo *Ulysses* and the short story 'Two Gallants' in *Dubliners*, and parallels have been drawn between Queneau's characters, Narcense and Potice, and Joyce's Lenehan and Corley, and between Pierre Le Grand and Leopold Bloom;[83] and Étienne's unpunctuated, stream of consciousness interior monologue (pp. 79–81) clearly has its roots in Molly Bloom's soliloquy. *Les Derniers Jours* has obvious affinities with *A Portrait of the Artist as a Young Man* through their youthful, studious and semi-autobiographical heroes, Vincent Tuquedenne and Stephen Dedalus. In *Zazie dans le métro*, the question-and-answer sequence involving Gridoux and Mado Ptits-pieds (pp. 98–8) corresponds to the passage where Bloom and Stephen arrive at Bloom's house in the 'Ithaca' section – the seventeenth chapter – of *Ulysses*.[84]

The richest vein of Joycean borrowings and allusions is to be found in the Sally Mara books. There are references to Joyce by name, both in *On est toujours trop bon avec les femmes* (*Sally Mara*, p. 245) and in *Journal intime* (*ibid.*, p. 189). Just as explicit is the password 'Finnegans Wake!' which the Irish rebels use – anachronistically – in the earlier novel. Less overtly, the rambling conversation during a drinking session in *Journal intime* – 'Nous nous mîmes à parler de choses et d'autres, de la situation financière en Finlande, de la teneur en vitamines du lard aux choux, de l'existence d'Homère et de Shakespeare, de la gueule du prince de Galles' (p. 104) – is reminiscent of Bloom and Stephen walking drunkenly to Bloom's house:

> Of what did the duumvirate deliberate during their itinerary?
> Music, literature, Ireland, Dublin, Paris, friendship, woman, prostitution, diet, the influence of gaslight or the light of arc and glowlamps on the growth of paraheliotropic trees, exposed corporation emergency dustbuckets, the Roman catholic church, ecclesiastical celibacy, the Irish nation, jesuit education, careers, the study of medicine, the past day, the maleficent influence of the presabbath, Stephen's collapse.[85]

In *On est toujours trop bon avec les femmes* the parallels go further.[86] The names of all the major characters of Queneau's novel – Corny Kelleher, Mat Dillon, Cissy Caffrey, Chris Callinan, Larry O'Rourke, Gallager, Mac Cormack and Gertie Girdle – as well as those of some of the minor figures, all occur in *Ulysses* or are recognisable corruptions of names in Joyce's novel. Almost every street, building and statue that Queneau mentions, from Eden Quay to the College of Surgeons to Nelson's Pillar, has its place in *Ulysses*. *On est toujours trop bon avec les femmes* also echoes *Ulysses* in its observance of the unities of time and place (which are never imposed with such rigour in Queneau's other novels), and, more decisively, in its allusions to sexual topics. Speculation on the sufferings of women, in Queneau's novel ('— Par exemple, quand elles accouchent, dit Gallager. On ferait une drôle de gueule si ça devait nous arriver [...]. — Nous, les hommes, dit MacCormack, on rouscaille quand il s'agit de souffrir. Les femmes, elles, souffrent tout le temps' p. 322) serves as a sort of coda to Molly Bloom's 'Nice invention they made for women for him to get all the pleasure but if someone gave them a touch of it themselves theyd know what I went through with Milly'.[87] Other parallel passages cover erotic clothing,[88] masturbation,[89] shaving (with overtones of castration),[90] and women's lavatories.[91] On close inspection, then, a novel which at first sight appears to be nothing more than an essay in the genre of the erotic thriller emerges as an intricate tissue of textual allusion and parallelism.

No one major theme links *Ulysses* and Queneau's fiction; and certainly, there is no such clear-cut connection as can be seen in the cases of *Hamlet* and *Bouvard et Pécuchet*. At the same time, Joyce's work enjoys a unique prominence by the very weight of Queneau's allusions. Perhaps there are two reasons for this. In the first place, Joyce, like Hugo, represents for Queneau the epitome of the 'classical' writer, whose own creations are built on those of the past.[92] As with Hugo, this fact alone is sufficient to ensure him a degree of importance in Queneau's works. But in addition, it is clear that Queneau owes Joyce a major – and very specific – technical debt, for Joyce's stylistic explorations and experiments with narrative structure were a vital source for Queneau's own (*Bâtons*, p. 42 and *Charbonnier*, p. 50). So perhaps the prominence of Joyce's work in Queneau's fiction is in essence the most appropriate form of homage which could be offered to a 'classic'.

Thus far, Queneau has been seen to integrate existing texts into his work in a variety of ways, but the role of these texts has always been a minor one. Despite the number of allusions to Hugo in *Loin de Rueil*, or to Joyce in *On est toujours trop bon avec les femmes*, 'Oceano nox' and *Ulysses* are not fundamental thematic preoccupations in these books: intertextuality of this sort is never more than one literary feature among others, and its aim generally goes no further than to reinforce the link between Queneau's texts and the tradition. But on some occasions Queneau gives the literature of the past a more serious task, and it is on these occasions, perhaps, that he best exemplifies the definition of intertextuality given earlier: 'Ce dialogue d'un texte avec tous les textes, avec l'histoire elle-même considérée comme un texte', utilising to the full the thematic or ideological content of his sources.

This can be seen to particularly good effect in *Saint Glinglin*, a work whose aura of myth, legend and archetype is significantly enhanced by its connections with earlier texts of a similar tenor. One important pattern of allusion is based on the Gospels. Beyond the obvious fact that Jean Nabonide becomes a Christ-like figure through his pseudo-crucifixion on the mast of the 'nasse-chuages', sacrificing himself for the salvation of the community, which is ensured when the fine weather is restored, his sister Hélène, 'en lui tendant au bout d'une perche une éponge imbibée de vitamines' (p. 266), recalls the Roman soldier who offered Christ a sponge soaked with vinegar, thus reinforcing the parallel. Elsewhere in the novel Pierre, like Christ a 'prophet without honour in his own country', is mocked by the audience whom he lectures in the attempt to convince them of the 'truth' he has learned in the Ville Étrangère. After the lecture, 'quand ils furent tous partis, Pierre découvrit qu'il était triste jusqu'à la mort' (p. 90), just as Christ in the Garden of Gethsemane tells his disciples: 'My soul is exceeding sorrowful unto death.'[93]

However, the text which is most closely linked with *Saint Glinglin* is not the Bible, but Freud's *Totem and Taboo*, and here the link is not so much textual as thematic.[94] On an anthropological level, both works deal with the beliefs and rituals of primitive societies. Both are particularly concerned with the function of the totem, which in Freud's terms may be a 'natural phenomenon (such as rain or water), which stands in a peculiar relation to the whole clan',[95] and which in Queneau's work revolves around the Urbinataliens' belief in the power of the 'chasse-nuages' to preserve the endless fine weather. Both, moreover, treat the question of taboo.

Transcending the opposing meanings of the word taboo – as 'sacred' on the one hand and 'forbidden' or 'unclean' on the other – and beyond the notion that a taboo finds its principal expression in prohibitions and restrictions, Freud suggests that 'anyone who has violated a taboo becomes taboo himself because he possesses the dangerous quality of tempting others to follow his example [...]. Thus he is truly contagious in that every example encourages imitation, and for that reason he himself must be shunned.'[96] This tendency is exemplified in *Saint Glinglin* by Pierre, who, precisely, violates a taboo by challenging conventional Urbinatalien attitudes to life in his public lecture (pp. 86–90), and whose potential danger to the community is suggested by the hostile reaction of the mayor, his father. The mayor, Nabonide (Kougard in *Gueule de pierre*), is in any case of great importance in his own right, as he illustrates clearly the ambivalence which Freud sees in the role of the ruler. Freud argues: 'The taboo does not only pick out the king and exalt him above all common mortals, it also makes his existence a torment and an intolerable burden and reduces him to a bondage far worse than that of his subjects';[97] and Queneau's ruler, although a tyrant, is also a servile figure through his enforced obedience to the 'printanier' ritual, in which he has publicly to destroy his own property in order to affirm his position.[98]

The most important parallel between the two works, however, lies in the link which Freud and Queneau both make between anthropology and psychology. Having discussed some of the strictly anthropological aspects of taboo, Freud continues: 'Anyone approaching the problem of taboo from the angle of psychoanalysis, that is to say, of the investigation of the unconscious portion of the individual mind, will recognize, after a moment's reflection, that these phenomena are far from unfamiliar to him.'[99] This correspondence is to be clearly seen in the close connection which exists between the attitude of primitive peoples towards their rulers – one alternating between adulation and fear – and the love–hate relationship which Freud discerns between son and father.[100] Pierre crystallises his ambivalent attitude to his father in a soliloquy, during the pursuit in the mountains:

'Oh! je te hais, mon père, je te hais immodérément, mon père!

....

'Je voudrais que tu meures, mon père, oui je veux que tu meures!
'Pourquoi donc étais-tu si puissant, mon père? pourquoi donc étais-tu si fort?
'Tu t'es dressé sur ma route et je ne te voyais pas.
'Tu m'as protégé lorsque j'étais enfant, mon père, mais tu m'as écrasé.
'Tu m'as soutenu lorsque je ne savais pas marcher, mon père, mais tu m'as humilié.
'Tu m'as conduit aux portes de la virilité, mon père, mais tu m'avais châtré'.
(p. 108)

Freud makes another equally important link when discussing the phenomenon of narcissism in relation to human thought-processes:

Primitive man and neurotics [...] attach a high valuation [...] to psychical acts. This attitude may plausibly be brought into relation with narcissism and regarded as an essential component of it. It may be said that in primitive men the process of thinking is still to a great extent sexualized. This is the origin of their belief in the omnipotence of thoughts, their unshakable confidence in the possibility of controlling the world and their inaccessibility to the experiences, so easily obtainable, which could teach them man's true position in the universe. As regards neurotics, we find that on the one hand a considerable part of this primitive attitude has survived in their constitution, and on the other hand that the sexual repression that has occurred in them has brought about a further sexualization of their thinking processes. The psychological results must be the same in both cases [...]: intellectual narcissism and the omnipotence of thoughts.[101]

There could be no better illustration of this 'intellectual narcissism' than that afforded by Pierre, sexually repressed, neurotically clinging to the notion that he is a genius, and incapable of a balanced view of the value of his ideas:

Le Génie étant une Réalité objective incontestable, mon père ne pourra plus me désavouer et je légitimerai mon ignorance de la Langue Étrangère par la manifestation de ma Génialité! Ainsi, je serai le premier homme de génie de la Ville Natale, et dans la voie la plus difficile, la plus ardue et la plus passionnante: la Métabiologie. Ce terme même que je forge à l'instant est une nouvelle preuve de ma géniale exaltation.
(*Gueule de pierre*, pp. 45–6)

Attention has been drawn to Queneau's practice of building a novel on a 'concealed model',[102] and the term seems wholly appropriate to describe the function of *Totem and Taboo* in relation to the Saint Glinglin trilogy. For here, more than in any other case of intertextuality discussed so far, Queneau adapts and absorbs from another text the very thematic patterns which lie at the heart of his own work.

In other cases, however, Queneau works not by using 'concealed' texts which contribute to his thematic patterns, but rather by the more overt method of resorting to direct quotation.[103] And the effect is normally a serious one which has little in common with the playful gestures in the direction of the literary heritage. At one point in *Un Rude Hiver*, Mme Dutertre is to be found reading *Le Journal d'un Bourgeois de Paris, sous Charles VI et Charles VII*:

> Item, en ce temps estoient les loups si affamés, qu'ils desterroient à leurs pattes les corps des gens qu'on enterroit aux villaiges et aux champs; car partout où on alloit, on trouvoit des morts et aux champs et aux villes, de la grant pouvreté, de cher temps et de la famine qu'ils souffroient, par la maudite guerre qui toujours croissoit de jour en jour de mal en pire.
>
> (p. 168)

The passage presents obvious parallels with the situation in *Un Rude Hiver*: war, scarcity, misery and death; but more than that, it induces Mme Dutertre to speculate on the processes of history and man's ignorance thereof: 'Ce n'était pas drôle l'Histoire, songeait Mme Dutertre, arriverait-on jamais à sortir de là, elle en désespérait. Et dire qu'il y avait seulement trois ans, il y avait encore des tas de gens qui non seulement se croyait heureux mais encore pensaient que ça durerait tout le temps comme ça' (*ibid.*, pp. 168–9). In this way, too, then, Queneau uses intertextuality – 'Ce dialogue d'un texte [...] avec l'histoire elle-même considérée comme un texte' – to raise issues central to his own works.

Direct quotation has its greatest impact in *Les Enfants du limon*. As much as anything else, the novel is an account of Chambernac's great work *L'Encyclopédie Des Sciences Inexactes*, an anthology of the works of the 'fous littéraires' of nineteenth-century France – eccentrics whose ideas owe nothing to the past and are ignored by posterity, hence the definition: 'Un "fou littéraire" n'a ni maîtres ni disciples' (p. 121).[104] A large proportion of the text is given over to the various 'fous littéraires', such as the self-proclaimed messiahs Paul Lacoste and his cousin Jacob-Abraham Soubira (p. 229) and Constant Cheneau (p. 233), or Monfray, 'roi provisoire de l'intelligence humaine' (p. 239); more especially, there are extensive quotations from their works: from Monfray's 'Ordonnance' and 'Proclamation' (pp. 239–41), from J. J. B. Charbonnel's *Histoire D'Un Fou Qui S'Est Guéri Deux Fois Malgré Les Médecins Et Une Troisième Fois Sans Eux* (pp. 246–9) and the writings of Hersilie Rouy (pp. 259–60) and others. If all these quotations were simply obscure literary curiosities, then *Les Enfants du limon* would be part indigestible anthology and part narrative, with no linkage between the two, no 'dialogue' between the texts.[105] There is, however, no question of the extracts from *L'Encyclopédie Des Sciences Inexactes* being artificially hedged around with an alien story-line in order to give the spurious impression of a novel, for, contrary to appearances, the *Encyclopédie* forms an integral part of the whole novel structure. At the end of the novel, Chambernac abandons the *Encyclopédie* to Queneau himself, telling him: 'Refaites avec ces vieux papiers un livre neuf si vous en éprouvez la nécessité' (p. 315), and through this episode Queneau reaffirms his personal authorship of the novel, asserting beyond any doubt that he is using the texts of the 'fous littéraires' rather than being used by them.

The *prière d'insérer* to the first edition of the novel claims that between the three groups of characters in the novel, between the themes presented by the 'fous littéraires' and the events of the narrative, 'il s'opère des échanges et se forme des harmonies comme des dissonances, qui donnent au livre son unité'.[106] The claim can be easily justified. As to the links between the characters and the themes of the 'fous littéraires', the most apparent is an exaggerated sense of self-importance – which in Chambernac's view amounts to madness: 'J'ai examiné tous les fous, les miens pas les autres, et voici ce que j'ai constaté: la folie est l'auto-déification d'un individuel dans lequel ne se reconnaît aucun collectif' (p. 294).[107] In common with, for instance, the messianic Lacoste and Soubira, major characters in the novel have this sense developed to a high degree. Chambernac's general comment on messianic figures is that: 'Tous ont cru en leur mission, mais l'histoire seule est juge' (p. 233). Now Chambernac, too, considers his life in these terms: 'Quant à moi, ma mission est de sortir de l'oubli ces esprits égarés et d'en faire des exemples

pour les temps à venir' (pp. 233–4), and so does Agnès
Coltet: 'Elle aussi croyait dans sa mission' (p. 270). Agnès's
mission, as she sees it, is to liberate the French nation by
means of her political party, the 'Nation Sans Classes'. As
Berthe puts it, 'elle se croit Jeanne d'Arc' (p. 183) – which
could pass as a conversational commonplace, were it not for a
reference in Chambernac's book to one Amélie Seulart, who,
in 1870, 'avait déclaré "prendre domicile officiel à l'hospice
de la Salpêtrière, refuge des femmes aliénées pendant que les
armées des rois souilleront le sol de la mère patrie". Amélie
Seulart, qui prétendait être Jeanne d'Arc réincarnée' (p. 280).
Agnès's overdeveloped sense of mission, it is implied, takes
her to the brink of madness, and much the same could be said
of Chambernac. Indeed, on several occasions it is clear that
other characters regard him as being mad (e.g. pp. 290, 300).
But Chambernac eventually comes to understand the logical
conclusion of his obsession, and refrains from undertaking a
private publication of his encyclopedia after all the publishers
have refused it, 'car il risquait ainsi en mettant en circulation
un livre qui ne rencontrait qu'indifférence, d'entrer lui-même
dans la catégorie des "fous littéraires"' (p. 313). Chambernac, then, pulls back just before the point at which intertextuality closes in completely on itself and where controlled
dialogue turns into manic monologue. Having reactivated
the words and ideas of the 'fous littéraires', he narrowly
escapes replicating their mentality.

As the *prière d'insérer* suggests, there are also links between
the texts of the 'fous littéraires' and certain developments in
the narrative. For example, the theory propounded by Lady
Newborough, Baroness of Sternberg, according to which
Louis-Philippe was the son of an Italian jailer called Chiap-
pini (p. 237), and Hersilie Rouy's claim to be the daughter of
the duchesse de Berry (p. 255) connect with the cases of
illegitimacy and disputed parenthood concerning both
Clémence, the illegitimate daughter of Jules-Jules Limon,
and Robert Bossu who, it eventually emerges, is the natural
son of Chambernac. Similarly, J. J. B. Charbonnel's reflexion:
'Ne faut-il pas [...] que l'esprit du malade aide la science?'
(p. 249) has direct relevance to the scientific and intellectual
explorations of the asthmatic Daniel.

The writings of the 'fous littéraires' are not the only example of direct quotation in *Les Enfants du limon*, for here again Queneau makes extensive use of the Bible.[108] Early on in the novel, Salomon Hachamoth is seen taking stock of his situation, personal and professional, and his musings on the intelligence immediately evoke a biblical text from the book of Proverbs – traditionally attributed to King Solomon (cf. p. 61: Proverbs, 19. 14). When his thoughts turn to his business career, which now seems futile since he is childless, the words of Ecclesiastes are recalled: 'J'ai vu que tout travail et toute habileté dans le travail n'est que jalousie de l'homme à l'égard de son prochain. C'est encore là une vanité et la poursuite du vent' (p. 63: Ecclesiastes, 4. 4). Later, Hachamoth's questioning of Agnès concerning her self-appointed task of single-handedly rescuing the French nation from disaster gives rise to a quotation from the book of Judges, describing Deborah as prophet, judge and effective leader of the children of Israel (p. 218: Judges, 4. 4–5).

The biblical texts quoted in *Les Enfants du limon*, then, serve not simply to reinforce particular incidents, but to develop and amplify major preoccupations of individual characters. And the Bible and the work of the 'fous littéraires' have a still more important role, for between them they form the connecting link between the activities and ideas of a collection of bizarre individuals and a cultural background against which these can be understood. Avoiding the dangers which Chambernac understood just in time, and to which the 'fous littéraires' by definition succumbed, Queneau succeeds in integrating personal creation and literary heritage in such a way as to do justice to both.

If intertextuality seems the best term available, still no word fully describes Queneau's varied use of the texts of the past. His techniques can, however, be limited to a specific area which is bounded at one extreme by casual parody and at the other by the wholesale assimilation of key ideas and themes. The variations to be found within this area preclude any simplistic evaluation. Attempts have been made to interpret Queneau's intertextual techniques as nothing more than an extension of his formalism, promoting the notion of literature as a totally hermetic, self-generating process; but

while certain casual allusions could be understood in this
way, those with a more serious specific application to human
life – to Freud, or Flaubert, or the Bible – could not. As
Simonnet points out, even parody – the lighter side of
intertextuality – has its value in this respect, introducing as it
does 'une distance de l'auteur à l'égard du thème qui est
objectivé et dépouillé de son poids de faux sérieux' and at the
same time involving 'une critique de la philosophie scolaire et
livresque qui est comme une préface à la sagesse véritable'.[109]
Elsewhere, the texts which Queneau integrates into his own
have been represented as the indispensable keys to the
'meaning' of Queneau's works.[110] In fact, no work – not
even *Saint Glinglin* – can be understood exclusively in terms
of source-texts. If Queneau's intertextuality lends some
weight to both of these critical extremes, it rarely justifies
either. But what it does do is to lead away from the idea that
Queneau's works are purely formal structures and towards
the notion that, while remaining autonomous constructions,
they can and do embody enduring themes of profound
human and philosophical importance.

Just as, on one level, Queneau's work is an exploration of the
modes of communication which go to make up language, so,
on another, it serves to examine the resources and potentialities of the formal system which generates literary works.
Initially the system appears as a self-contained entity, marked
by a formal control which finds its fullest expression outside
the fiction, in the narrative schemes and rhetorical constructs
of Oulipo, the Ouvroir de Littérature Potentielle. It is also,
obviously enough, presented openly as a gratuitous creation
with no necessity beyond its formal constraints, and an
artificial one, constantly emphasising its affiliation to a long
reflexive tradition stretching back through Diderot's *Jacques
le fataliste* and the burlesque novels of the seventeenth
century to the origins of literature itself; as Queneau pointed
out, there is a sequence in the *Odyssey* where Ulysses hears his
own story being sung by a bard (*Charbonnier*, p. 60). But to
recognise the artificiality of literature is not to negate it, and
in Queneau's case it is, on the contrary, a way of conferring a
certain status on what he writes. As Roland Barthes notes,

his work depends precisely on a balance between what it denounces and what it leaves in place:

La spécialité de Queneau, c'est que son combat est un corps-à-corps: toute son œuvre *colle* au mythe littéraire, sa contestation est aliénée, elle se nourrit de son objet, lui laisse toujours assez de consistance pour de nouveaux repas: le noble édifice de la forme écrite tient toujours debout, mais vermoulu, piqué de mille écaillements; dans cette destruction retenue, quelque chose de nouveau, d'ambigu est élaboré, une sorte de suspens des valeurs de la forme: c'est comme la beauté des ruines.[111]

Further, Queneau's fictional practice points ahead clearly to the work of later writers: his willingness to abandon all preconceptions, to re-appraise every traditional element of narrative and to borrow from other arts all show him to be a significant precursor of the 'new' novelists of the fifties and sixties, as Alain Robbe-Grillet, for instance, has readily recognised.[112]

It does not, however, follow that Queneau's fiction is by definition hermetic, incapable of ever referring to anything outside itself. If, in the first instance, it may appear simply as a collection of literary artefacts, it is far too diverse a creation to be encompassed by such a description: 'Un roman de Queneau, c'est un objet, une sorte de sculpture, une œuvre d'art infiniment complexe et qu'on peut regarder de mille façons, un jardin-labyrinthe, une pyramide aux dimensions ésotériques, le poème du dernier grand rhétoricien.'[113] Queneau's methods of structuring, patterning and shaping his works and his experiments with literary genres and artistic forms inevitably form a central part of the experience of reading any of his texts, and they demand to be considered in their own right. But if they do not in themselves constitute a content, neither do they exclude the possibility of one – as Queneau has made abundantly clear:

Je sais en principe ce que j'ai à dire, et ce que je veux dire, seulement je veux le dire de cette façon-là et avec cette structure, cette armature qui me paraît apporter une rigueur plus grande à ce qu'on a l'intention de dire, de façon que cela ne s'écoule pas comme ça, à droite et à gauche, d'une façon informe.   (*Charbonnier*, pp. 53–4)

Moreover, Queneau's use of the texts of the past is a positive indication that his fiction can refer to subjects outside itself, that it can have a 'content', in the conventional sense of the term, that it is capable of encompassing a 'reality', even if it proclaims its independence from it. To deny all this would be to restrict the writing of fiction more than Queneau himself is prepared to do.

3　The fictional world

From realism to fantasy

'CE SONT plutôt des cadres qui sont imposés à un sujet qui se développe, qui pourrait apparemment s'exposer avec moins de rigueur. Ensuite les deux, le sujet et la forme, sont absolument imbriqués, mais on peut quand même les distinguer' (*Charbonnier*, pp. 52–3). Queneau is here discussing the novels whose composition inspired him at the beginning of his career, such as *Sanctuary* and *Lord Jim*, but his words are equally relevant to his own fiction. If he adopts an elaborate formal technique, then this is a sort of scaffolding – a framework which, by definition, supports something inside it. Equally, if intertextuality can function as a reminder that Queneau's writings inevitably belong within the confines of literary tradition, it can also involve basic human questions which fall outside the strictly literary context. For whatever technical and formal differences separate Queneau from more traditional novelists, his works, like theirs, have a recognisable content. No less than his predecessors, Queneau invents and portrays living situations in which characters move about, events take place and thematic preoccupations are developed. Some critics refer to the 'universe' or 'world' of Queneau's fiction,[1] while one has written an article describing the characteristics of 'the Queneau country'.[2]

Queneau does tend to favour a particular level or area of society: one which is to be found in, for instance, *Pierrot mon ami*, *Loin de Rueil*, *Le Dimanche de la vie* and, as he has noted himself, in *Zazie dans le métro*: 'Je vois bien, évidemment, qu'il y a dans *Zazie dans le métro* des personnages ou des situations qui se trouvent dans d'autres de mes livres. C'est en effet un peu le même monde, la même sorte de gens [...]. Et toujours les mêmes endroits.'³ Given the full range of his output, however, it is perhaps more accurate to talk of 'fictional worlds' rather than of a single 'world', for there is little common ground between, say, the realistically drawn student milieu of *Les Derniers Jours* and the mythical society of *Saint Glinglin*, or between the Dublin portrayed in the Sally Mara books and the Paris of *Zazie dans le métro*.

The freedom and the playfulness which characterise Queneau's work mean that he is not committed to any one specific way of representing his subject-matter. Since he is attempting not to reproduce any given reality, but simply to create self-sufficient works of literature, he is in a position to exploit a whole range of fictional registers, from the factual and realistic to the outlandish and fantastic; and, further, he is free to switch from one register to another within the same novel. The lesson which one reviewer derived from *Zazie dans le métro* was that 'a fiction, which, far from representing reality actually suspends it, is the one place where emperors and gamines, the historical and the imaginary, meet as equals'.⁴ In *Les Enfants du limon*, the diabolical Purpulan, who belongs firmly in the realm of fantasy and whose death at the end of the novel defies any realistic explanation, nevertheless lives and moves in a milieu which is rendered almost entirely in realistic terms. On the other hand, *Les Fleurs bleues*, a novel based on the totally unrealistic idea of one of its central characters travelling through seven centuries of time, can still surprise its reader by passages of realistic description. There can be no question of classifying individual novels as, for example, realistic, fantastic or mythical. It is, however, possible to distinguish the various levels of 'reality' contained in Queneau's fiction as a whole, ranging from those rooted solidly in experience of verifiable fact to those deriving above all from the imagination.

Queneau never regarded his personal life as a particularly important source of material for his fiction: 'Je grince des dents quand des gens pensent que je fais ceci ou cela [...] pour en faire ensuite un morceau de roman. Quelle idée de

profane. Comme si on ne pouvait pas vivre comme un autre'
(*Contes*, p. 148).[5] At the same time, the link between a work
and its author can be of some value: 'Le rapport de l'homme à
l'œuvre, quoiqu'on en pense dans un esprit classique, ce n'est
pas une recherche méprisable' (*Bâtons*, p. 131). Certainly it is
undeniable that Queneau used a considerable amount of
autobiographical matter in his early works,[6] and the general
effect is to lend the works in question a convincing flavour of
authenticity, especially as, in many cases, the autobiographical element can be verified from other sources.

Apart from *Chêne et chien*, the verse novel which is written
in the first person and describes Queneau's childhood and
schooldays and the 'retour à l'enfance' of his period under
psychoanalysis, the largest concentration of autobio-
graphically-based material is to be found in *Les Derniers Jours*
and in *Odile*. Between them, these two texts fill most of the
gap left in *Chêne et chien* between Queneau's final years at the
lycée around 1920 ('Alors je me mis au travail / et décrochai
plus d'un diplôme', p. 60) and the period following 1933
when he underwent analysis ('Je me couchai sur un divan / et
me mis à raconter ma vie', p. 63). The central character of *Les
Derniers Jours*, Tuquedenne, resembles the young Queneau
not only in his physical characteristics – long hair and weak
eyesight – but also in his passion for literature, philosophy,
billiards and cinema. His background, too, recalls that of
Queneau: he originates from Le Havre, and his parents
eventually sell their business there in order to live in the Paris
suburbs. The novel ends with Tuquedenne acquiring his
degree and waiting to leave for his call-up.[7] *Odile* begins,
precisely, with its hero's military service, which, like
Queneau's, takes place in North Africa. The story deals with
the experiences of Roland Travy, an amateur mathematician,
on his return to Paris: his encounters with various artistic
and political circles, his love-affair with Odile, whom he
eventually marries, and a crucial journey to Greece, all of
which relate directly to Queneau's career. With the exception
of these two novels, *Chêne et chien*, – and *Les Enfants du
limon* where Daniel's asthma recalls Queneau's own – he
makes little reference to specific events from his own life, and
he expresses misgivings about the amount of autobiographi-

cal material in his early work: 'Je n'ai écrit que deux livres qui soient des romans à clé. *Les Derniers Jours* [...] et *Odile*, qui raconte des histoires du groupe surréaliste. Je vous avoue que je trouve *Les Derniers Jours* trop autobiographiques.'[8]

Certainly, the self-revelation which the term 'auto-biography' usually implies is rarely apparent in Queneau's fiction. On the other hand, personal experience clearly provides a valuable source of fictional material, and not only in *Les Derniers Jours* and *Odile*. When asked whether all his books were 'livres à clé', Queneau, after denying the suggestion, added: 'Mais on trouve beaucoup dans la vie, autour de soi. On n'a guère besoin d'inventer, parfois.'[9] Thus in *Odile*, Anglarès, the flamboyant and authoritarian leader of the artistic groups, is clearly based on André Breton, and his associate Saxel is generally taken to represent Louis Aragon. However, Queneau's experiences furnish him not merely with personal details, but also – and more importantly – with a background of public events, of history. He describes in *Chêne et chien* how, during the First World War, the realisation came to him that historical developments ran a parallel course to the life of the individual: 'Le monde était changé, j'avais donc une histoire / comme la France ou l'Angleterre' (p. 58). Thus the personal life of the young Queneau is set against such occurrences as the coronation of George V, the events surrounding the theft of the Mona Lisa, and the sinking of the Titanic.

In his fiction Queneau makes repeated reference to historical events – battles, disasters and *faits divers* of all kinds. All help to situate a narrative in a historical context and thereby contribute, in another way, to the solidity of the world of the novel. Further, in Queneau's view, this use of history is not merely one of several ways of authenticating a fictional work; it is also the result of a conviction that history impinges constantly on private life. In an interesting discussion with Georges Charbonnier he divides novels into two broad groups; those deriving from the *Odyssey*, where the emphasis is on the progress and achievements of an individual seen as separate from his environment, and those written in the tradition of the *Iliad*, where the individual is never free of the influence of current events. Concerning the

latter, he insists: 'Il n'y a eu que de rares moments dans
l'histoire où les histoires individuelles ont pu s'écouler sans
qu'il y ait des guerres ou des révolutions [...]. L'*Iliade*, c'est
la vie privée des gens dérangée par l'histoire' (*Charbonnier*,
pp. 63–4). And the world in which Queneau began to write
his novels certainly allowed no respite from the pressure of
events. As he argued convincingly, even if the atmosphere of
the 'belle époque' or the 1920s allowed a little escapism, the
situation soon changed drastically and irrevocably:

Dès 1930, il fallut déchanter et le 6 février 1934 offrit aux romanciers un
incident qui figure déjà dans bon nombre d'œuvres antérieures à Munich.
Depuis, il s'est passé suffisamment d'événements pour que l'on conçoive
mal une œuvre quelconque, placée 'dans la réalité', qui non seulement
puisse les passer sous silence, mais encore ne soit obligée de leur attribuer
un rôle important et même prépondérant, même dans une histoire
d'amour, même dans un récit d'adolescence.   (*Bâtons*, pp. 197–8)[10]

The transition is precisely registered in *Les Enfants du limon*,
which begins in the hedonistic ethos which preceded the
Wall Street crash of 1929, and refers back explicitly to the
years leading up to World War I ('tout était calme, stable,
tranquille', p. 134), before plunging into the crises of the
early thirties. Increasingly, the characters are subjected to the
strains of financial mishap and political upheaval, until
Agnès is killed, in the rioting which took place on February
6, 1934 in the aftermath of the massive scandal surrounding
the swindler Serge Stavisky. Although this event has less
significance for the plot of *Journal intime*, it is specifically
mentioned twice: Sally Mara's diary entry for 7 February
1934 records that there has been 'du grabuge' in Paris (*Sally
Mara*, p. 27), and later she recalls having seen film of 'le 6
février à Paris' on a cinema newsreel (p. 50). Moreover, this
is not the only reference to current affairs in a book which at
first sight could not be more remote from them, for Sally's
first mention of the riots gives rise to a reference to General
Eoin O'Duffy and his fascist 'blue-shirt' movement, which
was attracting considerable attention in Ireland at the time
Sally was supposed to be writing.

Queneau argues that historical events should play a role
'même dans une histoire d'amour, même dans un récit
d'adolescence', and his own love-stories, *Odile* and *Un Rude*

Hiver, and his account of adolescence, *Les Derniers Jours*, all contain incidents from contemporary history. *Odile* has references to a meeting addressed by the one-time communist leader, Jacques Doriot (p. 24), and to a demonstration against the controversial death sentences passed on the anarchists Sacco and Vanzetti, in America in 1927 (pp. 121ff.), as well as more general allusions to the political situation in Europe and France's military campaigns in North Africa. The story of Lehameau's discovery of love, in *Un Rude Hiver*, is located in the carefully drawn milieu of Le Havre in the First World War, with its cosmopolitan wartime population and its thriving black market trade, and repeatedly refers to the general progress of the hostilities. In *Les Derniers Jours*, although historical events seem to impinge less critically on the characters' lives, allusions to them are, if anything, more frequent than elsewhere. Mention is made of, for example, Jack Dempsey's boxing win over Georges Carpentier, and a visit to Paris made by Charlie Chaplin, both of which occurred in the summer of 1921. Einstein's arrival in Paris in the following spring is also recorded, as are various public events which serve as a background to Tuquedenne's private concerns during the autumn of 1922:

A cette même époque, il entreprit de lire [...] les trente-deux volumes de *Fantômas*. Il courait les quais pour en acheter les exemplaires d'avant-guerre avec la couverture sur papier glacé. Rohel cadet l'ayant surpris dans cette recherche, se moqua de ses goûts démodés; car lui, il apprenait le russe et descendait dans la rue. Ainsi passèrent les premiers mois de cet hiver qu'illustrèrent les exploits des piqueurs, d'incompréhensibles et multiples explosions de poêles et l'arrivée au pouvoir de Mussolini.

(p. 179)

Moreover, it would seem that Queneau is not content simply to rely on random historical alusions. Not only do most of his works contain specific references to dates, places and incidents; but between them, these references represent, in a way which seems almost systematic, every period of modern French history.[11] *Le Vol d'Icare* is set in the Paris of the 1890s, where survivals from a past age, such as duelling, coexist with the novelty of the motor-car, and the literary world discusses the impact of the death of Edmond de Goncourt. The First World War is reflected in *Un Rude*

Hiver, while *Les Derniers Jours* covers the early 1920s. The late twenties, including the Wall Street crash, and the early thirties, with the presidency of Albert Lebrun, the rise of fascism and anti-semitism and, of course, the Stavisky riots, all feature in *Les Enfants du limon*. Even *Pierrot mon ami*, seemingly a novel untouched by history, has links with the thirties, through the scene of much of its action, Uni-Park – a clear echo of the funfair popular at the time called Luna-Park, especially as both are situated at the Porte Maillot; and the bogus fakir, Crouïa-Bey, alias Robert Mouilleminche, recalls a similar figure known as Birman (in reality a French national called Fossez) whose alleged occult powers won for him a considerable popular reputation in the early thirties. Most of the events of *Le Dimanche de la vie* take place in the years preceding the Second World War: reference is made to the Popular Front and the Spanish Civil War, to the rise of Hitler and to Munich, when public events and headline news come to assume a central importance for everyone, as Valentin discovers:

Les gens du quartier, n'ayant plus de nouvelles histoires à lui raconter que dans la mesure où ils participaient à la grande, ne venaient plus que rarement lui confier les détails de plus en plus menus d'une vie concassée par les manchettes de journaux.   (p. 198)

Zazie dans le métro is set in the post-war period, when strikes like the one which prevents Zazie from seeing the métro were notoriously frequent, and when austerity was still the rule – hence, in Turandot's café, the 'zinc en bois depuis l'occupation' (p. 24).

The sense of history is complemented by a strong sense of place, especially in the novels with city settings. Queneau's evocations are both selective and economical, rarely exceeding a few words and often foregoing visual description completely, but he is highly successful in creating mood and encouraging his reader to imagine physical details. In *Le Chiendent*, Paris is an abiding presence which menaces and oppresses its anonymous inhabitants: 'La silhouette indiquée se dégagea du mur d'une bâtisse immense et insupportable, un édifice qui paraissait un étouffement et qui était une banque' (p. 7). Urban architecture is a convenient metaphor for the depressing nature of the city as a whole: 'Il contempla la bâtisse et supputa le degré de sottise et d'abjection de l'architecte qui avait élaboré cette croquignolade' (p. 84).[12] In this environment, the individual is a powerless victim. The silhouette is described as being 'empochée par le métro' (p. 7) and 'avalée par l'ombre' (p. 9). The misery of the daily urban routine is emphasised in the opening pages of *Le Chiendent* as nowhere else in Queneau's work,[13] but if there is less apparent hostility to city life in his other novels, the urban setting recurs constantly. In *Les Derniers Jours*, Tuquedenne, although he is principally interested in the lay-out of Paris,[14] is nevertheless susceptible to the pervasive atmosphere of city life, particularly the magical sights and sounds of a Parisian twilight:

> Il n'aimait pas la ville, mais sa topographie. Il ne connaissait que le squelette et non la chair. Et cependant le crépuscule lui paraissait toujours une heure émouvante, lorsque glapissent les crieurs de journaux, lorsque les terrasses des cafés émergent, étincelantes, d'un brouillard tout truffé de mugissements mécaniques, lorsque le soleil, comme un gros ballon rouge, va se dégonfler derrière l'Arc de Triomphe, du côté de Saint-Germain-en-Laye.   (pp. 113–14)

Much of *Le Dimanche de la vie* is centred on the little streets of the twelfth arrondissement north of the Gare de Lyon, which form a closely-knit community within the urban mass; but early in the novel, when Valentin visits the capital, it is above all the furious bustle that Queneau emphasises:

> On marchait de tous côtés et sur la chaussée on roulait dans tous les sens. Une agitation anarchique faisait bouger spasmodiquement bêtes, moteurs et gens, et tous accompagnaient leur désordre de sons en général déchirants. Un aveugle barbu jouait de la flûte avec son nez, enfilant sur sa maigre mélodie les coinquements et les crissements d'hommes et de choses en chemin. On criait les journaux du soir avec tant de rage et d'énergie que Valentin crut que la guerre était déclarée.   (p. 68)

When Queneau shifts the action away from the city, it is frequently in order to situate it in the nearby suburbs. It is with some justification that he has been nicknamed 'le parfait banlieusard'.[15] For much of *Le Chiendent* the scene alternates between Paris and Obonne or Blagny/Blangy. If the environment away from the city centre is different, the landscape is no more inspiring, as Narcense discovers during his journey to Obonne:

Dans le train, il regarda par la portière un paysage qui lui parut atrocement désespéré. Les locomotives lui plaisent, mais ces masures, ces taudis. Maintenant une série de villas conventionnelles. Ça dure depuis quelque temps; il y a quelques arbres par-ci par-là; puis des terrains vagues, une cité ouvrière, de nouveau des petits lotissements semés de cabanes, une usine par-ci par-là [...]. De nouveau des petits lotissements semés de clapiers, puis des terrains vagues.   (p. 118)

Loin de Rueil is identified more closely with the outskirts, and notably with Rueil itself: 'cette commune passablement suburbaine' (p. 28). The suburbs emerge here as an indeterminate zone, set midway between city and country and partaking of both; such is the impression from a *bateau-mouche* on the Seine: 'Les usines travaillaient paisibles, les arbres du Bois s'agitaient dans le vent. Ce furent des suburbanités exquises' (pp. 85–6). Much of *Pierrot mon ami* is set just outside the western limits of Paris where the same juxtaposition of the mechanical world and a persistent, residual nature is further elaborated:

De ce côté, la Seine n'est pas à plus de dix minutes de marche des fortifications, dont la sépare une région de manufactures de moulins à café, d'usines d'aéroplanes et d'ateliers de réparation de voitures de marques peu ordinaires. L'avenue droite et large ne se pave que par instants. Des herbes poussent tandis que ronronnent les moteurs [...]. On entendait la clameur de la circulation sur la route nationale. La berge était couverte de plantes poussiéreuses et vivaces.   (p. 75)

The bulk of Queneau's fiction is set in or near Paris, but he also, on occasion, uses the provinces as a realistic setting. In *Pierrot mon ami*, events move away from Paris to the south; much of *Les Enfants du limon* has as its background small provincial towns such as La Ciotat; and the initial stages of *Le Dimanche de la vie* take place in Bordeaux. However, apart from Le Havre, in *Un Rude Hiver*, the provincial setting is usually assumed rather than evoked. His preference for Parisian settings is clear.

Above all, however, Queneau's most characteristic *milieux* are typified by their utterly convincing evocation of the circumstances of daily life. Reflecting on the experiences which had contributed to his fiction, he once commented: 'La plus importante des leçons, c'est, je crois bien, en me promenant dans les rues populaires que je l'ai reçue, dans les kermesses, autour des appareils à sous.'[16] It comes as no surprise to find the photographer, Brassaï, who specialised in just this sort of subject, recalling accompanying Queneau to a street dance in the suburbs.[17] For in many ways Queneau puts into words the scenes which Brassaï recorded – cheap cafés and bars, young toughs, snatched kisses on fairground swings. Certainly this is the very stuff of *Pierrot mon ami*, whose hero is a champion at pinball and works in the fictitious version of Luna-Park.[18] Here Queneau captures the peaceful mood of the place in the early evening, before the arrival of the crowds and the subsequent frenetic activity:

Seules, les autos électriques à ressorts commençaient à se tamponner sur la piste du Skooter Perdrix. Les autres manèges, quoique déserts encore, ronflaient du souffle de leurs orgues, et leurs musiques nostalgiques contribuaient certes à développer la vie intérieure des employés du Palace de la Rigolade. A sa caisse, Mme Tortose tricotait.   (p. 8)

The cinema, too, has many charms for Queneau. In *Un Rude Hiver* he re-creates, in loving detail, the atmosphere of a picture-house in the days of silent films. The scene is the Omnia-Pathé in Le Havre in 1917, and a whole performance is reproduced, from the numerous national anthems, played at the beginning for the benefit of the different nationalities present in the audience, through the Pathé-Journal and an interval to a documentary: 'La nuit se fit de nouveau et ah fit le poulailler qui, de nouveau déçu par un documentaire sur l'équitation exprima en oh sa consternation. Cependant, indifférents à l'effet produit, des chevaux noirs dansaient sur l'écran' (p. 50). The proceedings are completed by the adventures of Nick Winter, detective, another interval and a final film. Queneau characteristically presents the experience of the cinema as a heterogeneous one, embracing both the films themselves and the behaviour of the spectators. Another attempt to render the complexity of the experience is to be found in the description of a visit made to Rueil Palace by the young Jacques and Lucas; as before, events on the screen are juxtaposed with events in the auditorium, and the realistic effect is more than tinged with comedy, as when the pianist arrives:

La mère Béchut se montre enfin aux applaudissements de l'assistance et assommant un vieux piano elle exécute de douze fausses notes dans la clé de sol un morceau de musique sautillant et pimprené qui fut peut-être célèbre. Puis vient le documentaire, la pêche à la sardine. Les gosses ça les emmerde la docucu, et comment. De plus ils n'ont pas des bottes de patience. Conséquemment s'agite la salle et bientôt les cris s'enflent au point que les rares adultes présents ne pourraient plus goûter les harmonies béchutiennes même s'ils le désiraient les imbéciles.   (*Rueil*, p. 38)

But the effect of many of Queneau's settings is their very banality, their established place in a seemingly immutable ritual. Hence, for the commuters of Obonne, the day begins with the train to Paris; and Queneau's mockery only serves to underline the utter predictability of the whole exercise:

Chantant sa petite chanson habituelle, tututte, le train entre en gare avec beaucoup d'entrain. Les journaux se replient et leurs possesseurs se précipitent avec courage dans une effroyable mêlée; chacun essaye de conquérir sa place habituelle. Lorsque tout le monde est casé, on clôt le récipient. Et de nouveau, le train joyeux repart vers la grande ville.   (*Chiendent*, pp. 25–6)

And in *Le Dimanche de la vie*, once the day's work is done, a visit to the local café is indispensable:

Le sergent Bourrelier poussa la porte du café des Amis et il entra, suivi du soldat Brû. Ils s'installèrent à leur place habituelle et, sans qu'ils lui eussent rien demandé, Didine leur apporta le tapis vert, les cartes grises, un pernod pour Arthur et le vin blanc gommé du soldat Brû.   (p. 31)

The tone of conventional realism is however one element among others: Queneau's use of a range of different registers is of at least equal importance, and reveals more characteristic, even idiosyncratic aspects of his technique.

He sometimes makes transitions from the recognisable 'real' world to a world of his own invention so delicately that the reader will scarcely realise – if at all – that they have taken place. For example, he introduces into *Pierrot mon ami* topographical details which do not correspond to the reality of the area around the Porte Maillot, where much of the action is set; however plausible they may sound, the 'avenue de Chaillot' (p. 57) and the 'boulevard Victor-Marie-Comte-Hugo' (p. 144) do not exist outside the confines of Queneau's novel.[19] Similarly, in *Le Dimanche de la vie*, mention is made of the 'cimetière de Reuilly' (p. 82); but there is no cemetery of this name, although there exists, at the end of the rue de Charenton, where the action is taking place, a cimetière de Bercy. For all their delicacy, modifications of this sort play an important role: one critic has described Queneau as 'un réaliste, une sorte de Meissonnier, qui gauchit très légèrement, d'une manière à peine perceptible', adding 'cela suffit pour faire tourner la soupe, pour tout basculer dans la division ou l'insolite'.[20]

This latter quality of 'strangeness', in fact, is as typical of his fiction as any other element; as Claude Simonnet puts it: 'Il apparaît de façon évidente, à la lecture de n'importe lequel des livres de Queneau, que la transposition et l'éclairage du réel s'effectuent sous le double signe du banal et de l'insolite.'[21]

The 'insolite' manifests itself in forms which are in themselves outlandish, even if the background against which they appear remains basically realistic. This is the case with Bébé Toutout, the white-bearded dwarf who, in *Le Chiendent*, inflicts his diabolical, parasitic presence on Étienne Marcel and his family in the humdrum surroundings of suburban Obonne. Although Bébé Toutout seems, at first sight, to be more a refugee from a children's fairy story than an integral part of Queneau's novel, he in fact represents a compromise between realism and outright fantasy which is in keeping with the mood of the novel as a whole.[22] Purpulan, in *Les Enfants du limon*, belongs in the same category; he, too, is a self-confessed demon, and explains how, after receiving his early instruction from his father – 'C'était un pauvre diable comme moi et qui appartenait au plus bas ordre de la hiérarchie infernale: un prolétaire de démon' (p. 32) – he comes under the influence of Bébé Toutout himself. Bébé Toutout instructs Purpulan in the 'art' of parasitism to such good effect that he is able to exploit Chambernac until the very end of the novel, when the schoolmaster finally manages to dispense with him. Queneau describes in detail the bizarre spectacle of Purpulan, who has been thrown into the Seine, gradually melting:

Il commençait à fondre avec un petit crépitement, le même bruit que font les pommes de terre frites qu'on trempe dans l'huile bouillante; mais il fondait comme du sucre. Il fondait même assez rapidement. Déjà les

moignons de ses jambes s'étiraient comme de la guimauve. Puis bientôt ce
fut au tronc de disparaître.   (pp. 310–11)

Bébé Toutout and Purpulan are both unreal figures set in a
basically realistic context: they are representatives of a supernatural plane of existence, but they do not shift the main
body of the action onto that plane. The same could be said of
the near-human animals of Queneau's short stories: the
horse in 'Le Cheval troyen', which buttonholes a couple in a
cocktail bar and engages them in conversation, or, in 'A la
limite de la forêt', Dino, a talking dog who performs the trick
of disappearing by running around in ever-decreasing
circles:

Décrivant ainsi une spirale, il finit par n'être plus qu'une sorte de minuscule
atome canin tournant avec une vitesse grandissante autour de l'axe de
symétrie normal de la figure géométrique ainsi suggérée; et enfin, par un
passage à la limite, ce vibrion atteignant des dimensions indéfinies de
petitesse finit par disparaître.   (*Contes*, p. 79)

The same story, which is set in a remote country area, also
contains a mysterious, and possibly magical, character, in
père Blandi: 'Y en a qui le prennent pour un sorcier. Il remet
les os en place [...] et il enchante le feu. Il connaît les plantes
toutes par leurs noms, avec à quoi elles servent. On disait
même autrefois qu'il évoquait les morts' (p. 68). Whether or
not Blandi succeeds in calling up the dead, Julia and Valentin
perform the feat in *Le Dimanche de la vie*, when, by means of
table-turning, they communicate with Valentin's ancestor,
'Le Hussard Brû', who fought at the Battle of Jena
(pp. 124–6).

Occasionally, Queneau reverses the terms of this last
procedure, when, instead of putting 'unreal' figures in credible circumstances, he imposes fantastic situations on 'real'
characters. Towards the end of *Le Chiendent*, Étienne and
Saturnin find themselves translated from the urban – and
suburban – banality which has thus far surrounded them, to
the improbable cataclysm of the war between the Gauls and
the Etruscans, which ends with an apocalyptic encounter
between Étienne and Saturnin, and 'Missize Aulini', the
Etruscan leader, which is the final metamorphosis of Mme
Cloche. However, through the repetition of the two sen-

tences with which the narration began, the last words of the book represent a return to 'normality'. For the repetition serves not only to stress the circularity of the novel's structure, but also to show that the Etruscan war is not a culmination, but rather an exceptional event enclosed within the basic context of the commonplace. The final chapters of *Zazie dans le métro* contain a similar cataclysm. An exchange of blows between Gridoux and Mme Mouaque in the restaurant 'Aux Nyctalopes' expands into a battle of fantastic proportions involving diners and waiters, which Queneau describes in an exaggerated heroic style:

C'était maintenant des troupeaux de loufiats qui surgissaient de toutes parts. Jamais on upu croire qu'il y en u tant. Ils sortaient des cuisines, des caves, des offices, des soutes. Leur masse serrée absorba Gridoux puis Turandot aventuré parmi eux. Mais ils n'arrivaient pas à réduire Gabriel aussi facilement. Tel le coléoptère attaqué par une colonne myrmidonne, tel le bœuf assailli par un banc hirudinaire, Gabriel se secouait, s'ébrouait, s'ébattait, projetant dans des directions variées des projectiles humains qui s'en allaient briser tables et chaises ou rouler entre les pieds des clients.

(pp. 239–40)

After Gabriel and his friends have won this encounter, they are confronted by the army of another apocalyptic figure, Aroun Arachide, 'prince de ce monde et de plusieurs territoires connexes' (p. 247), who is a further incarnation of Trouscaillon, just as 'Missize Aulini' was another manifestation of Mme Cloche. However, *Zazie dans le métro* reverts to the realistic register when, at the very end, Zazie is taken by métro to meet her mother at the Gare d'Austerlitz and return home at the end of her weekend in Paris.

Another sort of fantasy which Queneau exploits, and one which stands quite independent of realistic background, is the free movement of the individual's imagination. Pierre Le Grand takes off into fantasy when his attention is drawn to the shoes a woman is wearing:

Il remarqua, sans le faire exprès, que ses souliers étaient éculés; ceux du voisin aussi et ceux-là encore; brusquement, il aperçut une civilisation de souliers éculés, une culture de talons ébréchés, une symphonie de daim et de box-calf s'amincissant jusqu'à l'épaisseur remarquablement minime des nappes en papier des restaurants pour pas riches. (*Chiendent*, p. 9)

Valentin Brû gives way to daydreams when trying to concentrate on the passage of time by observing the hands of a clock: 'Sans quitter l'horloge des yeux, il se voit allant prendre le balai dans la réserve. Il revient et, d'un seul coup, il nettoie Houssette. Il le pousse dans le ruisseau et le flot emporte l'épicier souriant. Valentin balaie ensuite les maisons, puis les trottoirs, puis le ruisseau lui-même' (*Dimanche*, p. 179). The dreams of the characters of *Le Chiendent* take up the final sections of the first two chapters of the novel. Étienne's dream is typical:

> Ici, le corps recourbé tel un fœtus, replié sur lui-même, les poings fermés, c'est un camarade d'enfance qu'il rencontre. Le camarade est habillé en ambassadeur. 'Que deviens-tu?' Il ne s'explique pas. Voici un autre ami d'enfance; chirurgien-dentiste, il a voulu cumuler ses fonctions avec celle de contrôleur des poids et mesures; aussi a-t-il fait faillite. Maintenant, ils sont tous trois nus, Étienne les emmène au bal des Quatz'Arts.   (p. 39)

The fantasies and dreams just considered do not merge with a realistic background; they are, on the contrary, distinguished from it. The fantasies of Pierre Le Grand and Valentin follow introductory clauses – 'Il aperçut', 'Il se voit' – which indicate both their relationship to their context and their separation from it. The dream sequences in *Le Chiendent*, placed in the italicised thirteenth sections of their respective chapters, are demarcated typographically from other parts of the narrative. In other cases, however, Queneau tones down the transition from a realistic to a fantastic register, so that the two are not immediately distinguishable. *Loin de Rueil*, particularly, shows this blurring of the differences between observed and imagined life. The young Jacques L'Aumône discovers that he is the offspring of an adulterous relationship between his mother and the poet, Des Cigales, and immediately imputes to himself a noble ancestry:

> Le jour où s'étant levé de table à hauteur de la salade il força le secrétaire de sa mère et y découvrit une correspondance prouvant nettement sa filiation adultérine et descigalienne, il n'en fut pas autrement étonné. Il se trouvait donc ainsi apparenté aux Broyes et aux Noyes. La généalogie aidant, il remontait aux ducs de Saint-Simon, puis à des bâtards royaux, à Philippe le Bel enfin qui plaisait bien à Jacques L'Aumône, surtout comme ancêtre. De là on parvenait facilement à Hugues Capet. Ainsi lui Jacques L'Aumône se trouvait être de sang non seulement bleu mais royal.

(pp. 34–5)

Fantasies such as this recur throughout the novel, as, for instance, when Jacques' absorption in films leads him to identify with an outlaw in a western, and then with a brilliant aircraft designer. Moreover, his different fantasies intertwine, as when, after the massive success he imagines in the aircraft industry, 'il remonte sur le trône des Laumoningiens et finalement on le proclame Régisseur du Globe' (p. 46).

These flights of the imagination make a strong claim on the reader not only by virtue of their frequency, but also because of their integration into the narrative. Introductory formulae such as 'Il imagina' are relatively uncommon, and the characteristic accompaniment to a passage of fantasy is some indication of the lack of surprise which it holds – for Jacques, at least. When the outlaw appears on the screen: 'Jacquot n'est nullement étonné de reconnaître en lui Jacques L'Aumône' (p. 39). At the same time, Queneau occasionally deflates the fantasy by an abrupt return to harsh reality, as when the film about the aircraft designer – and with it Jacques' daydream – comes to an end:

Cocufié, méconnu, ruiné, le pauvre inventeur meurt.
Revient la lumière.
— Tu chiales? demande Lucas.
— Moi? tu rigoles, répond Jacquot en reniflant.   (p. 46)

The final irony of *Loin de Rueil*, however, lies in the very confusion of fantasy and reality. Jacques' family, whom he left behind in Rueil when he embarked on his cinematic career in America, fail to recognise Jacques in James Charity, the Hollywood star whose film, *La Peau des rêves*, they see at the end of the novel. Whereas for much of the book daydreams and fantasies have aspired to the status of reality, in this concluding sequence real events are relegated to the level of the unreal.

In its own way, *Les Fleurs bleues* goes further than *Loin de Rueil* in obscuring distinctions between dream and reality. Its very title suggests detachment from the everyday world in which much of Queneau's fiction is set, and this is confirmed by its epigraph from Plato's *Theaetetus*, which may be translated as 'a dream for a dream', and by the *prière d'insérer*, which begins: 'On connaît le célèbre apologue chinois: Tchouang-tseu rêve qu'il est un papillon, mais n'est-ce point le papillon qui rêve qu'il est Tchouang-tseu? De même dans ce roman, est-ce le duc d'Auge qui rêve qu'il est Cidrolin ou Cidrolin qui rêve qu'il est le duc d'Auge?'

The novel consists, then, of two series of dreams; for most of the novel, the narrative alternates between the life of Cidrolin in 1964 and the world of the duke, who advances through the centuries, arriving eventually at the modern age. At the end of the novel, the two characters meet and the two series are, briefly, fused. The plane of solid, observed reality, on which the whole of *Odile* rests, which forms the basis for *Le Chiendent* and the point of departure for *Loin de Rueil*, does not exist here – or, at least, no reader can be sure of its existence. The transitions between the two series take place mostly when Cidrolin or the duc d'Auge falls asleep. (And, if the cinema was the basis of dreams in *Loin de Rueil*, here the relationship is reversed; when there is talk of presenting Cidrolin with a television set, 'On verra, dit Lamélie. Pour le moment le mieux c'est de lui laisser faire sa sieste: c'est encore son meilleur cinéma' (p. 62).) The following switch is typical:

Tandis qu'on nettoyait ses vêtements et qu'il mijotait dans l'eau chaude, le duc s'endormit.

Après avoir fermé le portillon derrière lui, Cidrolin regarda si des inscriptions souillaient la clôture qui séparait du boulevard le terrain en pente attenant à la péniche.   (p. 24)

The shifts are often so delicate that the reader cannot know for several lines that they have been made. In the following example, the first paragraph refers to Cidrolin on his barge and the second to the duc d'Auge, but by his use of personal pronouns Queneau prevents an immediate identification:

Il alla dans le carré regarder l'heure et, comme conséquence de cet examen, il s'étendit de nouveau sur sa chaise longue pour achever sa sieste interrompue.

Lorsqu'il ouvrit de nouveau l'œil, il aperçut autour de lui tout ce qu'il avait l'habitude d'y voir, les murs de sa chambre, l'étroite fenêtre qui y donnait un peu de jour [. . .]. Ce spectacle familier rassura fort le duc.
                                                                       (pp. 35–6)

The reader may even find that his problems increase, rather than decrease, as he progresses. Some way into the book, for example, when he will probably have accustomed himself to the movement from one sphere to the other Queneau introduces what can best be seen as a fake transition:

— Donne-nous, dit Albert, une bouteille de champ. Ma cuvée spéciale. C'est, dit-il à Cidrolin, la même que chez les Rothschild, Onassis ou des gens comme ça.

Onésiphore ouvre une petite trappe et disparaît. (p. 98)

The name 'Onésiphore' inevitably recalls l'abbé Onésiphore Biroton, chaplain to the duc d'Auge, who appeared in the previous chapter, so that the reader is effectively encouraged to expect a transition from Cidrolin and the 'Bar Biture', where the scene has been taking place. It soon emerges, however, that in this case Onésiphore is the barman at the 'Bar Biture', previously described at some length but hitherto unnamed, and that no transition has occurred.[23]

In other ways, too, *Les Fleurs bleues* stands at some distance from conventional realism. For one thing, the presence of the talking horses, Sthène and Stèphe, extends the vein of fantasy common to 'Le Cheval troyen' and 'A la limite de la forêt'. For another, elements of realistic detail such as the trappings of technology – mobylettes, transistor radios and television sets – are sometimes deliberately confused with the atmosphere of past ages to give obvious anachronisms, as in this early exchange between the duc d'Auge and Biroton:

— Je rêve que je suis sur une péniche; je m'assois sur une chaise longue, je me mets un mouchoir sur la figure et je fais une petite sieste.
— Sieste ... mouchoir ... péniche ... qu'est-ce que c'est que tous ces mots-là? Je ne les entrave point.
— Ce sont des mots que j'ai inventés pour désigner des choses que je vois dans mes rêves. (p. 38)

If, through the autobiographical, historical and realistic elements in his fiction, Queneau offers a reflection of a recognisable, credible world, and if the fantasy in his work lies at a tangent to normal life, then in the Saint Glinglin trilogy, as nowhere else, he creates a world parallel to the one in which his readers live. Parts of the trilogy, certainly, are inspired to some extent by real places; Queneau has stated that he wrote 'Les Ruraux'[24] at Varengeville, near Dieppe, in 1939, even though 'si je n'aimais pas la campagne normande qui m'entourait, je pensais encore davantage à la Touraine en écrivant mon chapitre.'[25] At the same time, the world of the trilogy is an autonomous one, without specific reference to the actual world, and a world whose characteristics are described in minute detail.[26] Queneau delineates its geographical aspects – its remoteness from the sea and its situation on a plain surrounded by mountains, the climate based on the absence of rain, and the terrain which this produces. The social organisation too, is carefully depicted: the taxation system, the lay-out of the Ville Natale, which reflects a strict social hierarchy (the notables live in the centre, the lower orders in the suburbs), the range of occupations attributed to the 'Urbinataliens', the hereditary nature of political functions. The life of the town is increasingly marked by outside influences – the growth of imports, the tourists, the cinema; on the meteorological level, it is affected by the unprecedented event of rain. The town has a traditional ceremony, the Printanier, in which, in conformity with prevailing superstition, vast amounts of pottery are destroyed in order that the prosperity of the town and the fine weather will continue. In addition, it is believed that the 'chasse-nuages', invented by one Timothée Worwass, helps to prevent the rain. However, when Pierre attempts to revolutionise the rituals of the town, rain sets in, and it is only after a number of drastic upheavals that the good weather is restored.

The world of the Saint Glinglin trilogy is an enclosed, consistent entity, with its own carefully described rules and rituals: a world comparable with the one its readers know, but not identifiable with it; a world inclining towards science fiction, and towards allegory and myth. Maurice Blanchot's comments on *Les Temps mêlés* put the whole trilogy in perspective:

Le monde de Raymond Queneau, même quand il a pris la forme d'une allégorie, reste mystérieux et caché [...]. Que signifient ces épisodes dont l'étrangeté n'est à aucun moment une raison de les soustraire à notre croyance et qui, par delà le sens allégorique qu'on peut leur prêter, continuent de solliciter le vague des esprits? On dirait que de tels mythes sont destinés à nous faire pénétrer les choses, non point en nous introduisant dans leur mystère, mais en nous laissant éternellement au dehors.[27]

Queneau's fiction operates over a very wide register, from the historical accuracy of *Odile*, through the mixture of

realism and fantasy in *Le Chiendent* and *Le Dimanche de la vie*
to the imaginative creations of *Les Fleurs bleues* and *Saint
Glinglin*; and if he tends to favour the centre of the range,
peopled by a 'menu peuple de boutiquiers et bistroquets, de
cartomanciennes et brocanteuses, de petits rentiers et petits
marlous',[28] he is no more limited to this area than to any
other. The essence of Queneau's fictional world is precisely
that, because his works are, in the first instance, self-sufficient
constructions, they are not restricted to any one use of
reality, or of fantasy. Queneau is characterised by variety
rather than by uniformity. Yet despite all the diversity of
presentation, the solidity of his world and the fascination
which it exercises constitute one of the fundamental experiences of every reader.

Social patterns; nature and culture

The fictional world Queneau creates is no mere
background, no flimsy décor on which attention can rest for
no more than a few brief moments between incidents. It is a
coherent and substantial creation with its own lines of force
and its own recurring patterns. Underlying the superficial
differences which separate, for example, the Paris inhabited
by Vincent Tuquedenne, the France in which Cidrolin and
the duc d'Auge have their adventures, and the dream-world
of Jacques L'Aumône, a complex network of processes is
discernible – processes which bear on all aspects of human
life. There are the influences which govern social and personal situations and those which condition the more abstract
features of existence. And to all of them Queneau pays due
attention.

As Queneau presents it, most behaviour – particularly in
public – is dominated by convention; the life of a community, in its most trivial as in its most solemn aspects, tends
to be regulated by a series of routines – from the train
journey to work in the morning to the perusal of the
newspaper before bed. Even so small a matter as the buying
of drinks is controlled in this way, as Valentin Brû discovers,
having just learned from his superior that he is being sought
as a marriage-partner:

Ce qui le tourmentait, il fallait qu'il rende à Bourrelier sa tournée et, s'il buvait un quatrième vin blanc gommé, ça l'enivrerait. Non seulement les usages le voulaient, qu'il réponde au verre par le verre, mais encore à un homme qui venait vous apporter un riche mariage tout cuit et pour ainsi dire sur un plat, il devait témoigner sa reconnaissance au risque même de l'ébriété.   (*Dimanche*, p. 37)

Blind adherence to convention can reach absurd lengths, as when it is decided that come what may, there must be a honeymoon and that Valentin should celebrate it alone, since his bride, Julia, is too busy to accompany him; as she argues: 'Faut reconnaître qu'un mariage sans voyage de noces, ça n'existe pas' (*ibid.*, p. 58). Ritual also predominates in more serious matters, as is apparent from the various funeral scenes, such as the burial of Narcense's grandmother in *Le Chiendent* or Nanette in *Le Dimanche de la vie*. And Queneau regularly heaps indignities on the ceremonies he describes, as, in this case, via an uncouth cinema audience in Le Havre:

Les actualités offraient en effet une cérémonie officielle à l'Université d'Oxford; le poulailler prenant les professeurs en toge pour des curés manifestait énergiquement ses convictions anti-cléricales sans d'ailleurs choquer le militaire anglais pour qui les sifflets n'avaient point cette valeur réprobative. Bref tout le monde était content sauf quelques bourgeois français qui comprenait eux, grâce à leur instruction.

                                                    (*Rude Hiver*, p. 49)

In general, religion consists of worthless ritual based on superstition. The most obvious religious celebration, Christmas, is the one which Queneau evokes most, and he presents it as a mere pretext for indulgence, gastronomic – 'Le baron Hachamoth fêtait la Noël comme un chrétien, c'est-à-dire que, ce jour-là, il s'abîmait le foie pour quelques semaines' (*Limon*, p. 216) – or sexual – 'Et nouél, quel beau nouél ce fut. Cette nuit-là, tant de couples firent l'amour que la ville entière semblait miauler' (*Chiendent*, p. 281).

In *Le Chiendent* he devotes several passages to the predictable and repetitive routine of the sea-side resort where Étienne and his family spend their holiday. But everyday life, too, is governed by convention rather than individual choice. An insignificant activity can assume the dimensions of an important event; Sunday, for instance, is the day of the family walk; here the banal rhythm of the prose, the mocking inversion of 'l'habituel itinéraire' and the future tenses conspire to stress the utter predictability of the exercise:

Le Bois, naturellement, est envahi. Des gens ont picniqué et le papier gras s'étale. On dort çà et là, des couples se chatouillent et des femmes rient très fort [...]. Étienne à son bras sent sa femme se pendre. Lui, conduit sa famille suivant l'habituel itinéraire. On ira jusqu'au vieux château; là, repos; puis on descendra jusqu'à la rivière, à la petite guinguette; limonade, et puis retour [...]. Mais il est temps de rentrer. La foule commence à se diriger vers la gare. 6h. ½. On attendra une demi-heure le dîner, puis la pipe, un dernier tour au jardin, la nuit, le sommeil. Demain, le travail recommence.   (*Chiendent*, pp. 38–9)

Convention and habit play a very evident role in determining the conduct of the community, channelling it into a number of clearly defined and often-repeated paradigms. On a more personal level, the life of the individual is shown to be moulded by the crucial influence of kinship. It is not by chance, for example, that the holidays in *Le Chiendent* are taken *en famille*, or that the description of the Sunday walk stresses that it is a family activity. Here and throughout his work Queneau shows that no character can be totally free of his family. This is most apparent in the Saint Glinglin books, where the Kougard/Nabonide dynasty is the focus of interest as well as supplying rulers of the Ville Natale, and in *Les Enfants du limon*, which is dominated by the Limon-Chambernac-Hachamoth family, to which all the major characters, except Purpulan, belong. But in all his fiction Queneau traces the relationships which link his characters to their families.

The usual effect of the family environment is to create tensions and conflicts, and patterns of flawed relationships occur in all his works. The antagonism between the brothers Thémistocle Troc and Peter Tom at Ernestine's wedding in *Le Chiendent* is a typical case, as is Sénateur Lehameau's coldness towards his 'poor relation', Lalie, whom he does not invite to the celebration of his fiftieth birthday; she laments to her husband: 'Voilà comment elle me traite ma famille, des cousins germains encore, ma seule famille. C'est tonteux, c'est tonteux' (*Rude Hiver*, p. 94).

Queneau devotes particular attention to strained relations

between parents and children, particularly fathers and sons. The alienation of the child described in *Chêne et chien* (see especially pp. 36, 46) finds echoes in the misery of the adolescent Vincent Tuquedenne: 'Il était seul, car les êtres humains chez lesquels il logeait ne constituaient pour lui aucune société. A côté de lui, en dehors de lui, ses parents menaient l'existence diminuée de fonctionnaires retraités, privés de toute raison d'être' (*Derniers Jours*, p. 70). Roland Travy fails to achieve the academic success his father demands and is disowned (*Odile*, pp. 35–6). Sally Mara's family is first weakened by the abrupt departure of her father, then disrupted by his return, when he assaults his children (*Sally Mara*, pp. 19, 106–7). Zazie describes her father's ill-treatment of her (*Zazie*, pp. 71–2) and reflects on her mother's reluctance to spend any part of a Parisian weekend with herself and Gabriel: 'C'est comme ça quand elle a un jules [...] la famille ça compte plus pour elle' (*ibid.*, p. 13). Most striking of all, perhaps, is the anguished relationship between Pierre and his father in the Saint Glinglin trilogy. The father's latent hostility towards his son, who is sent to the Ville Étrangère to learn the language but devotes himself instead to the exhibits in an aquarium, turns into open aggression when Pierre returns home to proclaim his discoveries in the field of 'metabiology'. At this stage Pierre finds himself formally renounced by his father, and the situation reaches crisis point when the latter interrupts his homecoming lecture to the 'Urbinataliens'. Soon afterwards Pierre confronts his father, asking him explicitly: 'Pourquoi veux-tu m'empêcher d'être moi-même' (*Gueule de pierre*, p. 158). The specifically sexual – and Oedipal – implications of the father's tyranny become clear from Pierre's subsequent meditation:

> "Tu étais mon père, tu voulais faire de moi un homme, disais-tu,
> Mais vraiment, oui vraiment, tu voulais que je sois un eunuque."   (*ibid.*, p. 189)

Other conflicts in Queneau's fiction may be forgotten or resolved, but such is the intensity of this one that it can only end in death, which occurs when the father, having fled, eventually perishes in the Montagnes Arides.

Patterns of marital discord are also frequent. The defect is sometimes due to a grotesque mis-match, such as the pairing of the young waitress Ernestine and the aged scrap-merchant, père Taupe, in *Le Chiendent*. In *Le Dimanche de la vie* there is a clear disparity between Julia and Valentin not only in terms of age (Julia is twenty or twenty-five years older than her husband) but in their behaviour towards each other: initially Julia treats Valentin like a child; later Valentin strenuously asserts his independence.

However, most marriages in Queneau's works are failures less because of their initial incongruity than because of a breakdown in communication – physical or temperamental. In *Les Enfants du limon* Gramigni and his wife have never been able to produce children (p. 17) and Astolphe is unable to consummate his (incestuous) union with Noémi. If virtually all the marriages Queneau describes fail in some way, that of Paul and Chantal must be the most comprehensive failure of all: 'Chantal faisait allusion aux mœurs des hommes, des hommes mariés, et singulièrement à celles du sien, Paul Boulingra: l'alcoolisme buté, la tabagie autistique, la paresse sexuelle, la médiocrité financière, la lourdeur sentimentale' (*Dimanche*, p. 14).

The infidelity of either partner may be a result of such discord – or, indeed, a cause of it. Madame Dutertre in *Un Rude Hiver* is one character among many who have discovered this to their cost: 'Mon mari était un salaud. Il me trompait avec la première venue' (p. 26). Petit-Pouce, one of Pierrot's colleagues at the funfair, is one of a series of unfaithful husbands, even if he does experience some regrets:

Durant les entr'actes, Petit-Pouce n'était pas tellement que ça un homme heureux. Parce qu'il était marié, très légitimement. Et il avait des remords. Des tout petits mais des remords tout de même. Alors tout en sortant de son larenqué, il n'en pressait que plus fort la jeune mamelle où se plantaient ses doigts.   (*Pierrot*, p. 23)

Queneau's female characters are just as capable of unfaithfulness as the men. Suzanne, the wife of Jacques L'Aumône in *Loin de Rueil*, reserves her favours for one Butard:

Il entra. Ils s'embrassèrent avec véhémence.
— Jacques est en train de faire le con, dit Butard lorsqu'il eut dégagé ses lèvres.
— Ne me parle de ce type-là, répondit Suzanne qui l'entraîna vers le lit.
                                                        (p. 133)

Not surprisingly Chantal reacts against Paul's many short-comings – notably by committing adultery with an army officer:

— Il ne me reste plus qu'à travailler encore plus durement, déclama Paul. Pour que notre fille ait une dot.
— Ce que tu es vieux jeu, dit Chantal en lissant ses bas au souvenir du capitaine Bordcille.   (*Dimanche*, p. 106)

Queneau's characters are always subject to specific pressures, just as they are firmly located in particular physical environments. Convention imposes patterns of habit on all aspects of their lives, and they encounter grave personal and emotional problems as a result of their inescapable relationships with other members of their families. The sociological features of Queneau's world, then, are just as characteristic as its geographical locations.

Despite the importance of the sociological dimension, however, there are fundamental qualities of Queneau's world which are to be found elsewhere. For Queneau not only traces patterns determining human behaviour but characterises the phenomena which, for him, define the very nature of existence within this world.

Queneau repeatedly emphasises the central theme of his poem 'Petite cosmogonie portative': that man is one small part of a much larger creation. And he never tires of stressing the links between the two. In *Pierrot mon ami* the visitors to a zoo are seen not as creatures different in kind from those they have come to see, but as 'primates bavards en complet veston ou en culottes courtes' (p. 216). Here, as elsewhere, man is presented as one element in the continuum of living beings: as one among the many manifestations of life itself. Thus in *Le Dimanche de la vie* Valentin refuses to eat oysters because they are living creatures – and therefore belong to the same order as humans: 'C'est vrai, quoi, c'est vivant une huître. Autant que moi. Y a pas ddifférence. Y a qu'une seule différence: entre les vivants et entre les morts' (p. 112). The epigraph Queneau retrospectively applied to *Gueule de pierre* is a quotation from Goethe: 'Il s'était aperçu qu'il y a dans la nature humaine quelque chose d'analogue aux corps les plus bruts et les plus obscurs'[29] – which well conveys the metaphysical bent of the first part of the trilogy. On the basis of his observations in the aquarium in the Ville Étrangère Pierre comes to extend his conception of life beyond the usual understanding of the word; and this is what he so desperately wants to explain to his father:

Je voudrais lui faire comprendre que la vie, ce n'est pas quelque chose d'entièrement assimilable aux diverses facultés de compréhension de l'homme, et que les valeurs éthiques ou esthétiques qu'on lui attribue n'appartiennent pas à toutes ses formes et par conséquent encore moins à la Vie en Soi.   (*Glinglin*, pp. 26–7)

The differences between human and marine life are clearly immense in terms of intellect, vision, hearing, digestion; but for Pierre the common links are far more significant: both belong to one and the same basic category. The idea is further developed in *Les Temps mêlés*, when Pierre's brother Paul speculates on the points of comparison between man and plants (pp. 52–3), so that vegetable and animal existence are seen to form part of the same all-encompassing concept.

'C'est la Vie et non son expression baroque dans un patois barbare, c'est la Vie elle-même qui est le sens de mon activité' declares Pierre (*Gueule de pierre*, pp. 29–30), who thereby gives his own intonation to an unmistakable refrain which reverberates throughout Queneau's fiction. In *Le Chiendent* Étienne hears it: 'Une petite phrase se met à lui galoper dans la tête: "C'est ça la vie, c'est ça la vie, c'est ça la vie." La petite phrase devient d'immenses coups de cloche. Boum la vie, boum la vie, boum la vie' (p. 35). In the same novel Bébé Toutout 'se mit à raminagrober dans sa barbe: "Quelle vie, quelle vie, quelle vie"' (p. 45); and he is echoed by Des Cigales in *Loin de Rueil* (p. 201). In *Pierrot mon ami*,

Pierrot, tout en vidant sa bouteille de rouge, sentait son crépuscule intérieur traversé de temps à autre par des fulgurations philosophiques, telles que: 'la vie vaut d'être vécue', ou bien: 'l'existence a du bon'; et, sur un autre thème: 'c'est marant la vie', ou bien: 'quelle drôle de chose que l'existence'.   (p. 165)

All these characters are betraying some awareness, however vague, of their place in the order of things. Queneau, for his part, seeks to emphasise the fundamentals of the human situation. And since man's origins lie in the biological processes of evolution, Queneau returns again and again to the animal functions every human being must perform. Man can never completely transcend the animal state, as is confirmed in *On est toujours trop bon avec les femmes*, by the Irish rebels, at the very moment when they are revelling in the idea that they are making history:

> Dillon et Callinan allèrent chercher une caisse de conserves et des biscuits. Ils s'installèrent et commencèrent à mâcher en silence, comme des gens qui deviennent des héros et qui ne concèdent encore à la banalité de l'existence que ses banalités les plus extrêmes, telles que boire et manger, uriner et déféquer.   (*Sally Mara*, p. 289)

The novels contain frequent allusions to food; indeed some people seem to live to eat, which is why Paul Kougard, frustrated by the tedium of rural life, describes those he meets as 'bipèdes [...] enfermés dans les limites de leur digestion' (*Temps mêlés*, p. 46). The guests at the wedding of Taupe and Ernestine do show themselves to be reasonably civilised individuals, but for them eating is an indispensable preliminary to the more elevated activity of conversation:

> Passant de l'animal au social et de la gloutonnerie au bavardage, chacune des quinze personnes énumérées plus haut commence à s'apercevoir de nouveau de la présence de quatorze autres [...]. C'est seulement maintenant que les langues que nouait la faim vont se délier; c'est seulement maintenant que les bouches vont s'ouvrir pour autre chose que pour absorber, c'est seulement maintenant que l'estomac calmé va laisser le cerveau faire un peu d'exercice.   (*Chiendent*, pp. 182–3)

And similarly an ironic comment in *Les Enfants du limon* points out that beneath its apparent sophistication, a round of drinks serves a thoroughly primitive need: 'Et maintenant c'est au tour des cinq de se tremper les lèvres dans des faux-cols bien tièdes et de reprendre ainsi contact avec la civilisation occidentale' (p. 28).

As for 'uriner et déféquer', Dillon and Callinan are by no means the only ones who need to relieve themselves at crucial moments. Gertie Girdle's plight in *On est toujours trop bon avec les femmes* is entirely due to her being trapped in the lavatory when the Eden Quay post office is seized by the Irish rebels, who subsequently take her prisoner. The narrator of 'Une Trouille verte' describes how after relieving himself in the small hours of the morning he is so afraid of malign spirits that he spends the rest of the night in the water closet.

Whatever lofty aspirations the human race may cherish, Queneau perpetually recalls that in physical terms man is an animal much like any other. And as well as underlining the biological attributes of human beings he further blurs the distinction normally made between man and other creatures – by ascribing human qualities to animals. He does this both in terms of fantasy, through his portrayal of talking horses in 'Le Cheval troyen' and *Les Fleurs bleues* and of Dino, the magical dog in 'A la limite de la forêt', and in a more realistic manner through Laverdure, the talkative parrot in *Zazie dans le métro*. The best example is doubtless that of Mésange and Pistolet, who accompany Pierrot on a long road journey through France. For several pages, until a waitress in a restaurant is reluctant to serve them, the reader has no real indication that they are anything but human. Throughout the journey they behave in a thoroughly human way: they not only eat in restaurants but sleep in beds, and when confronted by a hotel keeper 'Mésange la salua d'un coup de chapeau plein de dignité. Pistolet la regarda plein d'indifférence, de son œil bistre et glauque' (*Pierrot*, p. 169). During a conversation between Pierrot and a restaurateur, 'Pistolet, que la conversation ennuyait, s'était endormi. Mésange avait sorti un cigare de sa poche, l'avait allumé et fumait placidement' (p. 167). Only considerably later does it become clear that Pierrot's travelling companions were, in fact, a wild boar and a monkey (p. 204).

But even aside from their affinities with the animal kingdom, the characters are in constant danger of falling below a properly human level – of becoming, to use a favourite word of Queneau's, 'abrutis'. For him, this conveys not merely its most usual meaning of general stupidity, but also its original sense of specifically brutish mindlessness: a predominance of lower functions over higher ones. The idea is forcefully expressed by Paul in his bitter meditation on the countryside in *Les Temps mêlés*:

Dans le ciel luisent les planètes et les étoiles éperdues de géométrie, mais du sol arable se dégagent des masses globulaires et obscures, des poches d'encre qui montent vers les cimes. La nature entière s'abîme dans un affreux marasme. Tout sombre dans l'abrutissement.   (p. 47)

This total eclipse of the mind, of higher human instincts, is a rare event in Queneau's fiction, but he insists that man always has a latent tendency towards it. Père Taupe seems to reveal this at his wedding: 'Quant au père Taupe, il se confine dans un silence souriant dont on ne saurait dire s'il mime la dignité ou s'il exprime l'abrutissement' (*Chiendent*, p. 181). In *Gueule de pierre*, Pauline, the grandmother of the Kougard children, who lives out her animal-like existence in the depths of the country is described in similar terms (p. 174). And while alcohol accentuates the 'abrutissement' of a primitive individual such as Pauline, it can also debase a more sophisticated character, like the intellectual Roland Travy in *Odile*: 'Émergeant de l'abrutissement spiral de l'ivresse, je me passai une main tremblante sur ma figure décomposée, hésitant à prendre le rasoir' (p. 130).

Travy regrets his 'abrutissement' and seeks to put it behind him, but other characters are positively eager to accept the animal side of their nature. Agnès de Chambernac for a time devotes herself exclusively to the care of her body, following the régime of sunbathing and swimming which was coming into vogue at the beginning of the period covered by *Les Enfants du limon*. The final simile neatly captures the implications of her choice:

Elle avait acquis [. . .] un corps souple et musclé, rebelle à toute maladie, habile à tout exercice, bronzé, seins petits et fesses dures, et c'est à ce corps qu'elle se référait pour orienter sa vie et pour stabiliser son âge, pour s'individualiser sans vieillir. Fière et sûre d'elle, elle allait calmement son chemin, comme une vache, broutant dans chaque instant son bonheur avec une réussite constante.   (p. 55)

In *Gueule de pierre* Pierre asks rhetorically: 'La vie animale serait-elle un perpétuel bonheur?' (p. 21). But humans who live close to nature can also achieve something of this happiness. Such, at least, is Dino's claim in 'A la limite de la forêt': 'Il n'y a que les animaux qui ne s'ennuient jamais, dit le chien, ou les individus qui ne se sont éloignés que de peu de la vie naturelle' (*Contes*, p. 65). Père Blandi, in the same story, is one such individual; for with his intimate knowledge of his rural surroundings he at least approaches the oneness with nature which animals enjoy.

Anyone living closer to the animal state than Blandi could scarcely be called human, and certainly no other character is by any means as integrated with the natural environment. Even Agnès eventually abandons her cult of the body to involve herself in the uniquely human activity of politics. Although man follows certain patterns of animal behaviour, he is obviously a very different being from other creatures. Whatever links Pierre Kougard may find to connect human beings and marine life, Bébé Toutout, for one, makes a very clear distinction between the two: 'Quand je dis la vie [...] je parle de la vie vécue par les hommes, par moi-même; pas de la vie en général, y compris celle des poissons, par exemple' (*Chiendent*, p. 239). Queneau is well aware that the human race has other defining characteristics than the purely physical ones, as he wryly shows in the poem entitled 'L'espèce humaine':

> L'espèce humaine m'a donné
> le droit d'être mortel
> le devoir d'être civilisé
> la conscience humaine
> [. . . . .]
> l'espèce humaine m'a donné
> ses trois facultés
> le sentiment l'intelligence et la volonté
> chaque chose de façon modérée.[30]

Man is an animal, but a moral and intelligent one, characterised by his aspirations and ideals: 'C'est vrai, comment vivre sans idéal? [...]. Sans idéal, on vit comme des animaux' (*Chiendent*, p. 194). For Queneau, man is above all the creature who cannot accept his situation as he finds it, who adapts, contrives, invents: the creature who is not satisfied with eating the fruit from the tree but instead concocts 'la brouchtoucaille'; who drinks, not the water from the pool but 'le fifrequet'. Man's animal qualities are certainly an essential part of his being, but they can also be seen as a precondition for the faculties and achievements peculiar to him: 'L'homme [...] est une espèce, une espèce animale même, et qui n'est sortie de l'animalité qu'en modifiant constamment son statuquo' (*Bâtons*, p. 92).[31]

To advance beyond the natural state man can either refine what nature provides, or else subjugate it totally. The former course of action is taken by some of Queneau's young female characters. Yvonne, in *Pierrot mon ami*, elaborates on nature by her earnest attempts to beautify her body:

> Yvonne devait le bouchonner, ce corps, le baigner, le doucher, le parfumer, lui donner la meilleure présentation possible, à lui aussi bien qu'à ses compléments, ongles, cheveux, sourcils. Il le fallait nourrir, avec grand appétit. Il le fallait vêtir, ce qui demandait choix et précision [...]. Ce n'est que lorsqu'elle dut attendre qu'au bout de ses doigts séchât un vernis plus noirâtre que sanglant, qu'Yvonne eut quelque loisir de penser à un autre être qu'elle-même.   (pp. 83–4)

And *Journal intime* traces Sally Mara's evolving attitude towards aids to beauty. Early in the novel she repeatedly rejects artificial adornments: 'Je ne me vois pas achetant une gaine ou me faisant friser. Je reste comme je suis, nature' (*Sally Mara*, pp. 134–5). Yet she succumbs to them eventually, and proclaims her delight in stockings, make-up and perfume (*ibid.*, p. 178).

In enhancing their beauty by cosmetic means Yvonne and Sally do no more than collaborate with the gifts of nature. The other course – man's attempt to impose his will even to the extent of violating his surroundings – is far more widespread. Pouldu in *Les Enfants du limon* explicitly condemns the ineptitude of the attempt to co-operate with the environment which he sees in signposted country walks during an excursion from La Ciotat (p. 30). In Pouldu's opinion man should not meekly work with nature, but rather mould it to his own needs – which is possible given the power of the human intellect, as manifested in technological achievement:

> Le seul contact véritable entre l'homme et la nature, c'est la science, la science qui transforme et qui détruit, la science qui rend habitable un désert ou des marécages, la science qui fait courir du fer sur du fer à travers les accidents géographiques les plus divers et qui fait voler de l'aluminium à travers les incidents météorologiques les plus variés, la science qui fait de l'essence de rose avec du charbon et du sucre avec des copeaux de bois. Voilà le seul contact véritable de l'homme avec la nature: un lac desséché, un désert irrigué, une mer domptée, une montagne coupée, voilà le contact

authentique de l'homme avec la nature, celui de l'action, de la destruction et de la transformation. (pp. 29–30)

A fable in *Les Temps mêlés* encapsulates the whole process. Queneau first evokes the might and splendour of a centuries-old tree, and then describes its fate after it has been struck down in a storm:

> Son tronc partit pour la scierie
> De ses planches on construisit
> une maison près des collines
> hutte cabane ou bien abri
> L'arbre dans les nuits citadines
> allait et venait bien qu'occis
> blanchâtre et lent comme la lune
> élancé comme un pilotis
> mât
>   poteau
>   ombre
>   infortune (p. 35)

When man asserts himself, nature must usually suffer. The conflict between the two lies at the heart of a long meditation by Paul, in *Saint Glinglin*. He can be distinguished not only from his brother Pierre, who seeks to establish the unity of all biological forms, and from the primitive père Blandi, who readily accepts nature unmodified by man, but also from Pouldu, whose views, if firmly stated, remain reasonably dispassionate. For Paul expresses his hostility to nature in the most violent terms. He is positively repelled by the country-side in which he finds himself: 'La cambrousse dans toute son horreur, le long drap d'ennui et de chlorophylle dans lequel s'enroulent jour et nuit les Ruraux' (*Glinglin*, p. 127). Indeed the loathing he feels is physical, and more precisely sexual, when he talks of 'les touffes ignoblement poilues des boqueteaux, l'érection grenue des grands arbres', of the 'vaches agrippées au sainfoin comme des morpions dans les poils pubiens' (*ibid.*). But for all its manic excess Paul's attitude is closest to that of Pouldu. What he finds most intolerable in the natural environment of the countryside is its utter mindlessness: 'Pour revenir aux hommes et aux animaux de par ici, évidemment je ne tremble pas de sympa-thie pour eux. C'est évidemment le minimum d'humanité

que l'on puisse trouver, et quant aux bœufs, coqs, et autres
abrutis, quelle misère évidemment' (*ibid.*, p. 133). To live so
far from human intelligence is to stagnate, and to be incapable of escaping from primitive, animal conditions; hence
Paul's language is charged with images of inertia and con-
finement:

La vie rurale n'implique qu'un accord naturel avec le cours des saisons; tout
ce qui dépasse cette routine ne saurait germer en elle [...]. Une humanité
engluée dans la boue des sillons et le fumier des champs ne dépassera pas
ses limites. Cernée par la passivité de la terre, elle s'incline, se couche et
somnole.   (*ibid.*)

For Paul, as for Pouldu, man assumes his full humanity by
transcending nature's limitations. And it is only by living in a
man-made environment that he can accomplish this:

Qui donc a jamais pu croire qu'il y aurait un rapport quelconque entre
l'homme et son milieu, un rapport naturel? Les seules harmonies véritables, l'homme les a créées. Les points communs, l'homme seul les a
touchés. L'esprit ne souffle que là où respire l'homme, mais l'homme
dégagé de ses contraintes biologiques et agricoles: l'esprit ne souffle que
lorsque la nature s'efface et disparaît. L'homme ne s'accomplit que dans la
ville.   (*ibid.*, p. 129)

Man fulfils himself by dominating his natural surroundings – by draining lakes, irrigating deserts or building dams
against the sea. But it is in his character not merely to impose
his will on existing creation, but also to create in his own
right – to invent. Indeed Pouldu touches on this when he
refers to the railway engine and the aeroplane. And Queneau
differentiates man still more clearly from other creatures by
emphasising this quality of ingenuity. Narcense's fantasy
about Péponas and his invention of the 'bilboquet', or cup
and ball, is a parable conveying the vital importance of
invention in general (see *Chiendent*, pp. 142–4). In *Le Dimanche de la vie* Queneau gives more concrete examples. When
Julie is calculating her debts, 'ses doigts traçaient avec une
application analphabète des signes que l'Occident doit aux
inventeurs de la gomme' (p. 16); and when Valentin earns
his living by selling frames for miniatures, Queneau uses the
occasion to reflect on technological progress:

La décadence de cet art, la miniature, décadence commencée avec la
découverte de l'imprimerie dont on ne peut fixer la date avec exactitude, du
moins en Occident, mais qui est certainement antérieure à la seconde

moitié du quinzième siècle, et achevée avec la découverte de la photographie qui remonte à l'année mil huit cent trente-neuf. (p. 119)

Le Vol d'Icare is set in the 1890s, a period when modern technology was fast superseding older methods; as Hubert Lubert observes: 'On va maintenant de Paris à Nice en moins de deux jours, la fée Électricité commence à illuminer les villes, qui sait peut-être un jour les campagnes, le télégraphe traverse l'Atlantique, on va diriger les ballons comme on conduit les chevaux, où le progrès s'arrêtera-t-il?' (p. 74).[32] And, of course, the novel ends with its hero's attempt to engage in the quintessentially modern enterprise of human flight. But it is *Les Fleurs bleues*, with its view of events over seven centuries which shows better than any other work by Queneau the crucial significance of inventions. As he has written elsewhere: 'La grande histoire véritable est celle des inventions; ce sont elles qui provoquent l'histoire, sur le fond des données statistiques, biologiques et géographiques' (*Bâtons*, p. 172).[33] When Onésiphore Biroton, the chaplain, expresses his horror of cannons, the duc d'Auge counters him by recalling the crucial role they can play in human affairs, pointing out that the Crusades would have turned out very differently if the crusaders had had the benefit of artillery (*Fleurs bleues* p. 85). In Queneau's view inventions reveal the greatest difference of all between man and the other creations of the natural world. For the rest of nature changes or stagnates, dependent on forces of evolution over which it has no control; man alone is capable of developing through his own efforts: only he can make his own history.

Appearance and reality

Among the projects which Queneau announced for the *Encyclopédie de la Pléiade* was a volume on 'l'Illusion, l'Erreur et le Mensonge' (*Bords*, p. 108), and when questioned about this extraordinary undertaking he explained: 'Le volume de l'Erreur examinera des procédés utilisés par les individus qui trompent le monde à dessein. Il y a toutes sortes de procédés: par exemple la prestidigitation qui est une chose extrêmement importante à mon avis' (*ibid.*, p. 117). Not surprisingly, perhaps, the volume never appeared, but the various problems of distinguishing between truth and falsehood or outward appearance and inner reality are a constant feature of Queneau's fiction and a decisive influence over the conditions of existence within it.

The simple example of inaccuracy in newspapers, which play an important part in the lives of most characters, in itself makes the point: 'Les journalistes arrangent toujours un peu les choses' (*Derniers Jours*, p. 88); 'Les journaux, ils romancent, je les connais' (*Pierrot*, p. 190). At the end of *Le Chiendent* the outrageous propaganda arising out of the war between the Gauls and the Etruscans, and clearly modelled on press campaigns in the First World War, stands as a vivid illustration of deliberate and crucial distortion.[34] In *Le Dimanche de la vie*, which has been termed 'le domaine des lacunes, des obscurités, de l'incertitude, le domaine de l'erreur et de la confusion',[35] the characters themselves sustain a general atmosphere of duplicity most obviously represented by the metre rule from which Julie, a haberdasher, has removed two centimetres (see pp. 45, 101). An encounter between Chantal and Bordeille is notable for the blatant attempts of each party to deceive the other. Chantal feigns interest in Bordeille in order to obtain information about her future brother-in-law, while Bordeille pretends to help Chantal so as to obtain her favours. When Chantal makes a joke, Bordeille's applause is completely artificial; and for both of them the split between thoughts and actions is complete:

En réalité, il ne la trouvait pas si bonne que ça, la calembredaine, mais voilà, il veut séduire. Chantal, elle, tient à accomplir correctement la mission que lui confia sa sœur.

— Comment cela peut-il se faire? demande-t-elle machinalement, absorbée par les plans d'action qu'elle essayait de se tracer.   (p. 28)

Chantal's husband Paul is also given to deceitful behaviour, conniving at Julie's shortened metre when he works as an inspector for weights and measures, and feigning affection for Julie in the hope of breaking her resolution to marry Valentin. The latter ploy is intended to keep Julie's inheritance for Paul's daughter – and therefore her niece – Marinette, who, given parents such as Chantal and Paul, is understandably described as 'perverse, fausse, menteuse, hypocrite, voleuse, tout' (p. 21). Even the basically innocent Valentin comes to realise the possibilities of deception, when he succeeds in misleading his wife:

S'il ne parvenait pas à lui donner des notions fausses sur la marche du commerce ou le nombre de tournées qu'il offrait et se laissait offrir, il avait fini par se convaincre qu'elle ne pouvait pénétrer à l'intérieur de sa tête et que, si la petite voix qui monte directement du fond de la gorge au cerveau sans passer par l'oreille disait noir, la haute voix pouvait déclarer blanc sans que Julia s'en aperçût. (p. 169)

The deception in *Le Dimanche de la vie* is either obvious, in the case of Chantal and Bordeille, or ineffectual, as with Paul, or harmless, as when practised by Valentin. But in other works the effect is more sinister. In the Saint Glinglin books Pierre is dogged by false and malicious rumours: 'Si mon père m'a si sévèrement jugé, c'est sur la foi de rapports inegzacts venus on ne sait d'où' (*Glinglin*, p. 41); 'Tu sais qu'il y a des tas de bruits qui courent sur nous – sur moi surtout, il est vrai' (*Temps mêlés*, p. 145). In the hope of gaining some financial reward Mulhierr gives Dussouchel, a visiting anthropologist, a wholly untruthful account of Kougard's death: 'Moi je vais vous dire: M. Pierre a tué son Père, il l'a jeté dans la Source, et, ensuite, il a supprimé M. Jean, son complice' (*ibid.*, p. 110). Elsewhere, disguise is a frequent variation on the theme. Brabbant, a confidence trickster in *Les Derniers Jours*, uses a series of false identities, posing variously as Martin-Martin, Tilleul and Blaisolle. Mme Cloche, in *Le Chiendent*, dresses up as a priest in order to obtain money from Taupe (pp. 229–32). And in *Pierrot mon ami* Jojo Mouilleminche convinces Mounnezergues that he is a royal prince called Voudzoï and subsequently passes himself off as Voussois, a dealer in circus animals, while his brother Robert takes the name Crouïa-Bey and works as a fakir in funfairs. 'Marceline', Zazie's 'aunt' is of course really a man, and although Zazie's mother is aware of this, others, such as the amorous 'Bertin Poirée', are certainly deceived (pp. 206ff.). As for the mysterious Peter Tom in *Le Chiendent*, his true identity remains uncertain but his powers are never in doubt. While waiting for his fellow wedding-guests:

Peter Tom l'Anachorète prend un *Paris-Midi* qui traîne sur table, en fait un cornet, place l'animal dedans, pose le tout sur le zinc, sort un pistolet de sa

poche, tire sur le journal, le déplie: le cobaye a disparu et *Paris-Midi* est
devenu *Paris-Soir* quatrième sportive. Les applaudissements crépitent, le
magicien salue et la noce n'est pas encore là.   (p. 173)

Peter Tom's importance stems wholly from the fact that he is
one of the 'individus qui trompent le monde à dessein'. It is
entirely appropriate that Queneau should make him a
conjurer.

However, Queneau develops the question of reality and
illusion far beyond the problems posed by liars, confidence-
men and conjurers. Although outside interference often
obscures the reality of a situation, other basic obstacles also
prevent Queneau's characters from understanding their
experiences. Frequently, for example, an individual's own
weaknesses are enough to mislead him totally. When the
short-sighted Pierrot calls on Mounnezergues, he spends
some time talking to a wax figure in the belief that it is his
host (*Pierrot*, pp. 149–50); Yvonne overhears a conversation
between Léonie and 'sidi Mouilleminche' and jumps to the
mistaken conclusion that the two have been lovers (*ibid.*,
pp. 87–8). A more important case is Mme Cloche's gross
misinterpretation of the situation and intentions of Étienne
Marcel and his family in *Le Chiendent*. Mme Cloche inter-
cepts a letter from Théo, the son of Étienne and Alberte, in
which he reproaches his 'enemy' Narcense for showing an
obvious interest in his mother. She completely misunder-
stands it, believing that Théo is a jealous husband threatened
by Narcense (p. 42) – which would not be serious in itself,
but becomes so when it leads on to a chain of damaging
misapprehensions. A snatch of conversation overheard by
her nephew leads Mme Cloche to interpret a random series
of trivial events as part of a sinister conspiracy:

Étienne Marcel veut s'emparer du trésor du père Taupe! Voilà pourquoi il
est venu manger des frites chez Dominique! Il n'y a pas d'autre explication.
Et il a un complice et peut-être que ce Meussieu Narcense est aussi un
complice. La pendaison de Théo, c'est une histoire de règlements de
compte. Entre bandits internationaux. Et le trésor du père Taupe doit être
important pour que des bandits de cette envergure s'en occupent.

(pp. 98–9)

The subsequent disasters of the novel come as a direct result
of Mme Cloche's failure to see a situation as it really is.

In many cases human beings alone are responsible for a misunderstanding, either because they actively promote confusion or because, through their own failings, they are unable to dispel it. But Queneau sometimes presents the problem so as to suggest that illusion and uncertainty are integral parts of his world, independent of human agency and ultimately impenetrable. The apocalyptic climax of *Zazie dans le métro* is dominated by the monstrous 'Aroun Arachide' who, with his army, besieges Gabriel and his friends in the night-club 'Aux Nyctalopes'. 'Aroun Arachide' (the name derives from Haroun al-Rashid, a caliph of Baghdad with a legendary penchant for disguises) is a protean figure, who has appeared earlier in the novel as Trouscaillon the satyr, Pédro-Surplus the flea-market trader and Bertin Poirée the detective. But this is no mere case of false identities, for 'Aroun Arachide' is explicitly designated as a generalised symbol: 'Prince de ce monde et de plusieurs territoires connexes, il me plaît de parcourir mon domaine sous des aspects variés en prenant les apparences de l'incertitude et de l'erreur qui, d'ailleurs, me sont propres' (p. 247). The importance to be attached to this figure is clear; when questioned about the characters in *Zazie dans le métro*, Queneau commented: 'Le personnage essentiel du livre, c'est plutôt Trouscaillon.'[36]

Through the incident of the fire which destroys Uni-Park in *Pierrot mon ami* Queneau crystallises the idea that it may be impossible to determine the reality of a situation: that any number of interpretations may be equally valid – or invalid. One eye-witness claims the fire was the result of arson:

Comme il avait l'air très exalté, les gens qui l'écoutaient n'osèrent pas proposer des versions différentes, et ils commentèrent la sienne. Qui? Pourquoi? Comment? On épiloguait. Le directeur? Un ennemi? Vengeance? Intérêt? Complicités? On rappela l'incident de la veille au Palace de la Rigolade. On envisagea diverses hypothèses, mais à chacune quelqu'un se récria.   (p. 138)

It is still possible, at the end of *Pierrot mon ami*, that the true explanation of the fire at Uni-Park will never be known;[37] certainly, no final explanation is given, and Pierrot, who has been as closely involved with events as anyone, is quite incapable of understanding them. Queneau reads Pierrot's thoughts at this point:

Il voyait bien comment tous les éléments qui le constituaient auraient pu se lier en une aventure qui se serait développée sur le plan du mystère pour se résoudre ensuite comme un problème d'algèbre où il y a autant d'équations que d'inconnues, et comment il n'en avait pas été ainsi. [...] Il n'était point possible de savoir s'il y avait une énigme à résoudre ou s'il n'y en avait pas.

(pp. 210–11)

Much of the uncertainty and deception in Queneau's fiction can be dispelled. It is known that newspapers tell lies; Paul B— is an obvious hypocrite; and Mme Cloche is manifestly wrong in her assumptions. But Pierrot learns that in the very nature of things truth sometimes remains inaccessible. It is a conclusion to which Gabriel in *Zazie dans le métro*, would readily subscribe: 'La vérité! s'écrie Gabriel (geste), comme si tu savais cexé. Comme si quelqu'un au monde savait cexé. Tout ça (geste), tout ça c'est du bidon: le Panthéon, les Invalides, la caserne du Reuilly, le tabac du coin, tout. Oui, du bidon' (p. 20). Repercussions of this are to be heard in the novel, as in an apparently trivial discussion of what Mado Ptits-pieds should wear to celebrate her engagement. Marceline asks her: 'Pourquoi ne mettriez-vous pas votre veste amarante avec la jupe plissée verte et jaune que je vous ai vue un jour de bal un quatorze juillet' (p. 189), and yet minutes later Mado asks if she should put on 'ma veste vert pomme avec la jupe orange et citron du quatorze juillet?' (p. 190). There is no means of deciding between these two different descriptions of what must be the same garments. As one critic of the novel explains:

Toute chose est ici pourvue d'une double face, irréalisée, blanchie de cette lumière lunaire, qui est thème essentiel de la déception et thème propre à Queneau. L'événement n'est jamais nié, c'est-à-dire posé puis démenti; il est toujours *partagé*, à la façon du disque sélénien, mythiquement pourvu de deux figures antagonistes.[38]

In Queneau's fiction, then, there are situations where it is impossible to choose between two versions of the same set of circumstances. There may or may not have been arson at Uni-Park; Mado's outfit may consist of a purple jacket with a green and yellow skirt, or a green jacket with a skirt in orange and lemon. And it may not always be possible even to arrive at a choice between two possibilities. In *Odile* Roland Travy talks of a mathematical theory which denies that all propositions can ever be shown to be true or false, and that, in consequence, 'Entre le vrai et le faux le tiers n'est pas exclus' (p. III). And Travy's words seem to echo those of Étienne moving towards enlightenment in *Le Chiendent*: 'On croit voir ceci et l'on voit cela. On vous dit une chose, vous en entendez une autre et c'est un troisième qu'il fallait comprendre. Tout le temps, partout, il en est ainsi' (p. 127). Indeed the whole of *Le Chiendent* is pervaded by the notion that the world consists of a vast network of bewildering and ultimately incomprehensible phenomena. Étienne becomes increasingly attracted by this idea, and reflects on it at length towards the end of the novel:

Étienne se félicitait de ses immenses progrès dans le maniement des concepts [...]. Tout ce qui se présente, se déguise [...]. On croit qu'il se passe ceci et c'est cela. Toute action est déception, toute pensée implique erreur [...]. L'on peut douter d'une apparence et se gourer, car toute chose a de multiples apparences, une infinité d'apparences.   (pp. 222–3)

Étienne's attitude has led him to doubt everything he perceives: 'Étienne douta du monde. Le monde se jouait de lui' (p. 148). But in spite of his mistrust of outward appearances he remains for the most part convinced that some truth, some meaning lies behind these appearances: 'Il y avait un secret derrière ce port de pêche, il y avait un mystère derrière cette falaise, derrière cette borne, derrière ce mégot' (*ibid.*). Accordingly, Étienne remains convinced that there is something behind the blue door owned by père Taupe which inspires the elaborate treasure-hunt of the later stages of the novel. But this belief proves to be totally unfounded; Taupe's door conceals precisely nothing: it simply rests against a railway embankment at the bottom of Taupe's yard. Further, it has no real significance, except for the sentimental value it holds for Taupe as a reminder of a love affair from his youth (p. 246).

For all his professions of scepticism Étienne can still be deceived by outward appearances. Saturnin, on the other hand, is a consistent doubter. Even during the festivities at the wedding of Taupe and Ernestine he maintains his mistrust of appearances, surveying his fellow guests and reflecting: 'Ils ne se doutait pas que l'assiette pleine cachait une assiette vide, comme l'être cache le néant' (p. 182). And it emerges in due course that this observation derives from a

systematic view of things, when, in a passage translating
Plato's *Parmenides* into 'néo-français', Saturnin distinguishes
between various modes of being and non-being:

L'être est, le nonnête n'est pas,
L'être n'est pas, le nonnête est,
L'être est, le nonnête est,
L'être n'est pas, le nonnête n'est pas,
qui toutes révèlent un aspect de la vérité; même ensemble, toutes les quatre
è n'révèlent pas la totalité, puisque admettre qu'i n'y ait que quat' formules
possibles, ça s'rait admettre, primo une limitation et secundo la légitimité
du principe de contradiction que justement on a dit n'êt' pas légitime
quand i s'agit d'totalité.
C' qui fait qu'la vérité est encore ailleurs.   (pp. 257–8)

According to Saturnin's system the truth behind appearances is even more elusive than Étienne supposes, because for
Saturnin the truth is never revealed in its entirety, even when
misleading externals are stripped away. But Pierre Le Grand
represents the ultimate stage of doubt. Unlike Étienne,
Pierre is reluctant to believe that Taupe's door conceals any
truth or significance; when the subject is first introduced he
comments: 'Je doute qu'elle ait quelque valeur' (p. 93). And
unlike both Étienne and Saturnin, he is prepared to accept
that there is no truth or meaning behind phenomena:

— Pour moi, aussi, dit Pierre, les choses, le monde n'a pas la signification
qu'il se donne, il n'est pas ce qu'il prétend être; mais je ne crois pas qu'il ait
une autre signification. Il n'en a aucune.
— C'est comme ça que vous pensez? interrogea Étienne.
Moi, je disais: on croit voir une chose et on en voit une autre.
— Et moi je dis, on croit voir une chose, mais on ne voit rien.   (p. 127)

There are great and obvious differences between the trivial
deceptions of *Le Dimanche de la vie* and the uncertainties of
Pierrot mon ami, between the antics of 'Aroun Arachide' and
the speculations of Étienne, Saturnin and Pierre Le Grand.
But all of them, in their various ways, illustrate one of the
essential experiences to be derived from Queneau's world.

Dualism

The opening of *Le Chiendent* describes a man being
swept along by city crowds returning home after the day's
work: 'La silhouette oscilla bousculée par d'autres formes'

(p. 7). However, Queneau is quick to probe beneath the surface: 'Cette oscillation n'était qu'une apparence; en réalité, le plus court chemin d'un labeur à un sommeil, d'une plaie à un ennui, d'une souffrance à une mort' (*ibid.*). The theme of deceptive appearances is thus coupled with another vital notion – that suffering, pain, death are never far away. As Simonnet neatly points out: 'Le monde d'ombres et d'apparences [...] est aussi un monde de misère, de labeur et de mort. Un monde où le mal existe.'[39] The conflict between appearance and reality is paralleled by a further conflict between good and evil, understood in their broadest terms.

Writing of one of his acknowledged masters, Pierre Mac Orlan, Queneau notes that the 'forces of darkness' underlie all his work, and goes on to speculate: 'Ne serait-il pas un gnostique pour qui le Démiurge, créateur de ce monde, est essentiellement mauvais?'[40] The question might well be asked about Queneau himself, for most of his fiction is marked in some way by a gnostic view of the world, and some texts refer more or less explicitly to motifs drawn from gnosticism.[41] The name of Saturnin in *Le Chiendent* recalls that of the gnostic sage Saturninus, or Satornil, while Valentin Brû commemorates, in his Christian name Valentinus, one of the leading thinkers of the school, and Sophie Hachamoth of *Les Enfants du limon* is a clear echo of the Pistis Sophia, the gnostic myth of human imperfection. But his treatment of gnostic material goes beyond the cultural cross-reference of many of his exercises in intertextuality, to delineate another principal feature of the imagined creation of his fiction. The central tenet of gnosticism is that the material world is flawed, inadequate, inherently evil. And images of evil pervade Queneau's work from 'l'enfer de la banlieue parisienne' which surrounds the characters of *Le Chiendent*, to the beach covered with sunbathers which Clémence so much detests in *Les Enfants du limon*: 'C'est un vrai enfer ici: rouges comme des démons et noirs comme du charbon' (p. 36). The mental universe of the young Queneau is also populated by hellish, demonic figures, as in this extraordinary reversal of traditional Christian mythology in *Chêne et chien*, in the period covering his psychoanalysis:

La Science de Dieu: le soleil c'est le diable.
Comment expliquer une telle inversion?
Dans le Soleil règne le Mal:
c'est là que cuisent les démons.
[......]
'Un des satans de l'Univers,
partant, comme un vrai tartufe,
il porte le manteau de Dieu;
c'est un sépulcre blanchi,
plein d'ossements et pourriture.
Pour tromper les âmes, Satan
s'habille en ange de lumière.'   (p. 70)[42]

Of course the devilish dwarf, Bébé Toutout, figures promi-
nently in *Le Chiendent*, and in *Les Enfants du limon* there is his
successor, Purpulan. Bébé Toutout's main characteristics are
his sedulous parasitism and his ability to dominate people by
means of intimidation. In effect he is a living symbol of moral
cowardice. And he tells Narcense: 'Je vis de la lâcheté des
autres. Est-ce bête, hein, d'avoir peur? Qu'est-ce que ça
représente comme merdouille au fond de l'âme' (*Chiendent*,
p. 46). Étienne's weakness of character is suggested early in
the novel. At this stage most of his actions are performed
'sans conviction' and when he smokes his pipe 'la fumée
s'étale autour de sa tête sans avoir le courage de monter
jusqu'aux plus basses branches du Tilleul' (*ibid.*, pp. 37–8).
This hint of weakness is confirmed much later when the
dwarf installs himself in the Marcel household and tyrannises
the family. Théo, no less than Étienne, falls completely under
the sway of Bébé Toutout, who makes of him a mere puppet,
responding obediently to his every whim: succeeding or
failing in his school lessons and treating Étienne well or ill
according to the dwarf's decree (pp. 262–3). But Bébé
Toutout is not important merely as a function of human
cowardice; he is also an active force for evil, 'habile à la
bassesse et d'une menaçante méchanceté' (p. 262). Thus he is
able to avenge himself on Narcense for refusing to take him
seriously, promising him 'une sacrée crasse [...] une crasse
qui vous démolit pour la vie' (*ibid*, p. 47) – a promise which
is fulfilled at the end of the novel, when Narcense is shot as a
deserter (*ibid.*, p. 282).
        Bébé Toutout is nothing less than a personification of evil:

'parasite/et méchant jusqu'au bout des doigts' (*Limon*, p. 35). This description comes from Purpulan, his disciple, who has taken his lessons to heart: 'Ce n'était pas au bon cœur que, selon son maître, il fallait s'adresser, mais à la crainte, à la trouille et à la superstition' (*ibid.*, p. 15). And Purpulan appears, if anything, as an even more diabolical figure than his mentor:

S'il n'était ni nain, ni barbu, Purpulan possédait cependant certaines qualités de cet ordre qui lui permettaient d'espérer quelques succès dans cette branche de l'activité humain contemporaine si vilisée.
Il était beau, et il avait l'haleine fétide, plus sulfhydrique encore que sulfureuse, réalisant ainsi d'une façon concrète l'image terrifiante et louche d'un ange déchu.   (*ibid.*)

As he explains, his past life has been devoted to evildoing in various forms (*ibid.*, p. 32) and his subsequent acquaintance with Purpulan leaves Chambernac in no doubt as to his true nature: 'Il n'est pas de notre espèce; c'est un démon, un vrai' (*ibid.*, p. 310).

Other characters besides the specifically demonic ones actively promote the cause of evil. In the war at the end of *Le Chiendent* Mme Cloche, transformed into 'Miss' or 'Missize' Aulini, the queen of the Etruscan forces, is another malevolent force:

J'étais [...] la reine des pots de moutarde, l'impératrice des fonds de culotte et la déesse des bandages herniaires. J'inspirais les trouilles nocturnes et les poltronneries diurnes. Toujours de mauvaise humeur, je distribuais les boîtes de cancer. Je gardais les chiottes du jardin des Tuileries. J'étais la chiffonnière avorteuse, la maquerelle véroleuse, la portière lyncheuse.   (p. 293)

The allusion to Mussolini is one of several in which Queneau identifies representatives of evil in his fiction with historical tyrants. In *Saint Glinglin* the overbearing father is called Nabonide, after an emperor of Babylon; and the name 'Aroun Arachide' derives from Haroun al-Raschid, as the caliph Haroun al-Rashid was notorious not only for his disguises but also for having conducted a massacre of his fellow countrymen. For as well as symbolizing the deceptiveness of appearances, 'Aroun Arachide' is another personification of the power of evil. He, too, catalogues his hilarious manifestations with mounting relish:

Policier primaire et défalqué, voyou noctinaute, indécis pourchasseur de veuves et d'orphelines, ces fuyantes images me permettent d'endosser sans crainte les risques mineurs du ridicule, de la calembredaine et de l'effusion sentimentale [...]. A peine porté disparu par vos consciences légères, je réapparais en triomphateur.   (*Zazie*, pp. 247–8)

– as is confirmed in his final incarnation, as a prince of darkness leading the sinister militia who brutally kill Mme Mouaque.

Evil maintains an almost tangible presence in Queneau's world: its images – tyranny, squalor, disease, destruction – are omnipresent – and it constitutes an active, living principle embodied in formidable figures and dramatic scenes. But it does not follow that the forces of evil go unchallenged, much less that they are always victorious. Purpulan recognises that his powers have been impaired ever since he assumed human form: for, having signed his 'devil's pact' with Chambernac, he can no longer use at will 'les pouvoirs démoniaques dont il était affligé' (*Limon*, p. 76). Furthermore at the end of the novel Chambernac destroys him – spectacularly – in the Seine. Bébé Toutout, for his part, has little lasting effect on proceedings in *Le Chiendent*, while in the final analysis neither 'Missize Aulini' nor 'Aroun Arachide' leaves a permanent mark. And there is vigorous opposition to this latter pair: Étienne and Saturnin, in *Le Chiendent*, resist the Etruscan queen, and at the end of *Zazie dans le métro* 'Aroun Arachide' finds ranged against him a number of characters, including Gabriel, whose angelic name identifies him as an adversary of evil.

Evil is consistently counterbalanced by an opposing principle: Queneau's world is characterised by the coexistence of these two, rather than the predominance of either one. This is clearly reflected in the observations of Queneau in his childhood, as described in *Chêne et chien*:

> ... je m'effrayais du mélange
> de l'ordure et de l'innocence
> que présentait la Création.   (p. 37)

Often, indeed, the whole of life is represented as a tension between opposites, an endless set of dualities. Thus Pierre Kougard, in *Gueule de pierre*:

"Il y a une Vie de l'Ombre et une Vie de la Lumière, une Vie de Repos et une Vie d'Inquiétude,

"Une Vie du Passé une Vie de l'Avenir, une Vie du Fœtus une Vie de l'Homme, une vie de l'Océan une vie de l'Atmosphère." (p. 182)

And Pierre's ideas are but one reflection of the series of fundamental oppositions on which *Gueule de pierre*, and the whole Saint Glinglin cycle, are built: Ville Natale and Ville Étrangère, 'urbinataliens' and tourists, town and country, wet and dry weather. Chambernac and Purpulan find a further elaboration of this view of things in the writings of Pierre Roux, who sees dualism as underpinning both the physical world and the most respectable philosophical interpretations of it. Interestingly, the passage they quote begins with one of the key oppositions of the Saint Glinglin books:

Le sec et l'humide, ou le froid et le chaud, ou le repos et l'harmonie et le mouvement irrégulier, ou la lumière et les ténèbres, ou le pur et l'impur, ou la liberté et l'esclavage, ou le céleste et le terrestre, ou le bien et le mal, ou le léger et le pesant, ou l'éther céleste et l'atmosphère terrestre, etc. (ce qui est tout un); cette division en deux des éléments ou ce dualisme que l'hydrogène (ou alcali) et l'oxygène (ou acide) nous représentent, et qui a été le fondement de l'ancienne philosophie chinoise et de celle de Moïse et de toute la Bible, est la plus pure et véridique de toutes les philosophies.

(*Limon*, p. 149)

But for Queneau the essential duality is that of good and evil. Its implications are explored by Daniel de Chambernac, who is tortured by asthma – which serves as his own personal paradigm and leads him to ask questions about the nature of evil, its power and origins. On one occasion, when his pain is at its height, Daniel seems convinced that evil falls entirely outside the sphere of divine influence; and the magnitude of his suffering is matched by the power of the prose:

Le mal était si fort, sa puissance si fabuleuse qu'il arrachait à Dieu de larges pans de l'être. Une tache de sang tombée dans le domaine de l'existence s'élargissait graduellement lentement, sûrement, comme huile. Et ce sang n'était point celui d'Abel, mais celui du premier supplicié. Comme les chrétiens voient toujours saigner les cinq plaies du Christ, Daniel apercevait roulant du fond des âges un fleuve écarlate charriant du pus et des chairs hachées. Et qui ne venait pas de Dieu. Qui donc avait gribouillé sur le plan de la création avec cette encre immonde? Qui donc l'avait ainsi rayé?

(*ibid.*, p. 206)

Later, however, Daniel's reading of the Bible suggests to him that both good and evil stem from the same source: that one creator is responsible for these apparently conflicting elements. In the book of Isaiah, for instance, he reads of a God 'formant la lumière et créant l'obscurité, faisant la paix et créant le mal, moi, l'Éternel, faiseur de toutes ces choses' (p. 215).[43] Ultimately, Daniel's view is less of a flawed gnostic universe than of a manichean one, in which opposed forces sustain their endlessly renewed and never conclusive struggle.

Although neither of the two elements can ever win a definitive victory over the other, the forces of good, no less than those of evil, enjoy occasional triumphs. The Queneau of *Chêne et chien* is torn between the two:

> Chêne et chien voilà mes deux noms,
> étymologie délicate:
> comment garder l'anonymat
> devant les dieux et les démons? (p. 81)

Yet the conflict between the baseness symbolised by the dog and the virtue of the oak tree yields a temporary victory for the latter when the narrator succeeds in taming his viler nature: 'Le chien redescend aux Enfers. / Le chêne se lève – enfin!' (p. 84)

Queneau's fictional world is an arena for the perpetual conflicts of light and darkness, angels and devils, good and evil. But perhaps his most concise formulation of this dualistic view comes in a poem, 'L'explication des métaphores', in which all human life is presented as being encompassed by the activities of gods and demons, and its every feature checked by its opposite:

> A chaque nuit son jour, à chaque mont son val,
> A chaque jour sa nuit, à chaque arbre son ombre,
> A chaque être son Non, à chaque bien son mal,
>
> Oui, ce sont des reflets, images négatives,
> S'agitant à l'instar de l'immobilité,
> Jetant dans le néant leur multitude active
> Et composant un double à toute vérité.[44]

This view offers little chance of any resolution to conflict: rather, the opposed elements engage in a permanent antagonism. But in any case, in Queneau's fiction there is no attempt to seek a resolution; the conflict is not presented in moral terms, and far less is it analysed or defined with any precision. For Queneau's dualism serves its purpose not by addressing real life, but by serving as an artistic term of reference within the confines of his fiction: a pattern which imposes itself merely on his world and the lives of his characters. And as such it lies at the heart of his creation.

'Lui aussi [...] s'est posé les problèmes de l'existence même et de la technique du roman.'[45] Queneau is talking of Proust, but the observation applies equally well to himself. If the sustained exercise in communication and the endlessly inventive experimenting with literary form are more readily perceived elements of his work, they cannot be allowed to obscure the existence of the fictional 'world' or 'universe' which forms another 'layer of the onion' – one which, if the metaphor were to be pursued, would be found at a deeper level of his literary creation. With Queneau – as with most other novelists – language, style, structure, narrative strategy, sustain and promote this further, indispensable part of the reader's experience; as has been well argued:

More than any other literary form, more perhaps than any other type of writing, the novel serves as the model by which society conceives of itself, the discourse in and through which it articulates the world [...]. The basic convention which governs the novel – and which, *a fortiori*, governs those novels which set out to violate it – is our expectation that the novel will produce a world. Words must be composed in such a way that through the activity of reading there will emerge a model of the social world, models of [...] the relations between the individual and society, and, perhaps most important, of the kind of significance which these aspects of the world can bear.[46]

Not that the relationship between Queneau's fiction and the realities of the outside world or society is a particularly stable one: to borrow a phrase from Claude-Edmonde Magny, the texts are marked, rather, by a 'coefficient de stylisation variable'.[47] Magny's comments cover a general movement away from the exact reproduction of the visible world, which she sees as following in the wake of Gide's *soties*, especially *Les Caves du Vatican*, and of which she sees Queneau's novels, notably *Les Enfants du limon*, with its amalgam of the supernatural and the realistic, as striking examples. Beyond this, of course, individual works differ one from another in the manner and extent of their fidelity to life: *Odile*, with its sober authenticity, *Saint Glinglin*, pervaded by the atmosphere of myth or legend, 'A la limite de la forêt', in a spirit of timeless fantasy, each has its own particular identity. But whatever the surface disparities, Queneau's texts are all bound together by shared patterns and laws. If they lack the complete consistency of, say, Zola's Rougon-Macquart cycle, what emerges from them, nevertheless, is a remarkably unified view of the human condition, presented within a coherently organised setting. And, just as important, once the integrity and solidity of Queneau's fictional world is established, it is possible to approach a further set of questions concerning the values and modes of conduct which are to be found within it.

4　Values

'J'AI, comme on dit, une "formation" philosophique [...]. Mais je ne suis pas philosophe, sans
doute, car je me méfie comme de la peste des
systèmes – de tous les systèmes que le monde dément
régulièrement le lendemain.'[1] Queneau's attitude in philosophical matters is consistently sceptical, and with his scepticism goes a profound reluctance to make pronouncements
on serious subjects:

> Ce n'est pas rendre hommage au langage que de lui attribuer des fonctions
> qu'il ne doit pas avoir, et notamment celle d'escamoter les questions
> graves. Je préfère ne pas parler de ce sur quoi je ne sais pas parler, à
> supposer que je sache parler de quoi que ce soit.　　　(*Bâtons*, p. 44)

But for all his reticence, Queneau does not reject out of hand
attempts to codify and evaluate existence in philosophical
terms, and neither does he exclude them from his fiction.
If he stresses the fact that the quest for abstract values is a
difficult and inconclusive matter, he is also fully aware of its
importance. And although his fiction is never a vehicle for
ideological 'messages', his characters – major and minor –
define themselves most of all by their development *vis-à-vis*
some abstract value or principle. If, in Queneau's view, the
Iliad and its progeny reveal the impact of history on the
individual, the *Odyssey* and novels deriving from it are based
on the individual's personal or emotional evolution:
'*L'Odyssée*, c'est manifestement encore beaucoup plus per-
sonnel, c'est l'histoire d'un individu qui, au cours d'expér-
iences diverses, acquiert une personnalité ou bien affirme et
retrouve la sienne' (*Charbonnier*, p. 59). In this light,
Queneau's own works can all be read as 'Odysseys'.

Art and science

Despite Queneau's refusal to commit himself to specific philosophical positions, he attaches great import-ance to activities which have a potential value for humanity. Most obviously some of his articles – notably those he wrote for the review *Volontés* between 1937 and 1940 – amount to a profession of faith.[2] For apart from the well-known 'Tech-nique du roman' Queneau produced a whole series of theo-retical texts in which he expounded his basic concerns. Two closely allied themes immediately stand out: the significance of artistic creation, and the human value of knowledge.[3] In an article entitled 'Qu'est-ce que l'art?' he contends that all artistic activity derives its true value from being indissolubly linked with other aspects of life: 'L'art, la poésie, la littérature est ce qui exprime (les réalités naturelles (cosmiques, univer-selles) et les réalités sociales (anthropologiques, humaines)) et ce qui transforme (les réalités naturelles et les réalités sociales)' (*Voyage*, pp. 94–5). The terms of this argument are reminiscent of those of an early review in which he insists above all that scientific work should always be related to its human context, that 'la science est *aussi* une activité humaine, un phénomène social et historique' (*ibid.*, p. 22). The simi-larity of tone is in no way fortuitous. For beneath the obvious differences between science and art Queneau points to an underlying unity: 'La Science prise en elle-même comme connaissance se trouve dans la même situation que l'Art que l'on veut faire parfois aussi passer pour une sorte de connaissance' (*Bords*, p. 127).[4] For Queneau they are essen-tial activities of mankind, since they constitute the two aspects of man's creative impulse: the two fundamental responses the mind can make to the human situation. Repeatedly, throughout his fiction, Queneau examines the significance of these activities in the lives of his characters.

If, in Queneau's formulation, science is one essential char-acteristic of man's attempt to come to terms with existence, artistic creation is '*l'autre* activité humaine' (*ibid.*). It is commonplace to juxtapose the two – as Limon does, com-paring the scientific experiments of Daniel and Noémi with

Clémence's violin-playing: 'Limon rêve, sourit, ce sera tou-
jours ça: des dispositions pour les sciences; un ingénieur tout
trouvé. Mais tout de même, l'art c'est bien supérieur; il
regarde Clémence, attendri, admiratif' (*Limon*, p. 141). But
Queneau prefers to regard science and art as allied activities.
This explains his enthusiastic response to the work of
Raymond Roussel, in which he discerns 'une imagination
qui unit le délire du mathématicien à la raison du poète'
(*Voyage*, p. 39), or the formula Saxel uses in *Odile* to praise
Travy: 'Il est humain en tant qu'il est poète, dit Saxel
bienveillant, et poète en tant que mathématicien' (p. 47).

In Queneau's world, artistic activity and the search for
knowledge run parallel courses; and both pervade the lives of
his characters. As des Cigales puts it: 'Ça n'existe pas les gens
qui n'ont pas pondu un sonnet au moins dans leur vie' (*Rueil*,
p. 29). Writers – and would-be writers – are to be found
everywhere in Queneau's books. *Le Chiendent* describes in
detail the agonies of the concierge, Saturnin, as he struggles
to come to terms with an inner compulsion to write:
'Souvent il a l'impression que c'est très important ce qu'il a à
dire, parfois même que c'est ce qu'il y a de plus important au
monde – ce qu'il vient d'écrire, ce qu'il va écrire, ce qu'il a
dans la tête, quoi' (p. 120). The same novel also shows
Théo's attempts to master the sonnet-form (p. 137). In *Les
Derniers Jours* another adolescent, Vincent Tuquedenne, tries
his hand at avant-garde poetry (p. 24). Others are a little
more successful: despite his continuing obscurity, des
Cigales is apparently a poet of some standing within his own
district of Rueil; Hubert Lubert in *Le Vol d'Icare* is an
established author (while Icare himself composes a poem
(p. 155)); and Sally Mara (whose brother, Joël, is yet another
poet) overcomes her deep-seated inhibitions about her lack
of literary skill enough to produce *Journal intime* and *On est
toujours trop bon avec les femmes*.

There are numerous other manifestations of art, or 'l'art
avec un grand a', as Gabriel calls it (*Zazie*, p. 202). The
narrator of the short story 'Dino' paints gouaches 'où s'im-
mobilisait dans son oscillation la peau d'un chat épouvantail,
où se fixaient, épinglées et mourantes, des formes humaines
indécises' (*Contes*, p. 57). The duc d'Auge decides to take up

painting, explaining that his decision is the result of a dream in which he plays Correggio to Michaelangelo's Raphael: 'Dans ce rêve, Phélise, la plus jeune de mes filles [...] revenait de Rome et me racontait qu'elle y avait vu la chapelle Sixtine et je me disais en moi-même: et moi aussi je suis peintre' (*Fleurs bleues*, p. 218). Mounnezergues is the son of an expert maker of wax models who exhibited in travelling fairs and museums of anatomy (*Pierrot*, p. 64), and Mounnezergues himself practises his father's art (pp. 150–1); in the same novel, Léonie Prouillot was part of a dance act (p. 95); and 'Narcense, lui, est artiste; ni peintre, ni architecte, ni acteur, ni sculpteur, il joue de la musique, plus exactement du saxophone' (*Chiendent*, p. 18). In *Loin de Rueil* Camille trains to become a singer (p. 73), while Jacques L'Aumône leads a troupe of actors before graduating to a successful career in cinema. Jacques also claims to have practised 'la danse artistique' (p. 97), a field in which Gabriel himself is pre-eminent. Gabriel, of course, performs his act in a night-club for homosexuals, but he considers himself to be an artist as much as an entertainer; it is when his act is praised for its amusement value that he makes his famous reply: 'N'oubliez pas l'art tout de même. Y a pas que la rigolade, y a aussi l'art' (*Zazie*, p. 224). Others engage in pursuits even more unlikely and exotic than Gabriel's – among them a friend of Gabriel, the tourist guide Fédor Balanovitch, who takes delight in misleading his charges by contriving totally ficti-tious excursions around Paris. As Paul Gayot puts it: 'En son genre (un autre que Gabriel), Balanovitch est un artiste, héritier du Baron d'Ormesan dont parle Apollinaire, l'inven-teur de l'art de l'amphionie.'[5] In *Les Temps mêlés* Pierre emphasises the creative and aesthetic aspect of his attempt to reconstruct the ancient myths and traditions of the Ville Natale: 'Certes, j'utiliserai bien d'anciennes légendes, d'an-ciennes coutumes, d'anciens us, mais dans l'ensemble, je suis un créateur [...] un Fondateur [...] une sorte d'Architecte' (pp. 132–3).

However outlandish the pursuits of Queneau's artists, and however modest their scope, they all fall within the limits which Queneau attributes to artistic activity. Indeed the very range of these pursuits serves to show how far, in Queneau's world, art extends beyond the territory ruled by a defined number of muses. But in his fictional works, at least, Queneau is not seriously concerned with technical details. Rather he seeks to evaluate artistic creation as such and to consider how it affects the lives of individuals.

The advantages which the artist can derive from his art are obvious enough: for the diligent Mounnezergues it brings the satisfaction of a job well done, and for the homicidal duc d'Auge it provides much-needed therapy and sublimation of guilt.[6] Similarly with the reception of art: Gabriel's dancing brings pleasure to his audience, while cinema is a welcome form of escapism for the public at large; as des Cigales says: 'Cet art – car c'en est un – nous fait oublier les misères de la vie quotidienne' (*Rueil*, p. 44). At this level, the artistic experience is a refreshing and beneficial one.

However, the artistic process can all too easily degenerate into sterility. One obvious risk is stagnation, which threatens any artist who continually repeats himself rather than innovating. Fédor Balanovitch makes the point when discussing Gabriel's dance routine, which he has often seen: 'Il ne se renouvelle pas. Les artisses, qu'est-ce que vous voulez, c'est souvent comme ça. Une fois qu'ils ont trouvé un truc, ils l'esploitent à fond.' Then, no doubt remembering his own 'act' with the tourists, he adds: 'Faut reconnaître qu'on est tous un peu comme ça, chacun dans son genre' (*Zazie*, pp. 221–2). But for Queneau a far graver danger lies in the disruption of the equilibrium which he sees as the basis of all good art. For him artistic creation should derive from a balance or tension between the poles of 'inspiration' and 'technique'. In *Odile* he portrays a literary group which practises automatic writing in the belief that the subconscious is the true source of artistic inspiration. Clearly, the group seeks to abolish the tension Queneau values, for its aim is to cling to one pole – 'inspiration' – to the total exclusion of the other. Moreover, this one-sided attitude is not even conducive to the 'inspiration' so much prized by the group. A disenchanted member of the circle, Vincent N . . . , comes to realise that inspiration of this sort is a mere illusion:

On l'oppose à la technique et l'on se propose de posséder de façon constante l'inspiration en reniant toute technique, même celle qui consiste à attribuer un sens aux mots. Que voit-on alors? l'inspiration disparaître: on peut difficilement tenir pour inspirés ceux qui dévident des rouleaux de métaphores et débobinent des pelotes de calembours.   (pp. 158–9)

In Vincent's view the true artist recognises that the two poles are of equal importance and combines them in his work:

J'imagine au contraire que le vrai poète n'est jamais 'inspiré': il se situe précisément au-dessus de ce plus et de ce moins, identiques pour lui, que sont la technique et l'inspiration, identiques car il les possède suréminemment toutes les deux.   (p. 159)

Vincent's sentiments and his manner of expressing them echo precisely the opinions expressed by Queneau in an article attacking the Surrealists' obsession with automatic writing. The article is entitled, appropriately enough, 'Le plus et le moins':

Le poète n'est jamais inspiré parce que maître de ce qui apparaît aux autres comme inspiration [...]. Il n'est jamais inspiré parce qu'il l'est sans cesse, parce que les puissances de la poésie sont toujours à sa disposition, sujettes à sa volonté, soumises à son activité propre.   (*Voyage*, p. 126)

Queneau's emphasis on the need for balance between technique and inspiration stems from a general belief that all the diverse elements of a work of art should be reconciled and co-ordinated, so that no single one can predominate. The essay 'Qu'est-ce que l'art?' ends with a denunciation of the literary schools who have disturbed the equilibrium in one way or another; all are compared with makers of hats:

Les naturalistes ont été des chapeliers qui se sont contentés de prendre l'empreinte de la tête et s'en sont tenus là. L'art pour l'art a consisté à faire des chapeaux pour le musée de la chapellerie. Les poètes expérimentateurs se sont évertués à fabriquer des couvre-chefs systématiquement inutilisables. La littérature de parti a cru bien faire en plantant dans de vieilles casquettes ou de vieux bérets de petits drapeaux rouges ou tricolores.   (*ibid.*, pp. 95–6)

As against the imbalance inherent in enterprises of this sort, Queneau proposes a simple programme for the would-be-artist: 'Il s'agit de faire et de bien faire quelque chose qui vaille d'être fait. Un bon et beau chapeau par example' (*ibid.*, p. 96). And above all there is the need to reconcile the work of art itself and the human context from which it originates, and in which it must find its place. Art is ce qui occupe tout le champ de l'affectivité de la connaissance à l'action, prend ses racines dans l'une et s'épanouit dans l'autre. C'est ce qui manifeste l'existence et la fait devenir, la prolonge et la transmet.

(*ibid.*, p. 95)

Queneau's role as director of the *Encyclopédie de la Pléiade* is well known, but his novels also reveal an extensive knowledge of many academic disciplines. It has been noted that they deal with subjects as diverse as mathematics, entomology, sexology and mechanical engineering;[7] and Georges Bataille has written of *Gueule de pierre*: 'Je doute qu'il existe un livre de fiction aussi délibérément fabriqué à partir de la science.'[8] Anne Clancier begins her study of one of the later novels by pointing out: 'Il nous a déjà donné différentes œuvres dans lesquelles, sans en avoir l'air, les sciences [...] sont le ressort caché de l'action. Avec *Les Fleurs bleues*, il nous dévoile une véritable psychanalyse.'[9] Indeed Queneau has himself stressed the range of scientific interests to be found in his fiction and has hinted at their importance. In the first edition of *Les Enfants du limon*, under the heading 'du même auteur', he listed his previous novels according to particular categories: *Odile* belonging to that of mathematics, *Gueule de pierre* to cosmography, botany and zoology, and *Chêne et chien* to psychoanalysis.[10] Yet despite this formal classification, Queneau's fiction is rarely concerned with technical information or scientific theories as such. For here, as in his treatment of art, Queneau leaves aside the intricacies of particular activities; instead he concerns himself in general terms with how his characters seek knowledge, and with the influence the search has on their development as individuals.

Throughout Queneau's fiction, characters of every kind – young and old, laymen and experts – are engaged in the pursuit of knowledge. Valentin Brû, who at one point aspires to study for his baccalauréat (*Dimanche*, p. 133), has read 'de la première à la dernière page, les roses y compris, le petit dictionnaire Larousse français et encyclopédique, ce qui avait ouvert en lui les écluses du savoir' (*ibid.*, p. 64). The young Queneau, convalescing after a long illness, achieved the same feat:

Je paressais immensément,
épelant d'A à Z le *Larousse* prodigue
en faciles enchantements.   (*Chêne et chien*, p. 42)

During the wedding feast in *Le Chiendent* Thémistocle and
M.Pic parade their paltry knowledge of astronomical matters,
thereby provoking a discussion of the practical application of
astronomy (pp. 197–8); and Pierre Le Grand describes his
brother as a 'cantorien' (*ibid.*, p. 65)[11] and as a 'professeur de
mathématiques' (*ibid.*, p. 130). In *Les Derniers Jours* the contrast between the amateur scientist and the professional is
accentuated by the waiter, Alfred, who compares Einstein's
theory of relativity unfavourably with his own allegedly
scientific system for predicting the results of horse-races (see
pp. 30, 45–6, 66–7). The same novel traces Vincent
Tuquedenne's search for knowledge; in the spring of 1922,
'Il pataugea dans l'eau noire de l'érudition. Il ne lisait plus
que des catalogues de libraire, des bibliographies, des ouvrages de référence' (p. 53). As children, Daniel and Noémi de
Chambernac conduct a range of experiments in a garden
shed, and the description of the scene is perhaps a deliberate
reminder of the list of works 'du même auteur' referred to
earlier:

C'était un tout petit laboratoire, et bien primitif, quoique l'on s'y préoccu-
pât de toute science expérimentale. Ici, une pile au bichromate: physique;
là, du lait pourrissant avec de la craie (préparation de l'acide lactique):
chimie; ici, des haricots germant dans du coton: sciences naturelles.

                                            (*Limon*, p. 137)

Experiments in progress also feature in *Loin de Rueil*, when
Jacques L'Aumône surveys his laboratory with its array of
phials and test-tubes: 'Sur cette table des plantes qui sèchent
et là-bas les cages des animaux à empoisonner à tuméfier à
empester ou même à guérir' (p. 92).

In *Pierrot mon ami* Mounnezergues recounts in detail how
his interest in the Poldevian dynasty gives him an appetite for
knowledge. Once again, the list of headings sets a characteristic tone; and the whole passage captures the laborious
processes of the classic autodidact:

J'empruntai des livres à la bibliothèque municipale d'Argenteuil, et je
découvris que l'histoire ne se pouvait comprendre sans la chronologie et la
géographie, qui ne me parurent pas compréhensibles sans l'astronomie et

la cosmographie, et l'astronomie et la cosmographie sans la géometrie et
l'arithmétique. Je recommençai donc mon instruction ab ovo, ce qui veut
dire à partir du commencement en langue latine (mais c'est beaucoup plus
rapide et expressif – vous voyez, jeune homme, les avantages de l'instruction). Au bout de quelques mois, j'appris ou réappris les règles d'accord
des participes, la formule des intérêts composés, les dates cruciales de
l'histoire de France, les départements avec chefs-lieux et sous-préfectures,
l'emplacement de la Grande-Ourse et quelques tirades de nos classiques.

(pp. 68–9)

Mounnezergues, then, realises that different areas of knowledge are interdependent, and, more importantly, that a bare
minimum of instruction in certain disciplines is indispensable to anyone with a genuine desire to learn. His reference
to Latin recalls Purpulan's words in *Les Enfants du limon*: 'Je
sais bien qu'à notre époque on considère comme une grande
chose de savoir le latin, mais à mes yeux ce n'est qu'un
minimum' (p. 54).

Knowledge, learning, the acquisition of facts, attract a
striking number of characters. In many cases their search may
be modest, naïve, even bizarre to the point of absurdity, but
the diversity of disciplines explored serves above all to
emphasise the general nature of the undertaking. Whether
successful or not, the pursuit of knowledge is a central
human activity in Queneau's fictional world – a way in which
people attempt to give meaning to their lives. And insofar as
knowledge contributes to understanding, it is to be pursued
conscientiously. A subject can be mastered only when its
basic implications are understood. Viewed in this perspective, the quest for knowledge is both natural and, within
limits, valuable. In the words of Roland Travy: 'Quelle
satisfaction peut-on bien éprouver à ne pas comprendre
quelque chose?' (*Odile*, p. 29)

The pursuit of knowledge can, however, detract from life
rather than enhance it. Indeed, as soon as a body of knowledge is considered as an absolute, and regarded as its own
justification, to the exclusion of all else, it loses all real value.
This is the tenor of another of the essays written for *Volontés*,
'Richesse et limite', in which Queneau states bluntly: 'Les
connaissances (faits) sont mortes si elles ne sont pas animées
par une activité vivante qu'elles ne peuvent d'elles-mêmes
engendrer' (*Voyage*, p. 103). And this is borne out by the

experience of a number of Queneau's characters. Chambernac, for example, devotes years of his life to amassing information about the 'fous littéraires', and this all-consuming mania eventually takes the form of the *Encyclopédie Des Sciences Inexactes* which he attempts to publish. However, Chambernac's enterprise ends in failure, because he so presents his findings that they have no apparent relevance to any other aspect of life; and since no publisher will accept the work, the *Encyclopédie* is condemned to go unread. At the end of *Les Enfants du limon*, having lost all interest in the work, Chambernac hands over the manuscript to 'Queneau', who wishes to incorporate it in a book of his own. Chambernac now insists that it is not a present of any great value and renounces it completely, declaring himself well satisfied to be rid of it, as this will allow him to die in peace (p. 315). Chambernac, then, comes to realise the uselessness of any obsession with knowledge which has no human application.[12]

There is a more extreme case in *Gueule de pierre*, where Pierre Kougard is obsessed by biology: 'C'est aux Sommets de la Biologie que je parviendrai, moi. Tel est mon avenir: la Science de la Vie' (p. 13). His obsession leaves him with an apparently unshakeable belief in his own genius. Although he fails to impress either his father or the people of the Ville Natale with his ideas, his confidence remains undiminished, and at the end of the novel, after the death of his father, he explains his ambition to his brother Jean:

Je redescendrai, mon frère, enseigner ma Vérité. Je redescendrai vers la Ville apporter ma parole [...].

Du grand Kougard de pierre, mon frère, oui je ferai un dieu,
Un dieu qui garantira ma Vérité, qui garantira ma parole,
Et la Ville Natale aura son dieu, son dieu de pierre, et Moi
Je serai le premier parmi ceux qui vivent en bas, je serai le gardien de cette
Vérité.   (pp. 219–20)

Pierre, even more than Chambernac, is blind to the futility of his enterprise – which, however, is obvious to all in the sequel. Even as mayor of the Ville Natale he is unable to convince his people of his great 'truth' – unable to bridge the gap between his scientific discoveries and his personal situation. The later states of *Les Temps mêlés* show him still believing in the value of science but long since diverted from his own researches by the cares of office:

C'est beau la science. Ça reconforte. Ça développe les poumons comme la culture physique, laquelle est d'ailleurs une science. Pourquoi ai-je donc abandonné les chemins de la science? [. . .]. Je me suis égaré sur les chemins de la politique, et puis me voici Maire et Réformateur, mais plus jamais [. . .] je n'ai pu consacrer un instant à la réflexion méthodologique.

(p. 152)

From this point Pierre's fortunes decline steadily. Eventually he is banished from the town, and although, in *Saint Glinglin*, he is allowed to return, he spends the rest of his life in obscurity. Pierre is an unmitigated failure: his total commitment to science has been of no use to others and causes irreparable damage to himself.

The most memorable example of the sterile pursuit of knowledge is the career of Roland Travy, whose story is told in *Odile*. Travy first appears as a misanthropist whose only interest is the mathematical research to which he devotes all his energy. Just as Pierre aspired to some ultimate truth through biological research, so Travy makes the most ambitious claims for his work in mathematics, which, he insists, is no mere artificial construct, but rather an objective representation of the universe:

Ce n'est pas à l'architecture, à la maçonnerie qu'il faut comparer la géometrie ou l'analyse, mais à la botanique, à la géographie, aux sciences physiques même. Il s'agit de décrire un monde, de le découvrir et non de le construire ou de l'inventer, car il existe en dehors de l'esprit humain et indépendant de lui.   (pp. 27–8)

His devotion to mathematics leaves him with little time for normal human contacts, and when this is pointed out to him he replies bluntly: 'Je ne me soucie guère d'être bien humain' (p. 47). However, as the novel progresses, Travy's attitude changes. Through his relationships with his friend Vincent and with Odile – the woman whom, as he eventually realises, he loves – Travy comes to recognise his role and responsibility as a social being, and understands that his absorption in mathematics could never be of the slightest value; and finally he admits this to Odile:

Voilà des années que je m'illusionne sur moi-même et que je vis dans l'erreur [...]. Je me suis saoulé de chiffres; ils galopaient devant moi jusqu'à ce que la tête m'en tourne, jusqu'à la stupeur [...]. Depuis des années je m'abrutis à poursuivre des recherches qui n'ont ni queue ni tête ni corps.   (pp. 163–4)

More completely even than Chambernac or Pierre, Travy reveals through his personal development the utter futility of pursuing any activity in total isolation.

Queneau's fiction, then, reveals an awareness of the positive side of the quest for knowledge; but this awareness is tempered by the recognition that the quest is fraught with risks. His comments on *Bouvard et Pécuchet* – a text which long fascinated him, as witness the three prefaces he wrote for it – shed further light on the subject. He argues forcefully that despite the obvious comic element in Flaubert's presentation of his would-be polymaths, they are not primarily figures of fun, and that their activities and attitudes do have some validity (see *Bâtons*, pp. 101, 104–5). The argument applies equally well to characters of his own whose activities are not discredited even though presented in a humorous way. Queneau contends that Flaubert reserves his criticism for one particular excess, and supports this by invoking Flaubert himself: 'Je ne m'étonne pas de gens qui cherchent à expliquer l'incompréhensible, mais de ceux qui croient avoir trouvé l'explication, de ceux qui ont le bon Dieu (ou le non-Dieu) dans leur poche' (*ibid.*, p. 122).[13] There could be no more fitting comment on Pierre or Travy. On the other hand, in Queneau's view, 'Flaubert est *pour* la science dans la mesure justement où celle-ci est sceptique, réservée, méthodique, prudente, humaine. Il a horreur des dogmatiques, des métaphysiciens, des philosophes' (*ibid.*, pp. 121–2). Not surprisingly, his own fiction yields a similar reading.

The pursuit of knowledge is presented as one area in which human beings attempt to give meaning to life. But it is clear from the experience of those who undertake it that this pursuit is worthless as long as it is regarded as an end in itself. As Queneau puts it in the article 'Richesse et limite': 'On peut connaître un grand nombre de "choses": cela n'a aucune importance [...]. La personnalité humaine reste pauvre et

nue, cette richesse ne la vêt pas' (*Voyage*, p. 99). For knowledge to have real value – the metaphor of 'richesse' pervades
the whole article – it must be recognised as a means to an
end: as something to be used and then transcended:

[Les connaissances] constituent une richesse, c'est-à-dire, quelque chose
qui est à soi-même sa propre limite alors que la personne humaine vivante
détruit constamment ses propres limites. S'identifier à cette richesse, c'est
philistinisme, pédantisme, décadence et sécheresse. Rejeter cette richesse,
y renoncer [...] y demeurer au moins indifférent et la prendre pour ce
qu'elle vaut: c'est la seule vie de l'esprit, le désencombrement, l'activité
possible, la liberté.   (*ibid.*, pp. 103–4)

But if the compelling urge to seek knowledge never provides
an absolute value, it still plays a significant part in the life of
the individual. In the words of André Blavier: 'C'est que
l'encyclopédisme, besoin de savoir, ou de croire savoir, est un
virus humain [...]. Et Queneau, sans illusions pourtant, fait
sa place à l'intelligence humaine.'[14] As with 'l'art', so with 'les
connaissances': the ultimate aim is a balance which is all the
more precious for its very precariousness.

'Sagesse'

As Queneau presents them, the artistic impulse and
the search for knowledge are beneficial inasmuch as they have
the potential to enrich human existence. However, none of
Queneau's characters finds ultimate fulfilment through these
activities, which at best provide a modest degree of satisfaction and at worst lead to obsession of the most arid kind.
They reveal a further dimension to Queneau's world, for they
are serious attempts to invest life with some fundamental
value; yet they offer no such value in themselves.

However, Queneau's Odysseys have far broader terms of
reference: his characters embody many other, more general
principles. *Chêne et chien* describes how, through psychoanalysis, the adult Queneau identifies and transcends his
childhood traumas and accedes to maturity. *Les Fleurs bleues*
traces a comparable integration of personality, for the novel
can be seen as a series of events symbolising stages of a course
embracing the subject's Oedipal phase (in Auge's revolt
against the king), guilt and neurosis (in Cidrolin's self-

accusatory graffiti), and ultimate sublimation (with the destruction of the implacable superego, Labal, when a building collapses on him).[15] Cidrolin, living in the present, and the duc d'Auge, moving through history, can be seen as representing the component parts of a single identity: Cidrolin's name conceals within it the 'id', while that of the *duc* is in effect 'ego' backwards.[16] The meeting of the two, which occurs towards the end of the novel when the duc d'Auge arrives in the present age, suggests that a conflict within the personality has been resolved.[17]

Étienne Marcel, in *Le Chiendent*, represents the growth of human personality through the processes of perception and thought. At the beginning of the novel Étienne is a mere shadow, an anonymous 'silhouette [...] sans comportement individuel visible' (*Chiendent*, p. 7). He attains the status of an authentic individual only when he breaks through the deadening patterns of habit which have hitherto governed his behaviour. Only then can he perceive things for himself and thereby achieve a degree of real independence. The moment of the breakthrough comes when Étienne notices, in a shop-window display, two rubber ducks floating in a waterproof hat filled with water, having previously remained oblivious to the display for over two years. And this event brings about a dramatic change in Étienne, as he realises himself: 'J'ai découvert des choses à côté desquelles je passais chaque jour, sans les voir [...]. Tout d'un coup, ça a changé, du jour au lendemain' (p. 53). Before this, 'je ne pensais pas je n'existais pas pour ainsi dire' (p. 79). As his perceptions and thought-patterns develop, so the 'silhouette' evolves. In the eyes of the 'observer', Pierre, he becomes 'un être plat' (p. 11), then an 'être de réalité minime' (p. 33); soon he acquires a name (p. 35) and thereafter he attains 'la réalité tridimensionnelle' (p. 55). The ultimate stage of Étienne's evolution is a state of perpetual doubt in which he systematically puts into question anything and everything.[18] Progress beyond this extreme position would seem to be impossible, and indeed Étienne, far from progressing, returns to his starting-point, for at the end he retreats to the status of a silhouette. Before his final reversion to anonymity, however, Étienne embodies a resistance to stultifying routine which guarantees an authentic perception of the world.

The psychoanalytical framework of *Chêne et chien* and *Les Fleurs bleues*, like the phenomenological pattern in *Le Chiendent* – the evolution of Étienne – following as it does an initial moment of illumination, is the first illustration of a major theme which is developed in subsequent novels – a theme for which, as suggested earlier, the term 'philosophical' seems quite inadequate: 'L'illumination d'Étienne correspond à l'accession à une sagesse qui dépasse la simple réflexion philosophique, au sens habituel et scolaire du mot.'[19] If 'sagesse' – or 'wisdom' – itself lacks precision, it at least points away from the notions of doctrine or academicism implied by 'philosophy', towards simpler, more intuitive qualities. The expression owes much of its currency to an article by Alexandre Kojève entitled 'Les romans de la sagesse', which examines the heroes of *Pierrot mon ami, Loin de Rueil* and *Le Dimanche de la vie* in the light of Hegel's understanding of wisdom as 'la parfaite satisfaction accompagnée d'une plénitude de la conscience de soi'.[20] Other attempts have been made to evaluate the moral dimension of Queneau's characters,[21] but it is striking that practically all his major characters can be placed on a scale according to the degree of moral maturity – of the 'sagesse' – that they reveal. At the bottom of the scale are those whose conduct and sense of values are manifestly deficient because of their inability to come to terms with the world. Higher up are to be found characters who revise their values and gain in maturity as they reconcile themselves to their circumstances. And at the top of the hierarchy is a small group of figures who have no need to develop, because they already have the lucidity and serenity others lack – who, in the words of one critic, 'd'emblée [...] surabondent en sagesse'.[22]

The figures at the bottom of the scale are marked by their extreme selfishness. Paul B— in *Le Dimanche de la vie* devotes his life to his own advancement, both social and material. He is obsessed by the idea of becoming a member of the *Légion d'honneur* (pp. 193, 195–6); and in the years leading up to the Second World War he abandons his position as a (highly dishonest) inspector of weights and measures in order to make his fortune in the flourishing armaments trade (p. 190). However, Paul's mercenary instincts avail him little: his ambition is fruitless in its own terms as well as worthless according to any scale of moral values, and he ends the novel no further advanced than when he began. Mme Cloche is another embodiment of egocentricity and greed. Her plot to deprive père Taupe of his supposed 'wealth' via marriage with Ernestine ends in failure, as it is bound to do – but not before Narcense, Saturnin and others are heavily implicated and Ernestine dies in suspicious circumstances. Yet in her moment of failure Mme Cloche can see no further than the frustration of her gross materialistic desires:

C'en était fini de ces festins longs et copieux dont elle promettait de gaver sa vieillesse; c'en était fini des jeunes gens aimables qui l'auraient fait danser dans les boîtes de nuit; c'en était fini des voyages; auto et des robes du soir décolletées, maizoui, maizoui, maizoui et des petits chiens de luxe horriblement laids et chers et des bijoux véridiques [...]. Découvrir un trésor, un vrai, et se le voir souffler, quelle dégoûtation.

(*Chiendent*, p. 214)

In as far as *Le Chiendent* has a plot in any conventional sense, it is that of the pursuit of Taupe's 'treasure' which occupies many characters in the later stages of the novel. Indeed the image of the treasure-hunt effectively conveys not only the naked greed of all the characters at the bottom of the hierarchy, but also a more general perversion of values, which, as Queneau pointed out elsewhere, is embedded in our very language:

Depuis la Renaissance en Occident, la richesse est considérée, à la fois comme l'origine et l'expression de toute supériorité [...]; non que l'on jauge nécessairement la capacité, le talent, le génie d'après 'l'argent gagné' [...] mais l'on utilise fréquemment dans ce domaine des termes relevant de l'autre catégorie, on parle volontiers 'd'abondance' et de 'richesse' [...] trahissant ainsi l'embargo du commerce sur l'esprit.   (*Voyage*, p. 97)

Whether 'l'embargo du commerce sur l'esprit' manifests itself in the crude terms of Mme Cloche's ambitions, or whether it takes a more subtle form, the danger is the same. For in Queneau's world those who devote themselves exclusively to personal gain remain caught in a trap of their own making.

Other characters acquire some degree of maturity and wisdom – but only when they have overcome their own egotistical desires. For renunciation is what characterises all those who belong to the second level of the hierarchy. This is explained in an article entitled 'Le mythe et l'imposture', which also exploits the metaphor of wealth:

> L'acquisition de biens [...] est un obstacle à toute compréhension véritable. Plus exactement: ce n'est pas tant l'acte de l'acquisition [...] que le fait de la possession, la passivité de la conservation. Et c'est par un acte que ce fait, cette possession sont dépassés: par le renoncement, non par un abandon morose qui serait une ruine, mais par une pauvreté qui est une aisance, une aisance dans l'action.   (*Voyage*, pp. 152–3)

A number of characters, drawn from varying spheres of activity, reveal this process at work by their abandoning of their respective obsessions. Jacques L'Aumône in *Loin de Rueil*, having realised the futility of his existence, attempts to shed the ambitions of wealth, fame and nobility he has previously cherished in a process of complete renunciation. He comes to envisage his destiny in chilling terms as

> l'équivalent de la préparation culinaire des lapins et des lièvres, écorchement, dépiautement, éjection des viscères, avec comme but dernier l'innocence absolue et gratuite de l'idiot privé de l'impatience coutumière à ceux de son espèce quant à la réalisation des besoins physiologiques élémentaires.   (p. 165)

In the event Jacques' aspiration turns out be be nothing more than a passing fancy, and his old ambitions soon reassert themselves. But other characters undergo a decisive and permanent change. Roland Travy's life is transformed when he finally understands the immaturity of his obsession with mathematics and acknowledges his love for Odile. In a figurative sense *Odile* traces Travy's progress from childhood to adulthood, for in the opening section, describing his military service, Travy claims that his life really began then, when he was twenty. It was only towards the end of the novel that Travy emerges from the self-absorption of his infancy: 'Mon orgueil de ne pas vouloir suivre une vie commune n'était qu'enfantillage puisque je la suivais, cette voie, et que j'aimais' (p. 183). Moreover, Travy's change of direction represents a cure, as well as a new-found maturity. His elopement with Odile coincides with a heavy cold which leads to fever. Odile, alone, cures him, and immediately after his cure he completes the formalities necessary for their marriage, noting: 'Je crois bien que c'était le premier acte social que j'accomplissais' (p. 148).

The case of Travy closely resembles that of Bernard Lehameau in *Un Rude Hiver*. Both turn from selfish obsession to love for another, and both are cured physically as well as mentally. The parallel is all the clearer for Travy's observation that when he felt his attitudes changing, it was as if he was losing the outward appearance he had thought of as his own – 'celui de stropiat qu'abîme le malheur' (*Odile*, p. 157). At the beginning of *Un Rude Hiver* Lehameau is an embittered figure, robbed of most of his family by a fire, disillusioned by current developments in the First World War – and crippled by a wound sustained in battle. His hatred of all that surrounds him is a mania which fills his life just as mathematics filled that of Travy. An afternoon stroll in Le Havre near the beginning of the novel serves to illustrate his initial disposition:

Sur le quai des Casernes, le lent flâneur croisa un groupe de morveux à moitié ivres, de francs bandits de quatorze ans. A les voir, il éprouva une joie bien vive, comme un élu devant le spectacle des damnés au dire de certaines religions. C'était là le plus grand profit de ses promenades à travers les quartiers pauvres, il récoltait de la haine.   (pp. 27–8)

As with Travy, it is love that transforms – the love of a very young girl called Annette. As his love for her grows, so his wound begins to heal. Early on in the novel he is unable to walk quickly (p. 27), whereas later, in the company of Annette, he manages to break into a run. This same occasion is when Lehameau first declares his feelings for the girl, in terms such as to establish her as a counterweight to the cold and dark – metaphorical as much as real – of the Le Havre winter:

Tu es tant de choses pour moi, tu ne peux pas savoir tout ce que tu es pour moi, tu es une flamme qui m'éclaire, une petite flamme dans la nuit, tu es quelque chose d'inouï, je ne saurais pas t'expliquer ça: une merveille.
(pp. 115–16)

Soon after this he announces that his leg will be completely healed. He amazes his long-standing acquaintance, the shopkeeper Madame Dutertre, by his new attitude of tolerance and optimism:

—Alors, finit-elle par dire, vous ne haïssez plus les pauvres, ni les misér-
ables, monsieur Lehameau?
—Ni les Allemands même, madame Dutertre, répondit-il en souriant. Pas
même eux. Pas même les Havrais, ajouta-t-il en riant.
—Il faut alors que vous soyez devenu un bien grand sage, dit Mme
Dutertre.   (p. 174)

Travy and Lehameau both leave behind an old obsession
in favour of a new and positive attitude. Other characters
develop according to a process at once simpler and more in
keeping with the spirit of Queneau's world: abandoning an
attitude they come to see as useless, but without seeking
another attitude to replace it. At the end of *Les Enfants du
limon* Chambernac is not setting out on some new path, but
simply ridding himself of the encyclopedia to which he has
devoted so many arid years of his life. The career of Robert
Bossu, Chambernac's illegitimate son, reveals a similar progression. Early in the novel the ebullient, self-centred Bossu
harbours the ambition of reaching a position of social emi-
nence, thereby overcoming the 'injustice' which ordained his
lowly status. He determines to educate himself, with the
ultimate aim of becoming a radio engineer. Although he falls
short of his ambition – he in fact becomes a pimp, bearing
the name Toto-la-Pâleur-de-vivre – he acquires enough
knowledge to impress his acquaintances, who, ironically
enough, nickname him 'l'Aristo' (p. 175). Yet by this stage
Bossu is becoming increasingly aware of the folly of his
aspirations:

Il se souvenait d'un temps où l'ambition gonflait ses veines et où il pouvait
commencer chaque phrase par moi je, sans avoir honte de sa vanité. Son
père lui mit dans la tête qu'il avait de l'avenir; il n'en doutait pas. C'est en
triomphateur qu'il avait pris le train pour Paris. Et puis voilà, il maquer-
eaute piètrement derrière la place de la République.   (p. 176)

Eventually, towards the end of *Les Enfants du limon*, Bossu
resigns himself to his situation and rejects the urge to succeed
which has motivated him hitherto: 'Il ne pensait plus à
devenir ingénieur, ni à se faire passer pour tel; il s'était
débarrassé de toutes ces imaginations [...]. Il flottait à la
surface des événements, plus léger qu'une peau de banane'
(p. 292). Similarly, Agnès de Chambernac, who at one time
sees her role as that of a latter-day Joan of Arc destined to

liberate France, comes to acquire an attitude of calm resignation (p. 282). And her brother Daniel eventually renounces his fanatical questioning of divine providence. His evolution, too, takes the same form:

Puis il comprit sa vanité: primo de croire qu'il était seul à se faire une idée juste de Dieu, et ensuite qu'il pouvait s'en faire une idée juste [...]. Il était tout humble maintenant, comme il avait toujours été. Il se reconnaissait dans sa petitesse et s'amusait que son infimité se soit gonflée de quelques onces de néant.   (p. 293)

The characters in the middle ranks of the hierarchy are all shown to resolve an inner conflict by rejecting some previously-held principle. They all come to learn that the values they used to proclaim do not meet the needs of real life. Typically, the change which comes over these characters takes them from self-will to passivity, or from the ambition of deciding their own fate to the acceptance of things as they are. However, the figures who best embody 'sagesse' are those who, whatever their past struggles may have been, reveal no inner conflict, no suppressed fears, no unsatisfied ambitions. They do not strain against their situation, but consistently succeed in accommodating themselves to it. In 'Le mythe et l'imposture', having condemned 'l'acquisition de biens', Queneau considers a contrasting attitude – that of 'quiétude', and quotes with approval Montherlant's aphorism: 'L'inertie est une vertu, en regard d'actes vains, comme l'apathie est une vertu, en regard de passions sottes' (Voyage, p. 153).[23] Such no doubt, would be the view of Queneau's 'sages', if they were willing or able to express themselves on the subject. They generally withhold their energies and emotions from worthless pursuits and often reveal the folly of their fellows.

Among the varied minor 'sages' are some whose wisdom is manifested in their ability to judge others. Zazie's principal merit lies in her skill in pointing out the pretensions of those around her. She is above all a figure of much-needed sanity in a confused world; in Queneau's words: 'Pour moi, c'est la personne normale.'[24] But it is her very grip on normality that explains her superiority to the unbalanced adults who continually try – unsuccessfully – to deceive her. Alfred, the waiter in Les Derniers Jours, also contrasts strikingly with the characters who surround him: 'Moi, je reste fixe au milieu des soucoupes et des bouteilles d'apéro et les gens tournent autour de moi [...]. Moi, je ne bouge pas, eux ils tournent et se répètent' (p. 93). While others spend their lives in the earnest pursuit of futile goals, Alfred is content to accept circumstances he cannot change: 'Je ne me mêle de rien et je laisse tout marcher comme ça veut' (p. 233).

There are others whose simple lack of greed or ambition puts them at the opposite end of the scale from the 'treasure-hunters'. Père Taupe, for one, refuses categorically to be compromised by possessions. Following some distant financial catastrophe he never again concerns himself with money: 'Depuis qu'il était ruiné, il ne redoutait plus la ruine. Parvenu au minimum de l'existence, il appréhendait de la dépasser [...]. Il se croyait heureux; il se croyait sage' (*Chiendent*, p. 89). By reducing the demands he makes on life, Taupe achieves genuine satisfaction such as is unknown to those around him, which is why his scrap-yard beside the railway embankment can be described without undue irony as 'un petit coin de paradis au milieu de l'enfer de la banlieue parisienne' (p. 112). Mounnezergues, in *Pierrot mon ami*, refuses all financial inducements to abandon the 'chapelle poldève', for which he maintains a stubborn and disinterested devotion (see, for instance, pp. 107ff.). Similarly Linaire, an old chemist in *Loin de Rueil*, wishes only to be left alone and thus to avoid the obligation of promoting a discovery he made as a young man: 'Oh mais je les connais, ils ne me laisseraient pas faire dès qu'ils commenceraient à entendre parler de guérison zou ils me feraient disparaître de dessus terre où j'ai bien du plaisir à être' (p. 123).

Simplicity, rather than intellectual distinction, is what characterises Queneau's 'sages', and never more so than in the case of Jean-sans-Tête in *Le Dimanche de la vie*. Jacques L'Aumône never attained 'l'innocence absolue et gratuite de l'idiot'[25] at which he aimed, but Jean spends his life in this rare and privileged condition. In conventional terms he is a simpleton, devoid of all orthodox accomplishments and credentials. Yet he alone can understand and respond to Valentin's personal evolution in the second half of the novel (pp. 174–7).

In addition to the lesser figures who reveal individual aspects of 'sagesse', Queneau has also created, in Pierrot and Valentin Brû, two major characters who embody 'sagesse' as such, combining complete simplicity with detachment from worldly obsessions, and possessing powers of perception and understanding far superior to those of their fellows. Pierrot steadfastly refuses to be downcast by misfortune, and is equally disinclined to aspire to great heights. Simply and unreflectingly, he accepts the quota of happiness which comes his way, as when he is offered a job at Uni-Park at the beginning of the novel:

Pierrot n'avait aucune idée spéciale sur la moralité publique ou l'avenir de la civilisation. On ne lui avait jamais dit qu'il était intelligent. On lui avait plutôt répété qu'il se conduisait comme un manche ou qu'il avait des analogies avec la lune. En tout cas, ici, maintenant, il était heureux, et content, vaguement.   (*Pierrot*, p. 22)

Pierrot is a passive figure, who never imposes his will on events, preferring instead to be carried along by them. Even when tempted to take matters into his own hands – when his favourite pinball machine has been tampered with, or when he is surprised to find his ex-employer, Crouïa-Bey, in Voussois's menagerie, 'Pierrot n'insista pas' (pp. 146, 205). Nevertheless, he is endowed with exceptional and precious qualities which are denied to those around him. Thus his powers of observation allow him to perceive the 'chapelle poldève' when others fail to do so (see, for example, p. 59). Moreover, while other characters in the novel are inextricably caught up in the passing of time, Pierrot can remain untouched by it: 'De temps à autre, Pierrot ferme les yeux, et il saute comme ça dix minutes, un quart d'heure. Quand il rouvre les yeux, tout est pareil' (p. 56). Pierrot, to borrow a phrase from Queneau's critical writings, enjoys 'l'intemporalité du sage et du saint'.[26] Similarly, he avoids the obsession with the past – and consequent inability to accept the present – which besets most of the characters, especially Léonie Prouillot, with her frantic attempt to trace a former lover who disappeared twenty years previously. From all such entanglements Pierrot, 'homme sans histoire, hors de l'histoire',[27] is totally free. Pierrot's 'sagesse' lies above all in his serene remoteness from the values that compromise others, which is crystallised when, late in the novel, he strolls past the shop-windows in his neighbourhood and views the cars, bicycles and postage-stamps on display: 'Il les examinait avec la sévérité du connaisseur dégagé de tous les soucis de la possession, mais avec la satisfaction que donne ce désintéressement' (p. 211).

Like Pierrot, Valentin Brû in *Le Dimanche de la vie* is a sage from the time he first appears, as a naïve, innocent individual, blithely unaware of Julia's admiring eyes on him. And Valentin even succeeds in enhancing his original 'sagesse' by the end of the novel. For one thing, he advances from his initial unawareness to a clear perception of events: the final scene has him in the role of the alert, objective observer, 'impassible et immobile', surveying the follies of his fellow-men (p. 251). But Valentin, too, reveals himself most of all in his freedom from conventional commitments. In common with Pierrot he remains detached from passing time: 'Il fixe une branche, un galet, mais il perd de vue le temps. Le temps a poussé l'aiguille de dix minutes sans que Valentin l'ait surpris. Et depuis la branche, le galet, il ne s'est *rien* passé' (p. 171). However, Valentin tries to go further, by clearing his mind of all unnecessary preoccupations: 'Couché sur le dos, il essayait maintenant de découvrir la différence qu'il y a entre penser à rien les yeux fermés et dormir sans rêves' (p. 170). He eventually claims to have succeeded in this attempt (p. 235), but immediately sets himself a still harder task of self-denial – that of becoming a secular saint:

> La chose lui parut d'autant plus facile que, ne croyant tout au plus qu'à un faux dieu, et encore si peu que rien, il pensait avoir un avantage immédiat sur ses collègues chrétiens candidats à la béatification, puisque l'espoir d'une récompense quelconque ne viendrait jamais jeter une ombre sur l'un quelconque des ses actes.   (p. 239)

Accordingly, he undertakes every kind of menial task, and disciplines himself so severely as to suppress all feeling of pleasure or self-satisfaction. By the end even the priest Foinard is forced to recognise the saintly qualities of Valentin's asceticism.

'Sagesse' lies within the reach of everyone – scrap-dealer, simpleton and fairground attendant included. Nevertheless, it remains the preserve of a small number of Queneau's characters. Further, no individual embodies it completely: even Valentin is to some extent contaminated by conventional behaviour, as when he contrives to deceive Julia (pp. 168–9). Perfect 'sagesse' is, no doubt, an unrealisable ideal. But if the ideal is never fully attained, it is at least symbolised – by the shadowy figure of the Arab in *Odile*. The Arab appears at every crucial point in Travy's story, from the opening on the road from Bou Jeloud to Bad Fetouh (p. 7) to the end of Travy's military service (p. 14) to the culmination of his stay in Greece (pp. 181–2). And the appearances of the Arab correspond not merely with phases of the narrative but also with stages in Travy's personal evolution. He is unable to attribute any importance to them early on, but when he becomes aware of the sterility of his life and of that of his literary friends, he begins to grasp the significance of the Arab. Thus when Vincent N... declares that 'le véritable inspiré n'est jamais inspiré: il l'est toujours', Travy immediately thinks of this figure: 'Rien ne me permettait de penser ainsi mais j'attribuais à cette image des significations multiples' (p. 159). The final reference to the Arab coincides with Travy's renunciation of his past and acceptance of his present situation: 'Il me semblait qu'à côté de moi venait de se placer cet Arabe que j'avais rencontré un jour, là-bas vers l'Occident, sur la route qui va de Bou Jeloud à Bad Fetouh' (p. 181).[28] The Arab is never more than a vision of Travy's, but his very abstraction is a guarantee of the ideal purity for which he stands. Whatever progress Travy makes, he knows that the perfection of the Arab will always elude him: 'Il y a un Arabe qui est seul et qui regarde ce que je ne sais pas voir' (p. 175).

'Sagesse' does not offer ultimate answers to the problems of the universe, for the simple reason that Queneau would never admit that such answers existed. Neither is it offered as a model for all to follow, since there is no didacticism in Queneau's fiction. Queneau presents it as the most valid response his characters can find to their situation: not merely a rejection of distorted, false or partial values, but a positive acceptance of real life in all its contradictory aspects. As he argued in one of his earliest, but most significant texts:

Accepter la réalité, c'est l'accepter dans sa *totalité*, le plaisir comme la
douleur, le bien comme le mal, le jour comme la nuit [...]. Il faut accepter
l'aspect négatif comme l'aspect positif des choses, et la première acceptation, en date comme en importance, est celle du sevrage, – de la peur et de
l'anxiété. Il faut accepter l'anxiété non la fuir ou la déguiser; et l'on
constatera alors que toute acceptation d'une perte devient alors un gain
[...]. L'on comprend alors que l'Enfer n'est que le lieu où se consume ce
qui a refusé de vivre d'une vie réelle, ce qui n'a vécu que d'une vie partielle.

(Voyage, pp. 172–3)

In this way – and only in this way – can opposites be
reconciled, and wholeness achieved; and only in this way can
the metaphor of wealth stand for real value. Such, for
Queneau, is the basis of 'une sagesse qui fut de tous les temps
et de tous les pays' *(ibid.)*. Such, too, is the soundest code of
conduct to be found among the inhabitants of his fictional
world.

Humour

The resignation which is a distinguishing feature of
'sagesse' often finds expression through laughter. Indeed,
many of Queneau's characters react to the most desperate
circumstances in this surprising way. At the height of his
religious crisis Daniel de Chambernac suddenly recognises
how presumptuous he had been in speculating on the nature
of good and evil, and bursts out laughing as he walks down a
city street *(Limon*, p. 293). Yvonne, in *Pierrot mon ami*,
recalls her feelings during a fairground boat-ride with an
admirer, and above all 'la peur qu'elle avait eue qu'ils ne
chavirassent avec la nacelle. Il y avait de quoi rire; et elle rit'
(p. 84). The expression 'il y avait de quoi rire' is a sort of
refrain which is heard in a number of crises. Jacques
L'Aumône describes how Camille has scorned him because
of his inability to realise his childhood ambitions: 'Elle me
rappelait que je me voyais déjà pape, académicien, empereur!
Et comme je n'étais rien de tout ça: il y avait de quoi rire'
(Rueil, p. 146). Similarly Roland Travy reflects on his wilful
alienation of Odile and comments: 'Je creusais un fossé, avec
des malices cousues de fil blanc. Il y avait de quoi rire: creuser
un fossé avec des malices cousues de fil blanc' *(Odile*, p. 167).
After such clear-sighted admission of personal failure,

a laugh is at first sight the most improbable response. In these situations, however, laughter is not the immediate or instinctive impulse with which, say, the uncomprehending crowd greets the Chinese at the beginning of *Un Rude Hiver*. On the contrary, it is the fruit of lengthy reflections on what has occurred, and thus indicates a certain degree of detachment on the part of the characters involved. They laugh because they refuse to be downcast by circumstances they can no longer redeem. Here, laughter provides a way out of crisis – as it does with even more effect at the end of *Le Dimanche de la vie*. In the final scene of this novel Julia is searching for her elusive husband, who has just been demobilised, and she eventually glimpses him among a crowd on a railway platform. Instead of attracting Valentin's attention immediately, Julia waits and observes his movements. And seeing Valentin offer his help to some girls attempting to climb through a carriage window, 'Julia s'étouffa de rire: c'était pour leur mettre la main aux fesses' (p. 252). At which point the book ends. Julia's laughter is doubly significant for occurring in the final line: although it might appear to be no more than a spontaneous reaction to a direct stimulus, it also represents Julia's response to her experiences during the novel as a whole – and particularly her attitude to the enigmatic Valentin. Julia has maintained only the most tenuous hold over him since their marriage, and now, when they might be reunited, Valentin is clearly being pulled in other directions. In this situation, which Julia may well regret but which she cannot retrieve, laughter serves as her best means of self-defence.

Pierrot mon ami, too, ends with laughter. In the epilogue, Mounnezergues nominates Pierrot as his heir, but when, two days after this event, Pierrot returns to the old man's house to collect the codicil to the will, everything has changed. He is greeted not by Mounnezergues but by Yvonne, who rejected his advances in the days of Uni-Park and now gives no sign of recognition. Mounnezergues has allegedly fallen ill and left for the country. His belongings have been relegated to dustbins, and the house is in a state of upheaval which parallels the change in Pierrot's fortunes. But Pierrot will not be unduly affected: 'Après un dernier regard

sur les deux poubelles, Pierre s'en alla. Arrivé au coin de la
rue, il s'arrêta. Il se mit à rire' (p. 221). This point, like the
end of *Le Dimanche de la vie*, is a culmination as well as a
conclusion, for the uncertainty and disappointment Pierrot
experiences here are characteristic of his state of mind
throughout the novel. Pierrot – 'qui avait eu une dure
enfance, une pénible adolescence et une rude jeunesse (qui
durait encore)' (p. 9) – is a modest, unpretentious individual
who quite innocently becomes implicated in a complex series
of events, including a mysterious fire, the search for a
long-lost lover, a property take-over, and sundry emotional
involvements. In the epilogue, which takes place the year
after these events, Pierrot looks back over his experiences
without being able to make any sense of them:

> Une sorte de courant l'avait déporté loin de ces rencontres hasardeuses où
> la vie ne voulait pas l'attacher. C'était un des épisodes de sa vie les plus
> ronds, les plus complets, les plus autonomes, et quand il y pensait avec
> toute l'attention voulue (ce qui lui arrivait d'ailleurs rarement), il voyait
> bien comment tous les éléments qui le constituaient auraient pu se lier en
> une aventure qui se serait développée sur le plan du mystère pour se
> résoudre ensuite comme un problème d'algèbre où il y a autant d'équations
> que d'inconnues, et comment il n'en avait pas été ainsi.   (p. 210)

Pierrot, who can neither understand events nor control
them, nevertheless protects himself by keeping his misfor-
tunes at arm's length. Hence his laugh at the end of the novel.

The resigned detachment achieved by Queneau's characters is an essential feature of his work. For it is through
their sense of humour that his characters can best confront
misfortune. For Gaëtan Picon, 'l'humour est à la fois le seul
écho qui reconnaisse la voix du néant, et la réaction saine et
franche qui le repousse'.[29] Considered in this way, humour is
based on a perception of the disparity between overweening
aspiration and depressing reality – a perception which
Queneau values above most others. And the awareness of
this disparity in all areas of life is typical of Queneau. As a
study devoted to his humour has stressed:

> Cette 'inconstance' déroutante l'humour la doit, au fond, à la profonde
> conscience qu'il a de la position de l'homme dans l'univers, position qu'il
> étudie amoureusement – dont il s'attriste et dont il rit. 'Rire c'est le propre
> de l'homme', et l'incarnation suprême de cette 'distinction', c'est pré-

cisément le créateur doué d'humour qui est capable de rire de ses propres misères.[30]

Queneau's protagonists reveal their sense of humour by accepting their own shortcomings. They contrast their own insignificance with the immensity of the world in which they live, and this gives rise to their laughter. Moreover it is a laughter in which Queneau, as author, can share; but Queneau's own humour extends far beyond that of his characters, to attain an immeasurably broader view of life. Thus whereas Pierrot, Julia and the rest see no further than the incongruity between themselves and all that surpasses them, Queneau perceives a second fundamental incongruity – between man and such things as are inferior to him. For Queneau, as for Pascal, man by his very nature stands midway between nothingness and infinity. As he puts it in 'L'explication des métaphores', man is as it were 'lost' between two extremes: on the one hand he is 'mince comme un cheveu, ample comme l'aurore', but on the other 'il n'est pas assez mince, il n'est pas assez ample'.[31] Awareness of this dual incongruity is the essence of Queneau's humour, which, in turn, pervades the whole of his fictional creation. As one of his most perceptive critics has argued: 'L'art de Raymond Queneau n'accepte de communiquer que sous une perspective d'humour et d'ironie.'[32]

By Queneau's own admission, his humour is instinctive and compulsive: 'Si je fais de l'humour, c'est, sans doute, que je ne peux pas m'en empêcher.'[33] But at the same time it is a process to which he devoted much serious thought. For humour, in his view, is potentially the most valuable of all human attributes. His most explicit statement on the subject comes in an article entitled 'L'humour et ses victimes', another of the 'prises de position' written for *Volontés*. Here he explains how humour, just like art or science, is vulnerable to abuse and distortion, and he distinguishes between what he regards as real humour – which always reveals a respect for human values – and the blinkered, self-justifying cynicism which discredits everything it encounters. Of the latter he writes: 'Il suffit de vivre conscient de la totalité humaine pour percevoir de l'évidence la plus convaincante qu'il n'y a là qu'usurpation et gangrène, absorption du grand par le petit, illégitime subversion de valeur' (*Voyage*, p. 81). Real humour, on the other hand, far from being a negative force, serves to put things in a proper perspective. Its ultimate significance, for Queneau, lies in its capacity to 'impos[er] le sérieux par le comique' (*ibid.*).

At the most obvious level Queneau's humour reveals a delight in evoking and describing simple comic situations – as in a memorable exchange between Trouscaillon and the cobbler, Gridoux, in *Zazie dans le métro*: Trouscaillon refuses to be put off by Gridoux's reluctance to sell him shoe-laces, and persists:

—Et une paire de souliers? Vous refuseriez de vendre une paire de souliers?
—Ah là! s'esclama Gridoux, là, vous êtes couyonné.
—Et pourquoi ça?
—Je suis cordonnier et pas marchand de chaussures. Ne sutor ultra crepidam, comme disaient les Anciens. Vous comprenez le latin peut-être? Usque non ascendam anch'io son pittore adios amigos amen et toc.

(p. 103)

The fantasy of Mme Cloche, disguised as a priest in search of money for a new church, shows Queneau's comic imagination at full stretch: 'L'eglise s'ra tout entière en ciment armé; à l'intérieur, y aura des fresques cubiques et la teuseufeu pour écouter l'pape. Et à l'entrée, y aura eau bénite froide et chaude' (*Chiendent*, p. 230)

The description of an extraordinary cabaret act in *Loin de Rueil*, involving the eating of a live lobster, is particularly rich in comic detail:

Une nouvelle roucoulade de l'orchestre indiqua l'arrivée d'un fait nouveau en l'occurrence un Indien Borgeiro habillé en marin on ne sait pourquoi et d'aspect considérablement barbare, à part ça. Après quelques bonds de droite et de gauche très chiqués le Borgeiro se précipita sur la bête et l'ayant habilement saisie lui sectionna le bout de la queue qu'il se mit à broyer grâce à une dentition particulièrement d'attaque. (p. 193)

Comic passages such as these, where to all appearances the humour has no serious implications, are to be found throughout Queneau's work. But despite their light-hearted tone they all reveal the same deep-seated sense of incongruity. The humour of Gridoux's retort lies in the juxtaposition of radically different sorts of languages; Mme Cloche's vision is humorous because of the startling contrast between hallowed ecclesiastical tradition and flashy modern gadgetry; and the spectacle of the Indien Borgeiro pushes incongruity to the extreme of grotesqueness.

In Queneau's work, however, this awareness of incongruity transcends the evocation of simply comic situations to convey something far more serious; as Queneau puts it: 'l'humour est la sobriété du rire' (*Voyage*, p. 87). For although in many cases incongruity serves the aim of provoking laughter for its own sake, the priorities are often reversed, so that the creation of laughter by comic effects brings the reader to an awareness of some underlying incongruity. And by inspiring this awareness, Queneau encourages his reader towards a more dispassionate and critical view of everything with which he comes into contact.

The detached, humorous perspective occasionally takes the form of satire. In *Odile* he describes the growing enthusiasm which Anglarès and his acolytes show for 'low-life' pursuits, and the description not only produces a comic effect but also serves to accentuate the shortcomings of those concerned:

Saxel, se faisant passer pour un collaborateur de *La Veine*, fut enchanté de faire la connaissance d'affranchis et de souteneurs; à tel point qu'à son tour il accompagna Oscar sur les champs de course et se mit à jouer aux cartes avec conviction. Il frisait l'enthousiasme, et d'autre part je triplai de prestige à ses yeux tant pour avoir d'aussi singulières relations que pour ne lui en avoir jamais parlé. La chose se sut également place de la République et aux Buttes-Chaumont. Anglarès prononça quelques mots favorables au lumpen prolétariat et Vachol se mit à apprendre la belote en cachette.

(p. 60)

Later in the same novel a meeting is planned between a large number of artistic and political groups, including:

les terroristes antifascistes promussoliniens d'extrême-gauche
les fruitariens antiflics
les metaphsychistes incoordonnés
les pararchistes disséminés
la ligue pour les barbituriques
le comité de propagande pour la psychanalyse par correspondance
le groupe Edouard Salton
les socio-bouddhistes dissidents (déjà cités)
les phénoménologues néantisseurs en inactivité

l'association des anti-intellectuels révolutionnaires
les révoltés nullificateurs intégraux
les syndicalistes antimaçonniques initiés
et trente et un groupements belges.   (p. 135)

Here the narrator ridicules the affectations of intellectuals by
the use of irony: he ostensibly accepts something from which
he in fact detaches himself. He notes with care the pursuits
which Anglarès and the others take up, and scrupulously
reproduces the list he receives of intellectual factions. But the
very neutrality of tone hints at a basic lack of sympathy with
the subject, and the bathos of the final items in both passages
totally undermines the pretensions of Anglarès and the rest.

The importance of irony in Queneau's work is clearly suggested by a reference in 'L'humour et ses victimes' –
'l'humour, c'est "dire une chose pour en faire entendre une
autre", sur le plan du comique' (*Voyage*, p. 87) – which is
really less a general definition of humour than a specific explanation of irony. And if satire is not often to be found in
Queneau's fiction outside *Odile*, it is nevertheless one aspect
of the irony which is an essential mechanism. Indeed it has
been argued that irony lies at the very heart of Queneau's
work: 'La démarche essentielle de Queneau s'appuie sur
l'ironie – mais l'ironie considérée étymologiquement comme
interrogation socratique, qui remet tout en question par le
biais d'une fausse naïveté.'[34] Seen in this light, Queneau
presents a constant challenge to all accepted norms – hence,
for instance, the perpetual questioning of the most banal
linguistic forms:

Il commença par employer exclamativement la deuxième personne du singulier de l'impératif présent du verbe tenir, puis énonça les syllabes composant le nom de la personne reconnue par lui.   (*Chiendent*, p. 90)

The effect of 'fausse naïveté' is often achieved by adopting the
point of view of the child uncompromised by the habitual
perceptions and second-hand values of the adult world. In
Chêne et chien he sees again through the eyes of his own childhood to recreate his alienating experience of his wet-nurse:

De cette outre de lait j'ai de la peine à croire
que j'en tirais festin
en pressant de ma lèvre une sorte de poire,
organe féminin.   (p. 31)

Obviously Zazie embodies a childlike vision which brings into question not merely language itself but all the conventions and preconceptions that language conveys and implies. And Zazie is to some extent prefigured, both in her language and in her rejection of superficial niceties, by the children Annette and Polo in *Un Rude Hiver*. But the most sustained use of the 'naïve' point of view is to be found in *Journal intime*, which consists purely of the experiences and reflections of its youthful 'authoress', Salla Mara. By the end of the book Sally has learned the secrets of sex, but at the beginning she is totally ignorant, and most of the succeeding narrative is characterised by its consistent ingenuousness. The phenomenon of animal reproduction remains a mystery to her even after she has witnessed it on her uncle's farm, and when she accidentally stumbles on her brother and the housekeeper at a crucial moment, her naïveté is such as to present this scene, too, as something alien to normal experience:

J'aperçus, écris-je, un magma corporel qui rythmait des soupirs [...]. [Mrs Killarney] se mit à compléter son activité par un commentaire parlé assez incohérent, mais dont il semblait résulter qu'elle allait passer de vie à trépas. Cependant, l'autre personnage répliqua, en jurant le tonnerre de God, qu'il éprouvait bien du plaisir, mais je ne reconnus ni la voix, ni le style de mon frère.   (*Sally Mara*, p. 170)

In this way Queneau is able to treat quotidian features of life as totally new experiences, and thus encourage his reader to perceive them afresh. In *Le Chiendent* he describes a funeral ceremony as seen by another ingenuous observer – this time a dog called Jupiter – and the effect, beyond the immediate comic impact, is to challenge any stereotype of such an occasion:

Autour d'un trou, tout le monde s'est arrêté. Au milieu du rassemblement, l'homme-femme gronde une chanson menaçante; les galapias agitent des théières fumantes. Deux ivrognes qualifiés descendent la boîte au fond du trou. Puis les invités jettent des gouttes d'eau.   (p. 49)

This detachment from the standard view of things is by no means limited to the occasions when Queneau adopts the standpoint of one of his unequivocally naïve observers. Sometimes he presents the familiar in an unfamiliar, or even absurd way, to show how the most banal of activities can be viewed critically – as when Paul and Julia, in *Le Dimanche de la vie*, exchange their ritual kisses on both cheeks, thus making 'le même bruit que font les flèches eurêka que l'on détache des cibles' (p. 45).

The commonplace view is continually being redeemed from banality by such means. An office secretary becomes 'une jeune personne qui dessine très vite des abrévations avec un crayon qu'elle ne peut s'empêcher de lécher parfois' (*Limon*, p. 63); and a ticket-collector is 'un homme dont la casquette galonnait et qui réclamait d'une voix rauque des morceaux de carbon à perforer' (*Chiendent*, p. 212). The effect is even greater when Queneau adds an imaginative touch to 'ingenuous' description, as when the Paris métro is presented in such a way that its ordinariness is left far behind; Étienne Marcel is seen entering

une sorte de tunnel, illuminé de place en place et dans lequel circulaient des séries de cinq véhicules attachés les uns aux autres et se déplaçant avec une certaine rapidité, rapidité qui naturellement n'atteignait pas celle du hourlouri en plein vol lorsqu'il fuit devant la tempête, mais qui dépassait cependant celle d'un cul-de-jatte remontant une rue en pente.

(*Chiendent*, p. 224)

What emerges from such passages as these is a constant refusal to take things for granted: an insistence on the potential strangeness of even the most ordinary aspects of existence, which encourages the reader to question his own assumptions and increases his awareness of his surroundings. And for at least one critic this quality is absolutely crucial:

La banalité de tout ce qu'on dit et qu'on fait [. . .] dès qu'on cesse de la subir pour la considérer, nous place en face d'un mystère. Qu'on se souvienne de Hegel: ce qui est trop connu, justement parce qu'il est trop connu, n'est pas connu. Mais dérangez un peu le trop connu, soulignez qu'il est trop connu: vous le rendez d'abord méconnaissable; et, précisément pour cela, ensuite, reconnu. N'avons-nous pas l'esthétique de Queneau?[35]

This well explains how, for instance, the first chapter of *Le Chiendent*, which consists mainly of accounts of commuter train journeys, suburban housing estates and boring family meals, is such a fascinating reading experience; or how a description of Ast sweeping out a garden shed (*Limon*, pp. 193–5) transforms the most trivial action into an event of a strange and rare beauty.

Clearly, Queneau's humorous vision of the world is too wide-ranging to allow simple definition and classification, for it both colours and shapes everything he writes. And this being so it also determines the experience of his reader, who, at the moment when he starts one of Queneau's texts, enters a new and unfamiliar world which will stay with him as long as he continues to read. From the beginning and throughout – appropriately enough given Queneau's emphasis on the visual, both literally and in metaphor – the reader is seeing with fresh eyes, and the effect stays with him to the end. As a critic wrote in 1953: 'Le roman terminé il ne reste plus à celui-ci qu'à prendre "l'histoire" à sa charge. Il écarquille un peu les yeux, le lecteur, comme à la sortie d'une salle de cinéma. Puis il recommence à marcher (dans tous les sens du terme).'[36] And strangely enough, the simile prefigures the experience of two characters in one of the later novels: 'Lalix et Cidrolin écarquillèrent les yeux lorsque la lumière se fit de nouveau et sortirent un peu éberlués du cinéma' (*Fleurs bleues*, p. 178). Like the cinema-goers, the reader has good cause to be wide-eyed, and it is understandable if his experiences leave him dumbfounded. After he has read Queneau, his view of the rest of the world can scarcely remain untouched.

Insofar as they eschew metaphysical declarations and moral lessons ('nulle œuvre n'est moins prédicante', according to one exegete),[37] Queneau's novels can scarcely be regarded as profoundly philosophical. At the same time, it is clear that the 'valeurs', literal and metaphorical, which pervade his essays and occasional writings, are also a vital presence here. His characters display a common need for a principle or code by which to regulate their lives, and artistic creation and the pursuit of knowledge – the fine details of which exercised Queneau outside his fiction – serve within it as effective general symbols for their quest. In the final analysis, however, the individual's worth depends on overcoming those impulses which alienate him from his situation, so as finally to accept existence as a whole rather than forever trying to alter parts of it.

Yet the ultimate value to be discerned in Queneau's fiction

concerns not the characters but the author himself. For if no lasting importance attaches to attempts to change the world, nothing matters more than to change the ways in which the world is perceived and understood. And this is what Queneau achieves in his manner of presenting his creation. For him, a detached, humorous vision counts far more than philosophical pronouncement precisely because he considers it a better way to avoid fixed attitudes and definitive judgements. His attraction to the 'fous littéraires', who by definition stand out against conventional wisdom, is another example of this attitude,[38] as is his commitment to 'pataphysics, the 'science of imaginary solutions', aiming to study the laws which govern exceptions to the rule, inspired by the example of Alfred Jarry.[39] And if Queneau's interest in 'pataphysics is generally seen as marginal to his fictional work, at least one critic has seen the link between the two, neatly characterising the 'discipline' as an attempt to 'décrire un univers que l'on peut voir et que peut-être "l'on doit voir" à la place de l'univers traditionnel' and claiming that Queneau has been practising it since his very first book.[40] Certainly, the sense that there are two ways (at least) of seeing everything is never better conveyed than when, in *Le Chiendent*, Saturnin confronts the dying Ernestine:

—Si on vit, c'est passqu'on meurt, vous avez dit ça spâ? demande Saturnin.
—Oui j 'l'ai dit.
—Vous auriez aussi bien pu dire le contraire, lui fit-il remarquer.
—J'suis d'accord, répondit Ernestine.
—Ah bon, fit Saturnin. C'est tout c'que j'voulais savoir.   (p. 207)

Inconclusion

Critical approaches

THE ATTEMPT has been made in this study to give separate consideration to different 'layers' of Queneau's fiction, in the belief that an appreciation of each individual level can contribute significantly to the understanding of Queneau's fictional work as a whole. It has also been attempted to go beyond the most widely discussed characteristics – whether on the linguistic or the formal level or elsewhere – in order to draw attention to some of the less well-known features, and thus to broaden existing views of the subject.

If different critical approaches tend to emphasise the diversity of Queneau's work, moreover, they need not obscure a fundamental consistency. For taken in conjunction they reveal a common pattern: in each case, Queneau can be shown to exploit his resources in a similar way. He shows an unfailing awareness of the limits beyond which any single element – linguistic experimentation, assimilation of other genres and art-forms, intertextuality or whatever – becomes an end in itself and fiction shades off into some other area of literary activity. Often, in his fiction, he operates very close to the limits – which explains why his work has so frequently been interpreted in exclusive terms – but he never oversteps them. However prominent 'le néo-français' in *Zazie dans le métro*, the work could never be seen as a mere exercise in verbal virtuosity, any more than *Un Rude Hiver* could be reduced to a realistic commemoration of Le Havre or *Pierrot mon ami* to a simple demonstration of the virtues of 'sagesse'. Far from precluding one another, the different elements of

Queneau's works are complementary; ultimately it is the balance between them, rather than the predominance of any one, which best characterises his fiction.

The primary aim of the study will have been fulfilled if, through its eclectic orientation, it helps to promote a more comprehensive analysis of the whole range of Queneau's fictional writings. At the same time the obvious constraints of such a method must be recognised. Clearly the sequence in which the material is presented could be different. The movement from one chapter to the next is based on a progression from the more generally accepted features of Queneau's fiction to those about which less agreement exists. But this is a question of convenience, not a necessary reflection of Queneau's work itself: these same chapters could be set out in any other order of priority. In addition, the 'layers' themselves – and therefore the scope of the individual chapters – could be defined in a different way: there are many overlaps, potential and actual. Humour is here presented as part of Queneau's basic world-view, but it is just as much a characteristic of his use of language; the intertextual techniques he adopts, notably the patterns of allusion to the Bible and to Freud, are at least as important for the values of Queneau's fictional world as they are for their function in acknowledging the literary tradition; the list could go on. The composition of each 'layer', then, is no less arbitrary than the order of their presentation; what often passes for a 'layer' of a literary work may be merely the result of a particular way of looking at the work: 'Ce qu'on appellera, pour plus de commodité, les "niveaux du texte" sont, en réalité, des niveaux d'analyse. Ces niveaux d'analyse sont eux-mêmes fondés sur des niveaux de perception de l'œuvre.'[1] Critical analysis involves extracting and isolating individual elements which, within Queneau's texts themselves, are always fused with others. If this is so, then the limitations of the metaphor of the onion become apparent (and that of the interweaving fabric of the text reasserts itself); for the 'layers' of the text isolated by the critics must then appear as arbitrary projections, devoid of the objectivity sometimes claimed for them. This, of course, was the primary implication of the 'Exercices de critique' of Robert Kanters. Finally – and crucially – it must be acknowledged that eclecticism does not equal complete comprehensiveness. Following, as it has set out to do, the paths of previous critics, this study has clearly left much ground uncovered. Given the scarcity, in Queneau criticism, of say, a Marxist critique, or a genetic approach, these have their place here merely as representatives of 'la critique que cela aurait pu faire'.

> Le lecteur croyait comprendre et tournait les pages avec satisfaction; puis il faisait tout autre chose [...] se trompait de livre, fouillait dans des boîtes pleines de clés d'où la bonne était absente [...]. On découvre alors que le livre voulait dire autre chose, que la clé ouvrait d'autres portes, que les petites cachettes ne valaient pas les grandes trouvailles.   *Morale élémentaire*, p. 73

Queneau and his reader

All critical approaches derive from the experience of reading Queneau's fiction, but never, either individually or collectively, can they fully represent it. By definition, no codification of the experience – however comprehensive – can convey the full complexity of the reader's involvement with Queneau's texts. It is appropriate to conclude, as it was to begin, by emphasising the importance of this relationship, precisely because it transcends the limitations of conventional critical analysis.

Both within his fictional works and outside them Queneau is constantly encouraging his reader to respond in the most open-minded way possible: to avoid narrow dogmatism at all costs. He also warns against exclusive interpretations in another way – by suggesting that his own works could very well have taken other directions or embraced other elements than those which actually characterise them. On occasion he does this by offering a possible addition to an already published work, as in the case of some fragments from an early version of *Zazie dans le métro* which present Marceline as 'un officier allemand planqué depuis 1942' with a keen interest in Clausewitz.[2] A more extreme example is to be found in 'Un conte à votre façon' (*Contes*, pp. 221–6), a do-it-yourself short story in which the reader dictates the course of events by choosing between a series of alternative possibilities.

But the most significant instances where Queneau under-
lines the arbitrary nature of what he writes occur in his main
fictional works. *Les Enfants du limon* has references to stories
about himself which Purpulan has to tell, but never in the
end does recount (pp. 35–6, 54); and in *Loin de Rueil* there is
a brilliant passage describing all the things that a 'citoyen
absolument quelconque', encountered in the street, does *not*
do (pp. 61–2).

It is clear, in the first chapter of *Le Chiendent*, that the
whole course of the novel is dependent on the whim of Pierre
Le Grand, and that his decision to persist in his study of
Étienne, in any case chosen at random out of thousands of
others, is a very casual one:

L'observateur mijote quelque chose; quoi, il ne le sait pas encore
lui-même. Mais il se prépare; soit qu'il continue l'étude du repéré, ainsi
qu'il le nomme, soit qu'il cherche quelque autre hasard, aussi vain, aussi
inutile. Après avoir hésité entre diverses occupations possibles, il opte
pour le pernod et la silhouette.   (p. 15)

Soon afterwards Queneau introduces, with appropriate
detail, one Potice, as if he is to play a significant part in the
novel, but then immediately has him killed in a road accident
(pp. 18, 28); and the reader is left to ponder on what might
have been if, like his companion Narcense, Potice had been
allowed to contribute his share to the remainder of the story.
Several very deliberate references are made to Pierre Le
Grand's elder brother, and the expectation that he will
eventually appear.[3] But in fact he remains permanently on
the periphery of the novel's landscape, from which the mist
never rises, and it is here that his real significance lies. For he
is not a real presence but rather a symbol of how *Le Chiendent*
could have been different. However, it is, of course, in *Pierrot
mon ami* that Queneau emphasises most forcefully the
'virtuality' of his fictional creation. Pierrot's meditations at
the end of the book, just before 'une sorte de brouillard'
returns to the setting (p. 211), reflect not merely his own
bewilderment in the face of a confusing situation, but also
the writer's recognition of the gap between what he might
have created and what he has actually written: 'Il voyait le
roman que cela aurait pu faire [. . .] et il voyait le roman que
cela avait fait' (pp. 210–11).

By the same token, any reading of Queneau, if it is to be in sympathy with its subject, must allow for a multitude of possibilities which it may indicate but to which it does not necessarily lead. The most fitting conclusion can only remain inconclusive,[4] rejoining its starting-point rather than suggesting a culmination – as do Queneau's own 'circular' novels. This also accords with Flaubert's dictum denouncing the folly of all attempts to 'conclure', which Queneau quotes with whole-hearted approval (see *Bâtons*, p. 124), or the line from Pascal which he endorses in one of his essays: 'A la fin de chaque vérité, il faut ajouter qu'on se souvient de la vérité opposée' (*Voyage*, p. 154). Anything more categorical would only betray Queneau's most characteristic position: 'Quand j'énonce une assertion, je m'aperçois tout de suite que l'assertion contraire est à peu près aussi intéressante, à un point où cela devient presque superstitieux chez moi.'

Chronology

Le rapport de l'homme à l'œuvre, quoiqu'on en pense dans un
esprit classique, ce n'est pas une recherche méprisable.

Bâtons, p. 131

There is no published biography of Queneau. Information on his
life and career is to be found in: Jean Queval, *Essai sur Raymond
Queneau*, pp. 201–9 and *Raymond Queneau*, pp. 147–66; Jacques
Bens, *Queneau*, pp. 7–35; Paul Gayot, *Queneau*, pp. 9–26;
Raymond Queneau plus intime (Bibliothèque Nationale, 1978);
André Blavier, 'Chronologie de Raymond Queneau', *Europe*, no.
650–1 (1983), pp. 130–48.

1903 (21 February)	Raymond Auguste Queneau born in Le Havre, only child of Auguste and Joséphine Queneau, haberdashers.
1908–20	Lycée du Havre, with contemporaries including Armand Salacrou, Jean Piel, Jean Dubuffet.
1913–17	Copious juvenilia (mostly unpublished). (See 'Bibliographie des œuvres complètes de R. Queneau jusqu'en octobre 1917', *Temps Mêlés Documents Queneau*, no. 150+3 (1978), pp. 46–9.)
1920	Baccalauréat, with options in Latin, Greek and Philosophy. Matriculation at the University of Paris.
1921	Move of family home to Epinay-sur-Orge in the southern suburbs of Paris.
1922	Two-month stay in Great Britain.
1923	Certificat d'études supérieures in general philosophy and logic.

1924	Certificat d'études supérieures in psychology and the general history of philosophy. Introduction, by Pierre Naville, to Surrealists including Breton, Aragon, Vitrac, Desnos; contributions to *La Révolution Surréaliste*.
1925	Certificat d'études supérieures in ethics and sociology; Licence ès Lettres.
1925–7	Military service with the 3ᵉ Zouaves in Algeria and in Morocco during the Rif wars.
1927	(Short-lived) employment as bank clerk at the Comptoir National d'Escompte in Paris. Renewed association with Surrealists, especially those of the rue du Château group–Prévert, Marcel Duhamel, Yves Tanguy.
1928	Marriage to Janine Kahn, sister-in-law of André Breton.
1929	Break with Breton and Surrealism.
1930–3	Study of 'fous littéraires'.
1931–3	Reviews for *La Critique Sociale*, journal of the Cercle Communiste Démocratique, under the direction of Boris Souvarine; association with Georges Bataille.
1932	Journey to Greece.
1932–9	Attendance at courses at the École Pratique des Hautes Études: Alexandre Kojève on Hegel; Henri-Charles Puech on Gnosticism and Manicheism.
1933	*Le Chiendent*.
1933–9 or '40	Course of psychoanalysis
1934	*Gueule de pierre*. Birth of a son, Jean-Marie.
1936	*Les Derniers Jours*. Move to Neuilly, his permanent home hereafter.
1936–8	'Connaissez-vous Paris?' column in the daily, *L'Intransigeant*.
1937	*Odile*; *Chêne et chien*.
1937–40	Co-founder of, and regular contributor to *Volontés*.
1938	*Les Enfants du limon*. 'Lecteur d'anglais' on the reading panel of Éditions Gallimard.

1939	*Un Rude Hiver.*
	Call-up, with rank of 'soldat de 2e classe'.
1940	Promotion to corporal; demobilisation.
1941	*Les Temps mêlés.*
	Secretary-General of Éditions Gallimard.
1942	*Pierrot mon ami.*
1944	*Loin de Rueil.*
	Member of the Comité National des Écrivains.
1944–5	Regular reviews for the Resistance newspaper *Front National.*
1945	Deputy director of the literary services of French radio. Director of the *Encyclopédie de la Pléiade.*
1947	*Exercices de style*; *On est toujours trop bon avec les femmes* (under the pseudonym of Sally Mara).
	Collaboration with René Clément on the scenario for the projected *Candide 47*, at the start of a long involvement with the cinema.
1948	*Saint Glinglin.*
1949	Exhibition of *Gouaches 1928–1948.*
1950	*Bâtons, chiffres et lettres*; *Journal intime* (under the pseudonym of Sally Mara).
1951	Election to the Académie Goncourt.
	Member of the Collège de 'Pataphysique.
	Co-founder of the Club des Savanturiers, for science-fiction enthusiasts.
1952	*Le Dimanche de la vie.*
	Member of the jury at the Cannes Film Festival.
1959	*Zazie dans le métro.*
1960	Co-founder of the Ouvroir de Littérature Potentielle, at the Décade Raymond Queneau at Cerisy-la-Salle.
1963	*Bords.*
1964	Member of the American Mathematical Society; growing interest in mathematical research.
1965	*Les Fleurs bleues.*
1968	*Le Vol d'Icare.*
1972	Death of Janine Queneau.
1973	*Le Voyage en Grèce.*
1976 (25 October)	Death of Raymond Queneau.

Notes

INTRODUCTION

N.B. Unless otherwise stated, place of publication of all books is Paris.
1 Jean-Louis Rambures, 'Le cas étrange de l'académicien Queneau', *Réalités*, no. 216 (1964), pp. 74–8 (p. 74). For another use of the same image, see Queneau's article 'L'amour, la peinture', *Les Lettres Françaises*, 17 mai 1946, p. 4.
2 Cf. Claude-Edmonde Magny, *Littérature et critique* (Payot, 1971), p. 384: 'Les critiques ne parlent jamais des difficultés qu'il leur arriva d'éprouver à lire, au moins au début, tel ou tel livre – comme si s'introduire dans un univers étranger était la chose du monde la plus aisée [...]. Qui [...] ne s'est senti submergé et comme enlisé au sein d'une œuvre romanesque pourtant accessible, perméable en toutes ses parties?' But cf. some interesting studies in the way novels begin, such as Bernard Alluin, 'Débuts de roman', *Bulletin de Recherche sur l'Enseignement du Français*, 24 (1980), pp. 51–61; Victor Brombert, 'Opening Signals in narrative', *New Literary History*, 11 (1980), pp. 489–502; Claude Duchet, 'Idéologie de la mise en texte', *La Pensée*, 215 (1980), pp. 95–108.
3 Iris Murdoch, *Under the Net* (London: The Reprint Society, 1955), pp. 277–8. *Under the Net* is in fact dedicated to Queneau, and *Pierrot mon ami* is mentioned as one of the favourite books of the novel's hero. For more on this connection, see Christopher Shorley, 'Irish Mist', *Temps Mêlés Documents Queneau*, no. 150 + 22–23–24 (1984), pp. 50–4.
4 On the concept of defamiliarisation, or *ostranenie*, as defined above all by the Russian Viktor Shklovsky, see, for instance, Ann Jefferson, 'Russian Formalism', pp. 19ff., in Ann Jefferson and David Robey (eds.), *Modern Literary Theory, A Comparative Introduction* (London: Batsford, 1982). For a fuller discussion of defamiliarisation in Queneau, see Stanley Fertig, 'Raymond Queneau et l'art de la défamiliarisation', *Temps Mêlés Documents Queneau*, no. 150 + 17–18–19 (1983), pp. 43–54.
5 Cf. Claude Simonnet, *Queneau déchiffré* (Julliard, 1962), p. 117.
6 Or, in Shklovsky's terms, defamiliarisation manifests itself on the level of language. See Jefferson, *op. cit.*, p. 20.

7   Maurice Blanchot, 'Chronique de la vie intellectuelle', *Journal des Débats Politiques et Littéraires*, 27 janv. 1942, p. 3.

8   Quoted in Jacques Bens, *Queneau* (Gallimard, 1962), p. 117.

9   Cf. Simonnet, *op. cit.*, p. 73 for this sort of demand on the reader in *Le Chiendent*; and Vivian Mercier, *The New Novel from Queneau to Pinget* (New York: Farrar, Straus and Giroux, 1971), p. 89 for similar comments on *Pierrot mon ami*.

10 Quoted in Bens, *op. cit.*, p. 118.

11 Quoted in Andrée Bergens, *Raymond Queneau* (Geneva: Droz, 1963), p. 69.

12 Cf. Paul Gayot, *Queneau* (Editions Universitaires, 1967), p. 80: 'Le "personnage" principal en est plutôt la Ville Natale [...]. L'histoire contée en *Saint Glinglin* est autant une crise sociale qu'une crise individuelle'; and Donna Clare Tyman, 'Queneau's Concept of Literature and its Illustration in some of his Works' (unpublished doctoral dissertation, University of London, 1973), p. 168: 'The novel is more the ancient history of the mind than the account of a primitive civilization.'

13 See Hubert Juin, 'La lecture, pour quoi faire?', *Les Lettres Françaises*, 14–20 sept. 1961, pp. 4–5. It should be noted that Queneau's challenge to reading reaches its logical conclusion outside his fiction, in experimental works such as *Cent mille milliards de poèmes* (Gallimard, 1961) and 'Un Conte à votre façon (*Contes*, pp. 221–6).

14 Cf. Hubert Juin, 'La lecture, pour quoi faire?', *Les Lettres Françaises*, 18–24 oct. 1961, p. 4: 'La lecture n'est aucunement un phénomène mécanique [...] mais une sorte d'improvisation personnelle, qui engage tout l'individu.'

15 Françoise van Rossum-Guyon, *Critique du roman* (Gallimard, 1970), p. 21.

16 Quoted in van Rossum-Guyon, *op. cit.*, p. 24n.

17 See, for example, Claude Simonnet's description of his study *Queneau déchiffré* as 'plutôt un exercice de lecture', in anon, 'Voilà vingt ans que j'épluche le même oignon', *L'Union de Reims*, 18 févr. 1962, p. 10.

18 There is very little criticism of Queneau's early work beyond a few perfunctory *comptes rendus*. It is claimed that the first serious critical article on Queneau dates from 1941; see Maurice Nadeau, 'A 30 ans l'auteur du *Chiendent* marche déjà à contre-courant', *La Quinzaine Littéraire*, 16 nov. 1976, pp. 4–6 (p. 4).

19 His first real recognition came with *Exercices de style* (1947), the popularity of which owed much to the music-hall adaptation performed by the Frères Jacques: see Étienne Boudot-Lamotte, 'Quelques souvenirs d'un lecteur et ami ...', *L'Herne*, no. 29 (1975), pp. 319–23 (p. 322). The first major fiction success was *Zazie dans le métro* (1959), of which 100,000 copies were sold in less than a year.

20 Malou Rorive, 'Les romans de Raymond Queneau: contingence, consubstantialité et sagesse' (unpublished *mémoire*, University of Liège).

21 Jean Queval, *Essai sur Raymond Queneau* (Seghers).

22 L. de Gérin-Ricard, 'Les Derniers Beaux [sic] Jours', Le Petit Marseillais, 25 nov. 1936, p. 6.

23 Robert Poulet, 'Faux snobs de l'ordurier', Carrefour, 20 mai 1959, p. 22.

24 'Criticus dissèque Queneau', Aux Écoutes du Monde, 17 avril 1959, p. 40.

25 Jacques Lemarchand, 'Si tu t'imagines à la Gaîté – Montparnasse', Le Figaro Littéraire, 17 févr. 1966, p. 14.

26 The articles in question – 'Écrit en 1937', 'Conversation avec Georges Ribemont-Dessaignes' and 'Connaissez-vous le chinook?' – all first appeared between 1937 and 1950.

27 'Errata' was first published in NRF, no. 196 (1966), pp. 627–9.

28 Stanley E. Gray, 'Beckett and Queneau as formalists', James Joyce Quarterly, vol. 8, no. 4 (1971), pp. 392–404 (p. 392). Cf. also J. Bersani, M. Autrand, J. Lecarme, B. Vercier, La Littérature en France depuis 1945 (Bordas, 1970), p. 396, and Walter Redfern, Queneau: 'Zazie dans le métro' (London: Grant and Cutler Ltd, 1980), p. 17.

29 Félicien Marceau, 'Queneau ou le triomphe de la grammaire', La Table Ronde, no. 53 (1952), pp. 137–41, (p. 138).

30 Anon, 'Voilà vingt ans que j'épluche le même oignon'.

31 Anon, 'The writing game', TLS, 25 May 1967, p. 438.

32 Richard Cobb, 'The writing game', TLS, 1 June 1967, p. 487 (a letter written in response to the previous item).

33 A representative selection of these is to be found in Bâtons, pp. 11–26, 35–94.

34 For example, 'Technique du roman' (Bâtons, pp. 27–33); 'La symphonie inachevée' (ibid., pp. 223–8); Charbonnier, pp. 47–56.

35 Pierre Léon, 'Phonétisme, graphisme et zazisme', Études de Linguistique Appliquée, no. 1 (1962), pp. 70–84.

36 Ernst Kemmner, Sprachspiel und Stiltechnik in Raymond Queneaus Romanen (Tübingen: Tübinger Beiträge zur Linguistik, 1972).

37 Régis Boyer, 'Mots et jeux de mots chez Prévert, Queneau, Boris Vian, Ionesco: essai d'étude méthodique', Studia Neophilologica, vol. 40, no. 2 (1968), pp. 317–58.

38 ibid., p. 357.

39 Gerald Prince, 'Queneau et l'anti-roman', Neophilologus, vol. 55, no. 1 (1971), pp. 33–40 (p. 39).

40 Ibid.

41 Albert-Marie Schmidt, 'Fantaisies du verbe et du moi', Réforme, 28 févr. 1959, p. 6.

42 See particularly Raymond Queneau (Oxford: Clarendon Press, 1976), pp. 6–7.

43 Paul Gayot, 'La Ville Natale – étude d'un milieu en crise', Cahiers du Collège de 'Pataphysique, dossier 20 (1962), pp. 5–13.

44 Notably 'De l'humour (?) à la sagesse', Temps mêlés, no. 50–2 (1961), pp. 36–52.

45 Stuart L. Johnston, 'Reflections on the philosophy of Raymond Queneau', French Review, vol. 29, no. 1 (1955), pp. 21–7.

46 Alexandre Kojève, 'Les romans de la sagesse', *Critique*, no. 60 (1952), pp. 387–97.

47 Jean Blanzat, '*Zazie dans le métro* de Raymond Queneau', *Le Figaro Littéraire*, 21 févr. 1959, p. 14.

48 Martin Esslin, 'Raymond Queneau, b. 1903', in *The Novelist as Philosopher*, edited by John Cruickshank (London: Oxford University Press, 1962), pp. 79–101 (p. 79).

49 See Simonnet, *Queneau déchiffré*, p. 12; Anne Clancier, 'Manuel du parfait analysé', *L'Arc*, no. 28 (1966), pp. 33–40 (p. 33); Paul Gayot, 'Petite cosmogonie "quenienne"', *Le Monde*, 26 oct. 1968, p. iv.

50 Cf. Bergens, *Raymond Queneau*, p. 15: 'Il se borne à imaginer des histoires à l'intérieur de l'absurde.'

51 Anon, 'The writing game'.

52 Tyman, 'Queneau's Concept of Literature and its Illustration in some of his Works', p. 22.

53 See, for example, William S. Bell's review, 'Andrée Bergens: *Raymond Queneau*', *Romanic Review*, vol. 56, no. 4 (1965), pp. 316–17.

54 As in Jürgen Pauls, '*Les Fleurs bleues*' von Raymond Queneau: Eine Analyse des Romans unter besonderer Berücksichtigung der Symbolik (Hamburg: Romanisches Seminar der Universität Hamburg, 1973).

55 As in André Targe, 'Poor Lehameau', *Silex*, no. 3 (1977), pp. 104–16.

56 As in Vivian Kogan, *The Flowers of Fiction: Time and Space in Raymond Queneau's 'Les Fleurs bleues'* (Lexington, Kentucky: French Forum, Publishers, 1982).

57 Robert Kanters, 'Exercices de critique', *L'Actualité Littéraire*, no. 56 (1959), pp. 18–19.

58 Maurice Nadeau, 'Pelons l'oignon', *La Quinzaine Littéraire*, 1er déc. 1968, p. 7. Cf. Roland Barthes, 'Style and its image', in *Literary Style: A Symposium*, edited by Seymour Chatman (New York: Oxford University Press, 1971), pp. 3–10 (p. 10): 'If up until now we have looked at the text as a species of fruit with a kernel (an apricot, for example), the flesh being the form and the pit being the content, it would be better to see it as an onion, a construction of layers (or levels, or systems) whose body contains, finally, no heart, no kernel, no secret, no irreducible principle, nothing except the infinity of its own envelopes – which envelop nothing other than the unity of its own surfaces.'

1. RAW MATERIAL

1 Emmanuel d'Astier and Michel-Antoine Burnier, 'De Queneau à Zazie', *L'Événement*, no. 27 (1968), pp. 22–5.

2 Cf. A. J. Greimas, *Sémantique structurale* (Larousse, 1966), p. 36, where the contrast is made between the two extremes of non-communication: the unchecked freedom of the schizophrenic and 'la parole totalement socialisée, itérative, le "tu causes, tu causes, c'est tout ce que tu sais faire" de Queneau,* et qui, elle aussi, est la négation de la communication, privée d'information'.

*The refrain of the parrot, Laverdure, in *Zazie dans le métro*.

3 Originally published in *Études de Linguistique appliquée*, no. 3 (1964), pp. 37–50. Reprinted in *L'Herne*, no. 29 (1975), pp. 55–60.
4 Éditions de l'Herne, 1971. Reprinted in *Contes*, pp. 227–34.
5 Preface to *Les Écrivains célèbres* (Mazenod, 1951), pp. 7–10 (p. 9).
6 d'Astier and Burnier, *art. cit.*
7 The reference is to J. Vendryes, *Le Langage* (La Renaissance du Livre, 1921), p. 325. In a later article, which develops a similar argument with reference to, for instance, the mute 'e', Queneau invokes later linguists, including von Wartburg, Thérive and Benveniste (see 'Écrit en 1955', *Bâtons*, pp. 65–94 (p. 94).
8 See Philip Morey, 'The treatment of English words in Queneau', *Modern Language Review*, 76 (1981), pp. 823–38 (p. 836).
9 Pierre Léon, 'Phonétisme, graphisme et zazisme', p. 79.
10 Yvon Belaval, 'Les deux langages', *L'Arc*, no. 28 (1966), pp. 14–22 (p. 15).
11 Pierre Léon, *art. cit.*, p. 79. It is impossible to accept Henri Peyre's assertion that 'the effect is entertaining for a while, then soon palls upon the reader as it becomes monotonously mechanical' (*French Novelists of Today*, New York: Oxford University Press, 1967, p. 354). Peyre seems more influenced by Queneau's propaganda than by his practice.
12 It has also been pointed out that with very few exceptions, Queneau does not resort to 'le néo-français' in his critical or technical (i.e. non-literary) writings. See Yvon Belaval, *op. cit.*
13 Stephen Ullmann, *Style in the French Novel*, second impression (Oxford: Basil Blackwell, 1964), p. 6. Cf. Michael Riffatere: 'Style is understood as the emphasis (expressive, affective, aesthetic) added to the information conveyed by the linguistic structure, without alteration of meaning. Which is to say that language expresses and style stresses' ('Criteria for style analysis', *Word*, 1959, pp. 154–74 (p. 155)).
14 'Quelques maîtres du XXᵉ siècle', *Les Écrivains célèbres*, tome III (Mazenod, 1952), pp. 228–33 (p. 233).
15 *Op. cit.*, p. 10.
16 Cf. *ibid.*, where Ullmann proposes three corresponding categories, based respectively on the sound, the word and the phrase.
17 Roland Barthes, *Essais critiques* (Seuil, 1964), p. 127.
18 Albert Doppagne, 'Le néologisme chez Raymond Queneau', *Cahiers de l'Association Internationale des Études Françaises*, no. 25 (1973), pp. 91–107 (pp. 92–3).
19 Philip Morey, *art. cit.*, counts about nine hundred examples including Queneau's poetry.
20 See his article 'Sur quelques aspects relativement peu connus du verbe en français', *Le Surréalisme Révolutionnaire*, no. 1 (1948), p. 36.
21 But cf. 'admirassions' in the Livre de Poche edition (1963, 1967), p. 141.
22 *Le Petit Robert* (1972).
23 Paul Gayot, 'A travers le Paris de Zazie et de Valentin Brû', *Cahiers du Collège de 'Pataphysique*, dossier 20 (1962), pp. 27–32 (p. 28).

24 Cf. Yvon Belaval, *op. cit.*, pp. 15–16: 'Il aurait pu opter pour les mots en désordre [...] il aurait pu, aussi, pousser jusqu'au lettrisme [...]. Queneau n'a pas tenté l'expérience.'

25 André Bay, 'A propos de *Pierrot mon ami* de Raymond Queneau', *Comœdia*, 19 sept. 1942, p. 2.

26 Jacques Brenner, 'Les mystères de Queneau', *Le Nouvel Observateur*, 25 nov. 1968, pp. 35–7 (p. 37).

27 See André Blavier, 'De l'humour (?) à la sagesse', *Temps Mêlés*, no. 50–2 (1961), pp. 36–53 (p. 52, note 10).

28 Stephen Ullmann, *op. cit.*, p. 2.

29 The most representative examples of this approach are to be found in Andrée Bergens, *Raymond Queneau*, pp. 196–212; Régis Boyer, 'Mots et jeux de mots chez Prévert, Queneau, Boris Vian, Ionesco: essai d'étude méthodique'; Ernst Kemmner, *Sprachspiel und Stiltechnik in Raymond Queneaus Romanen*, pp. 206–32.

30 Germaine Brée and Margaret Guiton, *An Age of Fiction: The French Novel from Gide to Camus* (New Brunswick, N.J.: Rutgers University Press, 1957), p. 170.

31 Claude Simonnet, *Queneau déchiffré*, p. 79. Cf also Yvon Belaval, 'Les deux langages'.

32 Gérald Antoine, 'Une intouchable: l'image chez Queneau', *Stanford French Review*, 1 (1977), pp. 153–65.

33 See Jean Paulhan, *Œuvres complètes*, t. 2 (Cercle du Livre Précieux, 1966), pp. 67–96; also C.-M. Lorin and A. R. Ratsimanga, 'Littérature malgache', in *Histoire des littératures*, edited by Queneau, t. 1 (Gallimard, Encyclopédie de la Pléiade, 1956), pp. 1469–1500.

34 'Quelques maîtres du XXᵉ siècle', p. 230. He is referring specifically to Henry James, Gertrude Stein and James Joyce.

35 For a further definition of decorum, see, for example, the article in M. H. Abrams, *A Glossary of Literary Terms*, fourth edition (New York: Holt, Rinehart and Winston, 1981), p. 41.

36 See, for example, Pierre Berger, 'Entretien avec Raymond Queneau, humoriste automatique', *La Gazette des Lettres*, no. 19 (1952), pp. 15–22.

37 Roland Barthes, *Essais critiques*, pp. 126–7.

38 Quoted in Claude Bonnefoy: 'Un illustrateur et un maquettiste – exercices de style avec Queneau', *Arts*, 27 nov. 1963, p. 5.

39 'La S.P.A.', *Le Nouvel Observateur*, 4 mai 1970, p. 41.

40 *Histoire des littératures*, t. 1: *Littératures anciennes, orientales et orales* (Gallimard, Encyclopédie de la Pléiade, 1956), p. viii.

41 His interest in the subject has attracted relatively little critical attention. Among the few accounts of it: Andrée Bergens, *Raymond Queneau*, pp. 65–7, 175–6; Jean Borie, 'Raymond Queneau: poésie et français parlé', *Romatic Review*, 57 (1966), pp. 41–55 (p. 51).

42 On the validity of the term 'non-verbal', see, for example, William C. Stokes, 'Sign languages and the verbal/non-verbal distinction', in *Sight, Sound and Sense*, edited by Thomas Sebeok (Indiana: Indiana University Press, 1978), pp. 161ff. For a theoretical discussion of the

relationship of verbal and non-verbal, see Michael Argyle, 'Non-verbal communication and language', in *Communication and Understanding*, edited by Godfrey Vesey (Hassocks/New Jersey: Harvester Press/ Humanities Press, 1977), pp. 63–78 (p. 71).

43 It is associated with Queneau in a variety of ways – from a famous early photograph from his military career in the Zouaves, showing him leaning on a broom, through his identification with the plant called 'le chiendent' (literally 'couch-grass' – and figuratively a 'snag' or 'hitch') also known in French as 'l'herbe à balai', to his answer to an interview question about his unfulfilled ambitions: 'J'ai toujours rêvé d'être balayeur' (Pierre Bourgeade, 'Queneaulogie', *La Quinzaine Littéraire*, 15 mars 1967, p. 28).

44 Dionys Mascolo, 'Zazie ou la philosophie dans le métro', *France-Observateur*, 12 févr. 1959, p. 24.

45 Examples of these have appeared in a variety of publications, e.g., *Opéra*, 7 févr. 1951, p. 3; *Topiques*, no. 7 (1952), pp. 4–5; *Cahiers du Collège de 'Pataphysique*, dossier 7 (1959), pp. 82–5. Most have been collected under the heading 'Sally plus intime' in *Les Œuvres complètes de Sally Mara*, pp. 345–60.

46 Queneau described the aim of Oulipo as being to 'proposer aux écrivains de nouvelles "structures", de nature mathématique ou bien encore inventer de nouveaux procédés artificiels ou mécaniques, contribuant à l'activité littéraire: Des soutiens de l'inspiration, pour ainsi dire, ou bien encore, en quelque sorte, une aide à la créativité' (*Bâtons*, p. 321). Queneau was a prominent member of the 'Oulipo' group from its formation in 1960 until his death. For further details see 'Littérature potentielle', in *Bâtons*, pp. 317–45; Paul Fournel, *Clés pour la littérature (Créations, re-créations, récréations)* (Gallimard, 1973).

47 See Claude Leroy, 'Étude sur la perte d'information et la variation de sens dans les *Exercices de style* de Raymond Queneau', in *Exercices de style*, 1963 edition, pp. 99–114; and P. Miclau, 'Structure et information dans *Exercices de style* de Raymond Queneau' in *Le Réel dans la littérature et dans la langue*, Actes du Xe congrès de la Fédération Internationale des Langues et des Littératures Modernes (Klincksieck, 1967), p. 221.

2. FORM

1 *Queneau déchiffré*, p. 52.

2 That of immobility or the failure to evolve; see Gayot, *Queneau*, pp. 71–2.

3 See, for one recent example among many, Seymour Chatman, *Story and Discourse: Narrative Structure in Fiction and Film* (Ithaca and London: Cornell University Press, 1978), pp. 43ff.

4 Of which, according to one review, the seventh and the thirteenth are structurally different from the rest. See 'The writing game', *TLS*, 25 May 1967, p. 438.

5 Simonnet, *Queneau déchiffré*, pp. 48–9.

6 See Malou Rorive, 'Les Romans de Raymond Queneau: construction, contingence et sagesse'. The first section of the mémoire is devoted to a meticulous analysis of the first chapter of *Le Chiendent*.

7 Rorive regards Dominique Belhôtel and his wife as an indissoluble couple and therefore as a unity (*ibid.* p. 18).

8 Rorive's last piece of evidence is a series of vertiginous calculations based on the train times mentioned in the first chapter, all of which would seem to be variations on the number forty-nine, i.e. the square of seven (*ibid.* p. 24).

9 For a fuller account of the pairings in *Le Chiendent*, see Simonnet, *Queneau déchiffré*, pp. 45–6.

10 For a detailed consideration of the exact relationship between Auge and Cidrolin, see Alain Calame, 'De l'inclusion dans *Les Fleurs bleues*', *Temps Mêlés Documents Queneau*, no. 150 + 2 (1978), pp. 11–14 (translated into English as 'Inclusion in *Les Fleurs bleues*' in *Prospice*, no. 8 (1978), pp. 72–4).

11 Marguerite Duras, 'Uneuravek', *L'Express*, 22 janv. 1959, pp. 27–8 (p. 27).

12 Cf. 'La répétition, suprême figure de style, règne. Je me demande si les exégètes de Queneau [...] ont su mettre en valeur ce phénomène central dans une clarté assez franche.' Jean Queval, 'Queneau, discours et rêve', *NRF*, no. 290 (1977), pp. 64–71 (p. 68).

13 On the derivation from 'chêne' and 'chien', see Noël Arnaud, 'Avènement d'un Queneau glorieux', *Temps Mêlés*, no. 5–6 (1953), pp. 45–50. Later accounts of Queneau's personal leitmotive are to be found in Simonnet, *Queneau déchiffré*, pp. 18–19; Gayot, *Queneau*, p. 77, and, most detailed of all, Val. Panaitescu, 'L'humoriste "chêne et chien" et sa mythologie', *Temps Mêlés Documents Queneau*, no. 150 + 2 (1978), pp. 18–35.

14 This question has been brilliantly discussed by Joseph Danan in his thesis 'Poétique du *Chiendent*', University of Rouen, 1970–1. Danan bases himself on the studies of paragrams by Jean Starobinski and Julia Kristeva, and refers to the implicit invitation to look for this sort of device: 'Tous deux, la narine frémissante, se mettent à guetter le mot-souche' (*Chiendent*, p. 184).

15 *L'Instant fatal* (Gallimard, 1966), p. 45.

16 Marguerite Duras, 'Uneuravek', p. 27.

17 Henri Peyre, *French Novelists of Today*, p. 435.

18 The quotation is adapted from Strabo, *Geography*, xiii, 598, line 36, in which reference is made to Aristotle's doubts as to whether the wall which the Achaeans built – and Apollo destroyed – in the *Iliad*, was ever more than a figment of Homer's imagination.

19 See Vivian Mercier, *The New Novel from Queneau to Pinget*, p. 102.

20 Gerald Prince, 'Queneau et l'anti-roman', p. 33.

21 Roland Barthes, *Essais critiques*, p. 125.

22 Jacques Bens, 'Etude sur Queneau/Chapitre IV: Les Hommes', *Temps Mêlés*, no. 50–2 (1961), pp. 17–24 (p. 18).

23 The actual distribution is shown in the appendix to Simonnet, *Queneau déchiffré* (pp. 165–81).

24 Guy Dumur, 'Les dimanches de Raymond Queneau', *Combat*, 28 févr. 1952, p. 7.

25 Vivian Mercier is one of very few commentators to note this. See *The New Novel from Queneau to Pinget*, p. 87.

26 See Jean Piel, *La Rencontre et la différence* (Fayard, 1982), p. 63. Piel describes *Les Derniers Jours* as a '"roman" qui n'ose pas dire son nom', suggesting that at the time of publication, Queneau was still sensitive to André Breton's much-quoted denigration of the genre in the first *Manifeste du surréalisme*.

27 See Donna Clare Tyman, 'Queneau: chêne et chien', *Temps Mêlés Documents Queneau*, no. 150 + 2 (1978), pp. 39–47 (p. 42).

28 Maurice Blanchot, 'Chronique de la vie intellectuelle', *Journal des Débats Politiques et Littéraires*, 27 janv. 1942, p. 3.

29 'Quelques maîtres du XXᵉ siècle', p. 230.

30 'Dino' was first published in *Messages*, no. 2 (1942), pp. 55–9; 'Panique' in the volume *Une Trouille verte* (Éditions de Minuit, 1947), pp. 21–32, and 'Le Cheval troyen', as a book, in 1948 (Éditions Georges Visat). Before their republication in *Contes et propos*, in 1981, virtually nothing had been written on them, according to Wolfgang Hillen's bibliography.

31 It has been suggested that it was originally intended as part of a larger work; see, for example, Claude Rameil, 'Bibliographie', *L'Herne*, no. 29 (1975), pp. 355–92 (p. 364); Jacques Bens, 'A la limite d'un roman', *Europe*, no. 650–1 (1983), pp. 77–82.

32 See, for example, E. K. Bennett, *A History of the German 'Novelle'*, revised and continued by H. M. Waidson (Cambridge: Cambridge University Press, 1961), Ch. 1.

33 For a fuller discussion of the treatment of the novel's antecedents in *Les Fleurs bleues*, see Vivian Kogan, *The Flowers of Fiction: Time and Space in Raymond Queneau's 'Les Fleurs bleues'*, pp. 71ff. Kogan concludes that Queneau's text is 'a fiction about the various ways in which we tell the stories we inherit and how we adapt and transform according to our purposes' (p. 125).

34 'Lettre du Deutérodataire Kirmu au Régent Tadjo', *Cahiers du Collège de 'Pataphysique*, dossier 20 (1962), pp. 43–6 (pp. 43–4). For other similar examples in Queneau's work, see Pierre Versins, 'Queneauctural', *Temps Mêlés* no. 50–2 (1961), pp. 28–9.

35 'La science-fiction vaincra', *Arts*, 29 oct. 1953, pp. 1, 4 (p. 4). See also another article by Queneau: 'Un nouveau genre littéraire: les science-fictions', *Critique*, no. 46 (1951), pp. 195–8, which is noted by Boris Vian in *Cinéma, science-fiction*, ed. Noël Arnaud (Christian Bourgois, 1978), pp. 81–2.

36 Quoted in Bens, *Queneau*, p. 118.

37 At the same time, explanations are possible; see especially Stephen Noreiko's hypothesis: 'We have [. . .] sufficient elements for supposing that after a riding accident while impersonating a foreign prince,

followed by a fake funeral [. . .] Voussois, through the intermediary of his brother, buys, or makes a semblance of buying, at about the time of his supposed death at Palinsac [. . .] Mounnezergues's vegetable garden, already promised to a "quidam", presumably Léonie's uncle, Pansoult, and has a memorial built, thus putting himself in a position ten years later to frustrate Pradonet's plans, and create his Jardin Zoophilique.' ('*Pierrot mon ami*: themes and an enigma', in *Mélanges de littérature française moderne offerts à Garnet Rees* (Minard, 1980), pp. 241–50 (p. 248)).

38 See Thelma M. Smith and Ward L. Miner, *Transatlantic Migration: The Contemporary American Novel in France* (Durham, N. Carolina: Duke University Press, 1955), p. 72. N.B. also pp. 65–6, where *Loin de Rueil* is judged to exhibit American influence.

39 Queneau admitted writing as Sally Mara 'pour faire comme Boris Vian' (quoted in Gayot, *Queneau*, p. 28).

40 The Sally Mara books have certainly attracted less comment than most of Queneau's other novels. Jean Queval was among the first to discuss them seriously – albeit briefly – in *Essai sur Raymond Queneau* (p. 205). More recently, however, some studies have appeared; see, for example, François Caradec, 'Queneau éditeur de Sally Mara', *Europe*, no. 650–1 (1983), pp. 91–5; Line McMurray, 'Le même et l'autre dans *Les Œuvres complètes de Sally Mara*', *Temps Mêlés Documents Queneau*, no. 150 + 20–21 (1983), pp. 9–18; Evert van der Starre, 'Sally Mara romancière', *ibid.*, pp. 85–109; and van der Starre, ed., *Études sur les 'Œuvres complètes de ~~Raymond Queneau~~ Sally Mara*', *Cahiers de Recherches Interuniversitaires Néerlandaises*, no. 10 (1984).

41 See, for instance, Paul Gayot, *Queneau*, ch. II for a general survey, or Noël Arnaud, 'Des goûts d'un satrape en couleurs', *Cahiers du Collège de 'Pataphysique*, dossier 20 (1962), pp. 47–58, for his painting.

42 'Je suis dans une situation . . .', *Temps Mêlés*, no. 50–2 (1961), pp. 9–12 (p. 10).

43 In the terms of C. S. Peirce's well-known typology, pictograms are icons, while language is made up of 'signs proper'. See, for instance, Jonathan Culler, *Structuralist Poetics: Structuralism, Linguistics and the Study of Literature* (London: Routledge and Kegan Paul, 1975), p. 16.

44 The pictograms in question are in *Bâtons, chiffres et lettres*, pp. 275–84; for further examples, see Queneau's 'Pictogrammes' in *Temps Mêlés Documents Queneau*, no. 150 + 8 (1980), pp. 21–37. The full import of these is suggested in an explanatory note: 'Queneau, comme Étiemble plus tard (*Le Jargon des sciences*) ne voyait de possibilité de communication universelle que dans le signe pictographique. Dans une note manuscrite, non datable, il énumère les "inventeurs": "Klee Miro Michaux moi-même"' (*ibid.* p. 54).

45 Quoted in Jacques Bens, *Queneau*, p. 12. On the musical origins of *Exercices de style*, see also Charles K. Keffer, Jr., 'Rencontre avec Raymond Queneau', *Romance Notes*, vol. 26 (1974), pp. 33–7 (p. 35). For technical discussions of the musical element, see Horst Petri, *Literatur und Musik. Form-und Strukturparallelen* (Göttingen: Sachse

und Pohl, 1964), pp. 25–8, and Helen M. Harbison, 'Le roman contemporain et la musique moderne', *French Review*, vol. 38 (1965), pp. 441–50 (p. 447).

46 See Florence Elaine Rechsteiner, 'Fallen Worlds and Artificial Temples: A Textual Analysis of Queneau's *Les Derniers Jours*' (unpublished doctoral dissertation, University of Utah, 1980).

47 See 'Miroir double', *La Quinzaine Littéraire*, no. 13 (1966), p. 27.

48 For a full account, see Ian Pilcher, 'Une source de la création littéraire: l'influence de la bande dessinée sur la composition des *Fleurs bleues*', *Temps Mêlés Documents Queneau*, no. 150 + 11 (1981), pp. 23–31.

49 'Quelques maîtres du XXᵉ siècle', p. 231.

50 On the dramatic qualities of *Le Vol d'Icare*, see Vivian Kogan, 'Raymond Queneau: Patapoetics of the Novel' (unpublished doctoral dissertation, Brown University, 1971), pp. 110–11.

51 Queneau's varied involvement with the cinema – his collaboration as writer – and occasionally actor – on a score of films, his writings on cinematic subjects, references to films in his novels, etc. – is charted in detail in *Raymond Queneau et le cinéma*, no. 10–11 of *Les Amis de Valentin brû*, published in 1980. For a discussion of some of the films in which he took part, see also René Micha, 'Le cinéma de Queneau', *L'Arc*, no. 28 (1966), pp. 59–68. Queneau's most explicit acknowledgement of his artistic debt to the cinema comes in an interview with Gabriel d'Aubarède, 'Raymond Queneau: l'ami des fous et des mots', *Gavroche*, 18 avril 1946, p. 4.

52 On the question of Queneau's originality in this matter, cf. another comment, also dating from 1944: 'Alors que la plupart des romanciers populistes et réalistes sont les héritiers plus ou moins évolués de la technique balzacienne, et qu'ils "mettent en scène", la technique de Queneau appartient à l'âge du cinéma' (Émile Danoen, 'Les lettres: Raymond Queneau romancier', *Combat*, 17 déc. 1944, p. 2).

53 For a fuller account of these two concepts, see James Monaco, *How to Read a Film* (New York: Oxford University Press, 1977), pp. 145–92.

54 Two commentators have noted the similarities between the technique of this passage and that used by Alfred Hitchcock in his film *Rear Window*. See Queval, *Essai sur Raymond Queneau* (1960), p. 153; and Gayot, *Queneau*, p. 99.

55 Marie-Claire Ropars-Wuilleumier, *De la littérature au cinéma* (Armand Colin, 1970), pp. 178–9.

56 Quoted in Gayot, *Queneau*, p. 30.

57 See, for example, Pierre Kast, 'Petite tyrannographie portative pour Raymond Queneau', *Les Cahiers du Cinéma*, no. 10 (1952), pp. 33–7; and Marcel Jullian, 'On n'est jamais assez infidèle aux bons auteurs', *L'Herne*, no. 29 (1975), pp. 313–16. Jean de Baroncelli makes the same point in his review of the film *On est toujours trop bon avec les femmes* in *Le Monde*, 15 juin 1971, p. 29.

58 d'Astier and Burnier, 'De Zazie à Queneau'.

59 'Miroir double'. The cartoon version is by Jacques Carelman and was published in 1966.

60 'Je suis dans une situation . . .', p. 10. Also in J[ean] G[uérin], 'Divers', *NRF*, no. 107 (1961), p. 935.

61 Jean-Louis Bory, *Tout feu, tout flamme* (Julliard, 1966), p. 130.

62 Claude Simonnet, 'La parodie et le thème de *Hamlet* chez Raymond Queneau', *Les Lettres Nouvelles*, no. 34 (1959), pp. 12–17 (pp. 12–13).

63 In J. Bersani, M. Autrand, J. Lecarme, B. Vercier, *La Littérature en France depuis 1945*, p. 392.

64 By Bersani, *ibid.*, p. 623.

65 The term 'intertextualité' is generally attributed to Julia Kristeva (see, for example, 'Bakhtine, le mot, le dialogue et le roman', *Critique*, no. 239 (1967), pp. 438–65 or 'Problèmes de la structuration du texte', in *Théorie d'ensemble* (Seuil, 1968), pp. 298–317 (p. 312). However, given the tendency to confuse 'intertextualité' with the simple tracing of sources, Kristeva subsequently proposed another term, 'transposition' (see *La Révolution du langage poétique*, Seuil, 1974, p.. 60). For later formulations, see Laurent Jenny, 'La stratégie de la forme', *Poétique*, no. 28 (1976), pp. 257–81, and, especially, Gérard Genette, *Palimpsestes* (Seuil, 1982). Before concentrating on 'hypertextualité', i.e. the systematic reference, in one text, to an earlier text, Genette surveys the current terminology in a field which he prefers to call 'transtextualité' (including 'citation', 'plagiat', 'allusion' etc.); but he is forced to admit that no single coherent terminology has yet been established (p. 7n. and p. 33). In what follows, therefore, none of the proposed critical models has been rigidly applied: the incidence of intertextuality in Queneau will rather be traced from its simplest and most superficial forms to the fullest and most complex integration of existing texts.

66 By Jean Queval at the colloquium 'Queneau et après' held at Rouen in November 1980. See *Les Amis de Valentin Brû*, no. 18 (1980), p. 59.

67 Cf. 'Ès uns escarbouilloyt la cervelle, ès aultres rompoyt bras et jambes, ès aultres deslochoyt les spondyles du coul, ès aultres demoulloyt les reins, avalloyt le nez, poschoyt les yeux' etc. Rabelais, *Œuvres complètes* (Gallimard, 1955), p. 85.

68 Pradonet quotes in passing the last two lines of one of the verses: 'Brigadier, répondit Pandore/Brigadier vous avez raison!'; Saint-Mouézy-sur-Eon and Saint-Flers-sur-Cavaillet, overnight stops on Pierre's journey south, derive their names from André Mouëzy-Eon, Robert Flers and G. A. de Cavaillet, all authors of musical comedies; and Pierrot sings 'l'air est pur, la route est large' (p. 159) – which comes from 'Le Clairon' by Paul Déroulède (1846–1914). See Noreiko, '*Pierrot mon ami*: themes and an enigma', p. 250, n. 14.

69 Cf. Du Bellay, *Les Regrets*, sonnet 31: 'Quand reverray-je le clos de ma pauvre maison,/Qui m'est une province, & beaucoup davantage'.

70 Cf. Molière, *Le Misanthrope*, 1. 314: 'Voyons, Monsieur, le temps ne fait rien à l'affaire'; and 1. 261: 'C'est à vous, s'il vous plaît, que ce discours s'adresse.'

71 See also *Bâtons*, pp. 135, 139, where Queneau refers to the list of 'literary geniuses' – from Homer to Shakespeare – which Hugo drew

up. The list is to be found in *William Shakespeare* (1864), première partie, livre deuxième, ch. III, 'Les Génies'. See Victor Hugo, *Œuvres complètes*, edited by Jean Massin (Le Club Français du Livre, 1969), vol. XIII, p. 189. For another view of the subject, see Victor Brombert, 'Hugo's Shakespeare', *Hudson Review*, 34 (1981), pp. 249–57.

72 Jean Roudaut, *Michel Butor ou le livre futur* (Gallimard, 1964), p. 234. Roudaut's quotation is from Butor, *Répertoire* II (Editions de Minuit, 1964), p. 240.

73 See Tyman, 'Queneau's Concept of Literature and its Illustration in some of his Works', pp. 102–3.

74 Cf. André Blavier, 'Deux sources de Queneau, l'une improbable, l'autre certaine', *Temps Mêlés*, no. 59–60 (1962), p. 50, who suggests another possible source in a story by E. Moerman in *La Lanterne Sourde*, no. 2 (1922).

75 See Tyman, *op. cit.*, p. 104. Queneau acknowledged his borrowings during an O.R.T.F. radio programme, 'Tels qu'en eux-mêmes', 4 July 1971.

76 For a detailed account of Apollinaire's influence, See Claude Debon-Tournadre, 'Présence d'Apollinaire dans l'œuvre de Queneau', *Revue d'Histoire Littérature de la France*, 81e année, no. 1 (1981), pp. 75–82. This covers intertextuality in Queneau's poetry as well as his novels, and Queneau's readings of Apollinaire.

77 *Le Chien à la mandoline* (Gallimard, 1965), p. 44.

78 Simonnet, 'La parodie et le thème de *Hamlet* chez Raymond Queneau', p. 15. The Freudian implications of the theme are discussed in André Targe, 'Poor Lehameau'.

79 Queneau had, however, alluded to *Madame Bovary* in *Le Chiendent*, notably in the ambiguous snatches of song rendered by père Taupe (p. 60), which echo the song of the blind beggar in Flaubert's novel. For a broad discussion of the relationship between the two writers, see Jean Queval, 'Queneau chez Flaubert', *Mercure de France*, no. 1157 (1960), pp. 8–28.

80 *Bouvard et Pécuchet* (Livre de Poche, 1959), p. 131.

81 It is worth noting that the Du Bellay poem mentioned earlier as the source of an allusion in *Les Fleurs bleues* itself begins 'Heureux qui, comme Ulysse, a fait un beau voyage'. N.B. also 'Sthène vient de relire tout Homère en trois jours' (*Fleurs bleues*, p. 129).

82 Notably in the 'Scylla and Charybdis' chapter, *Ulysses* (Harmondsworth: Penguin, 1969), pp. 184–218.

83 See Philip Handler, 'Joyce in France 1929–1959' (unpublished doctoral dissertation, University of Columbia, 1966), pp. 235–44.

84 See Bergens, *Raymond Queneau*, p. 210.

85 *Ulysses*, p. 586.

86 See Pierre-François David, 'Consubstantialité et quintessence d'une fiction dérivée', *Cahiers du Collège de 'Pataphysique*, dossier 20 (1962), pp. 15–20; also J.-M. Luccioni, 'Joyce chez Sally', *Etudes sur les 'Œuvres complètes de Raymond Queneau Sally Mara'*, pp. 22–34.

87 *Ulysses*, p. 663.

88 *Sally Mara*, p. 294; *Ulysses*, p. 366.
89 *Sally Mara*, p. 223; *Ulysses*, p. 367.
90 *Sally Mara*, p. 323; *Ulysses*, pp. 9–10, 594–5.
91 *Sally Mara*, p. 200; *Ulysses*, pp. 162, 692–3.
92 Queneau at one time planned to write an article on Joyce's links with Homer; see *Voyage*, p. 134.
93 Mark 14.34. More comparisons between *Saint Glinglin* and the Gospels are made in Margaret L. Eberbach, 'The Role of the Reader: A Study of Ten French Novels of the Twentieth Century' (unpublished doctoral dissertation, University of New York, 1963), pp. 260–1.
94 The links between the Saint Glinglin trilogy and *Totem and Taboo* have been stressed by Jean Queval in *Essai sur Raymond Queneau* (1960), pp. 49–50. Queval claims that although during the composition of *Gueule de pierre* Queneau was forbidden to read works of psychoanalysis, he remembered the general lines of *Totem and Taboo* well enough to use it as the basis for his novel. This explains both the close identification of themes and situations in the two works and the absence of quotation and verbal allusion.
95 *Totem and Taboo*, translated by James Strachey (London: Routledge and Kegan Paul, 1960), p. 2.
96 *Ibid.*, p. 32.
97 *Ibid.*, p. 50.
98 See Bergens, *Raymond Queneau*, p. 63 for a comparison of the 'printanier' and the Red Indian custom of *potlatch*, practised by the Kwakiutl tribe.
99 *Op. cit.*, p. 26.
100 *Ibid.*, p. 50.
101 *Ibid.*, pp. 89–90.
102 As in Stanley Gray, 'Beckett and Queneau as formalists', p. 402. Genette, in *Palimpsestes*, makes a helpful distinction between 'intertextualité', defined as the indiscriminate reference to many texts, and 'hypertextualité' , or systematic allusion to a single text (pp. 8, 16).
103 Direct quotation is a limiting case of intertextuality for Laurent Jenny, *art. cit.*, p. 258.
104 Cf. the definition attributed to Charles Nodier, who limited his list 'aux fous bien avérés qui n'ont pas eu la gloire de faire secte' (*Limon*, p. 51). For a comprehensive study of the subject, see André Blavier, *Les Fous littéraires* (Henri Veyrier, 1982).
105 Cf. Gayot, *Queneau*, p. 92, describing the story of the Limon family as 'la dorure destinée à faire avaler la pilule, le roman qui enrobe *L'Encyclopédie des Sciences inexactes*'.
106 Quoted in Bens, *Queneau*, p. 117. On the interweaving of the texts of the 'fous littéraires' and the rest of the novel, see Claude Simonnet, 'Note sur *Les Enfants du limon*', *L'Herne*, no. 29 (1975), pp. 192–4; Nicholas Hewitt, 'History in *Les Enfants du limon*: encyclopaedists and "flâneurs"', *Prospice*, no. 8 (1978), pp. 22–35; and Alain Calame,

'Raymond Queneau quadrateur', *Les Amis de Valentin Brû*, no. 15 (1981), pp. 33–40.

107   It might be noted in passing that the definition is also perfectly suited to Pierre Kougard in his intellectual narcissism.

108   See Marc-Daniel Marguliès, 'A propos des *Enfants du limon* de Raymond Queneau, essai d'interprétation arithmético-sémético-biblique', *Bulletin des Recherches de l'Université Aoyama-Gakuin de Tokyo*, 1 (1979–80), pp. 135–53.

109   Simonnet, *Queneau déchiffré*, p. 109.

110   As in Tyman, 'Queneau's Concept of Literature and its Illustration in some of his Works', pp. 222, 224.

111   *Essais critiques*, p. 125. The balance Queneau strikes can also be expressed as a reconstruction of the two alternatives open to the narrative artist as perceived by R. Scholes and R. Kellogg: 'In a brilliantly suggestive essay on "Art in a Closed Field", Hugh Kenner has said that for the narrative artist the limitations of language provide a "closed field" in which a large but finite number of elements are susceptible to infinite combinations and permutations. He suggests that a preoccupation with the finiteness of the elements, the "closedness" of the field, characterizes modern narrative. If Kenner's formulation is sound, we might make the further suggestion that again two alternatives, this time of essential philosophical attitude, face the narrative artist. He can accept his position with good humor and optimism and go ahead combining and permuting as brilliantly and meaningfully as it lies within his power to do, or he can combine and permute resentfully, demonstrating as he does so the hopelessness and meaninglessness of narrative art. Joyce exemplifies the former attitude and Beckett the latter.' (*The Nature of Narrative*, London, Oxford, New York: Oxford University Press, 1966, pp. 158–9)

112   See, for instance, *Pour un nouveau roman* (Gallimard, 1963), p. 177, and 'Quelques enfants du limon', *Le Monde*, 26 oct. 1968, p. iv.

113   Roger Grenier, 'Farces et satrape', *Le Nouvel Observateur*, 3 juin 1965, p. 19.

3. THE FICTIONAL WORLD

1   See, for example, Jacques Guicharnaud, 'Raymond Queneau's universe', *Yale French Studies*, no. 8 (1951), pp. 38–47; Robert Kanters, 'Queneau parle', *Le Figaro Littéraire*, 19 janv. 1963, p. 2; Pascal Pia, 'Grands travaux de 'pataphysique', *Carrefour*, 18 févr. 1959, p. 13.

2   Richard Mayne, 'The Queneau country', *Encounter*, vol. 24, no. 6 (June 1965), pp. 64, 66, 68–71.

3   Marguerite Duras, 'Uneuravek'.

4   John Sturrock, 'Free fall', *New Statesman*, 13 July 1973, p. 55.

5   The personal and autobiographical tone of the article in question, 'Le Café de la France', is in itself unusual.

6   On the autobiographical material in Queneau's fiction, see Gayot,

Queneau, pp. 10–11; and Noël Arnaud, 'Mais où est donc passé *Chêne et chien?*', *Temps Mêlés Documents Queneau*, no. 150+17–18–19 (1983), pp. 13–25.

7 Cf. Jean Piel, *La Rencontre et la différence*, p. 64: 'Le Vincent Tuquedenne des *Derniers Jours*, c'est, à s'y méprendre, le Raymond Queneau qui fut pendant cinq ans mon compagnon de tous les jours.'

8 Henri Kréa, 'Propos d'un Normand, *Le Nouvel Observateur*, 11 févr. 1965, pp. 20–1.

9 Pierre Berger, 'Entretien avec Raymond Queneau, humoriste automatique', *La Gazette des Lettres*, nouv. série no. 19 (1952), pp. 15–22.

10 Cf. also Queneau, 'Zazie dans son plus jeune âge', *Les Lettres Nouvelles*, nouv. série No. 2 (1959), pp. 5–7, where a similar point is made: 'Tout le roman contemporain est historique, les changements vont vite, ça marque. On ne peut pas montrer un type de quarante ans sans dire qu'il a été mobilisé, où, comment, son régiment, ses guerres, celle de quarante, l'exode, le six février, enfin tout le bordel infernal.'

11 See also Simonnet, *Queneau déchiffré*, pp. 33–4n.

12 Cf. Queneau's comments on humane town planning: 'Un effort pour rétablir un équilibre détruit par l'unique considération du gain immédiat et le mépris de toute valeur humaine. La ville actuelle est un cancer topographique' (*Voyage*, p. 179).

13 It is instructive to compare the criticism of urban conditions in *Le Chiendent* with Queneau's comments on Henry Miller: 'Les héros de Miller sont nos contemporains, c'est-à-dire des hommes jetés dans des situations contemporaines, j'entends: ordinairement avilissantes, et désespérées. Ce "héros" de Miller n'est pas l'homme en général, mais l'habitant de la grande ville cosmopolite' (*Voyage*, p. 74). For the evolution of Queneau's attitude to Paris as presented in his work, see François Caradec, 'Raymond Queneau 75012 Paris', *L'Herne*, no. 29 (1975), pp. 305–12 (p. 311).

14 The publication of *Les Derniers Jours* (in 1936) coincides with the period 1936 to 1938 when Queneau was presenting a daily quiz entitled 'Connaissez-vous Paris?' in *L'Intransigeant*.

15 See Bernard Pingaud, 'Le parfait banlieusard', *L'Arc*, no. 28 (1966), pp. 7–10.

16 Gabriel d'Aubarède, 'Raymond Queneau, l'ami des fous et des mots', *Gavroche*, 18 avril 1946, p. 4.

17 Brassaï, *Le Paris secret des années 30* (Gallimard, 1976), pages unnumbered. See also the English version, *The Secret Paris of the 30s*, tr. Richard Miller (New York: Pantheon Books, 1976).

18 Cf. his description of the helter-skelter in the real-life Luna-Park in 'Philosophes et voyous', *Les Temps Modernes*, no. 63 (1951), pp. 1193–1205 (p. 1194).

19 See Bergens, *Raymond Queneau*, p. 155.

20 Mathieu Galey, 'Un Meissonnier magique', *Arts*, 2 juin 1965, p. 8.

21 Simonnet, *Queneau déchiffré*, pp. 63–4.

22 Cf. Simonnet, *ibid.*, p. 74: 'Bébé Toutout est un personnage évidemment insolite et non réaliste; sa création peut s'expliquer pourtant par

une fantaisie poétique qui ne s'éloigne pas franchement du plan naturel.'

23 For a further discussion of the shifts between different narrative levels in *Les Fleurs bleues*, see Jean-Pierre Faye, 'Cidrolin sursautant', *L'Arc*, no. 28 (1966), pp. 11–13 (p. 12).

24 The second part of *Les Temps mêlés*, which is reworked as the fourth part of *Saint Glinglin*.

25 Émile Danoen, 'Secrets de fabrication: Raymond Queneau remet souvent à la Saint-Glinglin la suite de ce qu'il vient d'écrire', *Les Lettres Françaises*, 29 juill. 1948, p. 3.

26 See Paul Gayot, 'La Ville Natale – étude d'un milieu en crise', *Cahiers de Collège de 'Pataphysique*, dossier 20 (1962), pp. 5–13.

27 Maurice Blanchot, 'Chronique de la vie intellectuelle', *Journal des Débats Politiques et Littéraires*, 27 janv. 1942, p. 3.

28 Olivier de Magny, preface to *Les Derniers Jours* (Lausanne: Editions Rencontre, 1965), pp. 7–21 (p. 14).

29 Quoted in *Volontés*, no. 20 (1939), p. 14. The quotation is from *Wilhelm Meisters Lehrjahre*, book III, ch. XIV.

30 *L'Instant fatal* (Gallimard, 1966), p. 194.

31 Cf. Alexandre Kojève, *Introduction à la lecture de Hegel* (Gallimard, 1947), p. 11: 'La réalité humaine ne peut se constituer et se maintenir qu'à l'intérieur d'une réalité biologique [...]. Mais si le Désir animal est la condition nécessaire de la Conscience de soi, il n'en est pas la condition suffisante.' Queneau's interest in Hegel is often attested, notably in his presentation of Kojève's book and in his article 'Premières confrontations avec Hegel', *Critique*, no. 195–6 (1963), pp. 694–700. See also his article on Jean Tardieu in *Bâtons, chiffres et lettres*, pp. 177–8, and Pierre Macherey, 'Queneau scribe et lecteur de Kojève', *Europe*, no. 650–1 (1983), pp. 82–91.

32 The allegorical statue of 'la fée Électricité' was exhibited at the Exposition Internationale held in Paris in 1889; see Roger Shattuck, *The Banquet Years* (London: Cape, 1969), pp. 16–17.

33 See also *Une Histoire modèle*, pp. 91–2.

34 Cf. Queneau's particularly virulent denunciation of the press in *Le Voyage en Grèce*, p. 154.

35 Gayot, *Queneau*, p. 105.

36 Marguerite Duras, 'Uneuravek'.

37 But cf. the suggestion of Stephen Noreiko concerning the intriguing of Voussois ('*Pierrot mon ami*: themes and an enigma', p. 248).

38 Barthes, *Essais critiques*, p. 126.

39 Simonnet, *Queneau déchiffré*, p. 134.

40 Preface to Pierre Mac Orlan, *Œuvres complètes* (Évreux: Cercle du Bibliophile, 1969), pp. vii–xx (pp. xi-xii).

41 Gnosticism 'has come to serve as a collective heading for a manifoldness of sectarian doctrines appearing within and around Christianity during its critical first centuries' (Hans Jonas, *The Gnostic Religion: The Message of the Alien God and the Beginnings of Christianity*, second edition (Boston, Mass.: Beacon Press, 1963), p. 32). The major

discussions of Queneau's use of gnosticism in his fiction are to be
found in Simonnet, *Queneau déchiffré*, pp. 131–53 and in Tyman,
'Queneau's Concept of Literature and its Illustration in some of his
Works'. Simonnet indicates the allusions made in *Le Chiendent* to
gnostic numerology and mythology, and to gnostic teachers. Tyman,
too, lists gnostic motifs in Queneau's fiction, before examining in
detail the relations between the Saint Glinglin trilogy and gnostic
myths and cosmology. See also J.-H. Sainmont, '*Les Enfants du limon*
et le mystère de la rédemption'.

42 The description given here closely follows a text by one of the 'fous
littéraires', Pierre Roux, quoted in *Les Enfants du limon*, p. 152.

43 The quotation is from Isaiah 45:7.

44 *L'Instant fatal*, pp. 76–7.

45 'Quelques maîtres du XXe siècle', p. 229.

46 Jonathan Culler, *Structuralist Poetics*, p. 189.

47 Claude-Edmonde Magny, *Histoire du roman français depuis 1918* (Seuil,
Coll. Points, 1971), p. 215.

4. VALUES

1 Claudine Chonez, 'Instantanés: Raymond Queneau', *Les Nouvelles
Littéraires*, 4 sept. 1947, p. 6.

2 Cf. Georges Belmont, 'Queneau', *L'Herne*, no. 29 (1975), pp. 233–40
(p. 237).

3 The texts from *Volontés* are reprinted in *Le Voyage en Grèce*. The themes
of art and science are equally prominent in the later essays collected
in *Bords: mathématiciens, précurseurs, encyclopédistes* (Hermann,
1963).

4 Cf. Italo Calvino's comments on the passage leading up to this
quotation: 'Ce passage contient tout Queneau: sa pratique se situe
constamment à l'intérieur de deux dimensions simultanées, celle de
l'art (comme technique), et celle du jeu, sur un fond de pessimisme
gnoséologique radical. Convaincu que ce paradigme convient aussi
bien à la littérature qu'à la science, il se déplace avec aisance de l'une à
l'autre et peut les réunir dans un même discours.' ('Qui est Raymond
Queneau?', *Les Amis de Valentin Brû*, no. 15 (1981), pp. 5–22
(p. 14)).

5 Gayot, *Queneau*, p. 110.

6 See Vivian Kogan, *The Flowers of Fiction*, p. 126: '[The duke] begins to
negate his guilt by refuting the doctrine of original sin. He seeks to
prove man's innocence by creating evidence for the existence of
untainted prehistoric progenitors [...]. It may also be said that Auge
sublimates his guilt through art. For if art is a consequence of conflict
and guilt, it nevertheless offers a more noble and universal image of
persons. As Freud points out, the true artist knows how to give his art a
form that transcends its personal character.'

7 See Paul Gayot, 'Petite cosmogonie "quenienne"', *Le Monde*, 26 oct.
1968, p. iv.

8   Georges Bataille, 'La méchanceté du langage', *Critique*, no. 31 (1948), pp. 1059–66 (p. 1060).
9   Anne Clancier, 'Le manuel du parfait analysé', p. 33.
10 As Tyman pointed out in 'Queneau's Concept of Literature and its Illustration in some of his Works' (p. 100), the list could now be extended to include such classifications as anthropology, for *Les Temps mêlés* and *Saint Glinglin*, and linguistics, for *Journal intime*, and, perhaps, *Les Fleurs bleues*. André Blavier has also suggested additions to the list; see 'De l'humour (?) à la sagesse', pp. 37–8.
11 Cantor (1845–1918) was a Russian mathematician who helped to pioneer group theory.
12 In a way the *Encyclopédie* gains the relevance it had previously lacked when it is reworked in a literary form in *Les Enfants du limon*, for the novel does serve to set it in a human context.
13 The letter, written to Madame Roger des Genettes, dates from November (?) 1879: see Flaubert, *Œuvres complètes: Correspondance*, quatrième série (1869–1880) (Conard, 1902), p. 385.
14 Blavier, 'De l'humour (?) à la sagesse', p. 43.
15 See Anne Clancier, 'Le manuel du parfait analysé'.
16 See Alain Calame, 'L'inversion géométrique', *L'Herne*, no. 29 (1975), pp. 263–71 (p. 269).
17 See, for example, Jürgen Pauls, '*Les Fleurs bleues' von Raymond Queneau*, pp. 84, 105. It should, however, be noted that this is not a universally held view; cf., for example Alain Calame, 'De l'inclusion dans *Les Fleurs bleues*', *Temps Mêlés Documents Queneau*, no. 150+2 (1978), pp. 11–14, where Cidrolin is considered not to reintegrate his personality.
18 Simonnet (*Queneau déchiffré*, p. 100) detects in Étienne's development echoes of both the Cartesian *cogito* and Heidegger's idea that the very essence of the human condition lies in self-questioning.
19 Simonnet, *ibid.*, p. 133.
20 Kojève, 'Les romans de la sagesse', *Critique*, no. 60 (1952), pp. 387–97 (p. 389).
21 For example in Jacques Guicharnaud, *Raymond Queneau* (New York and London: Columbia University Press, 1965), pp. 34–43, where protagonists pursuing a fixed goal are distinguished from those who accept their fate with equanimity.
22 Blavier, 'De l'humour (?) à la sagesse', p. 47.
23 The quotation is from a lecture entitled 'La possession de soi-même'; see Montherlant, *Essais* (Gallimard, 1963), pp. 699–720 (p. 705).
24 Marguerite Duras, 'Uneuravek'.
25 Queneau stated in an interview with André Gillois that his favourite fictional hero was Dostoyevsky's 'idiot', Prince Myshkin, 'parce qu'il a un certain comportement dans la vie que je trouve éminemment sympathique, et qui n'a pas beaucoup d'équivalent dans la littérature' (quoted in Bens, *Queneau*, pp. 215–18 (p. 216)).
26 'Quelques maîtres du XXᵉ siècle', p. 232.
27 Gayot, *Queneau*, p. 103.

28 The sense of progress is enhanced by a pattern of imagery wherein clouds reflected in a puddle of water gradually disappear. At the time of the Arab's first appearance 'des flaques d'eau reflètent les derniers nuages' (p. 7); later the clouds are shown to be dispersing, and in the penultimate reference 'les nuages filent où le vent les pousse [...]. L'eau reflète le ciel' (p. 175). Queneau's attachment to the number seven is revealed once more in the number of times the Arab appears (see pp. 7, 14, 34, 129, 159, 175, 181).

29 Gaëtan Picon, *Panorama de la nouvelle littérature française*, new edition (Gallimard, 1960), p. 125.

30 Val Panaitescu, 'Le jeu des antinomies dans l'humour de Queneau', *L'Herne*, no. 29 (1975), pp. 139–47 (p. 140).

31 *L'Instant fatal*, p. 77. This notion of humour as the expression both of man's inferiority and of his superiority is also strikingly close to the ideas Baudelaire develops in an essay entitled 'De l'essence du rire et généralement du comique dans les arts plastiques': 'Comme le rire est essentiellement humain, il est essentiellement contradictoire, c'est-à-dire qu'il est à la fois signe d'une grandeur infinie et d'une misère infinie' (Baudelaire, *Œuvres complètes* (Gallimard, 1961) pp. 975–93. See also Baudelaire, *Selected writings on Art and Artists*, tr. P. E. Charvet (Cambridge: Cambridge University Press, 1981), pp. 140–61 (p. 148)).

32 Maurice Blanchot, 'Chronique de la vie intellectuelle: de l'humour romanesque', *Journal des Débats Politiques et Littéraires*, 2 sept. 1942, p. 3.

33 Pierre Berger, 'Entretien avec Raymond Queneau, humoriste automatique'.

34 Jean-Louis Bory, *Tout feu, tout flamme*, p. 129.

35 Yvon Belaval, *Poèmes d'aujourd'hui* (Gallimard, 1964), pp. 151–2.

36 Pierre Larue, 'Qui bien se pèse bien se connaît / Qui bien se connaît bien se porte', *Temps Mêlés*, no. 5–6 (1953), pp. 14–17 (p. 17).

37 Noël Arnaud, 'Queneau, l'humour et la 'pataphysique', *Magazine Littéraire*, no. 94 (1974), pp. 24–6 (p. 24).

38 Cf. Martin Esslin: 'The literary cranks are a fascinating illustration of Queneau's philosophy because they represent so many new patterns of the universe in a world that can be made to assume a different guiding principle according to the thinking of each differently oriented, or distorted, brain. Our normal universe is only one possible case in an infinity of others, just as Euclidean geometry only represents one possible case in an infinity of potential systems.' ('Raymond Queneau, b. 1903', p. 88).

39 Queneau was a member of the Collège de 'Pataphysique, set up as a sort of alternative Académie Française, from 1951. On Queneau's involvement with the Collège, see, for instance, Noël Arnaud, 'Queneau, l'humour et la 'pataphysique'; for a general survey of 'pataphysics, see Ruy Launoir, *Clés pour la 'Pataphysique* (Seghers, 1969).

40 Pascal Pia, 'Grands travaux de 'Pataphysique'.

INCONCLUSION

1 van Rossum-Guyon, *Critique du roman*, p. 40n.
2 Queneau, 'Zazie: Fragments d'une première version de *Zazie dans le métro*', *Biblio*, 28ᵉ année, no. 10 (déc. 1960), p. 7.
3 The first time the brother is mentioned Pierre fixes a rendez-vous with him (p. 15) but soon afterwards this is cancelled (pp. 21–2); later Pierre offers to introduce him to Étienne (p. 65), but the two never meet; and when, during the summer holiday section, Pierre goes to stay with him (p. 135), Pierre himself disappears from the action for a fortnight and gives only the briefest account of his stay when he returns (p. 146).
4 Claude Simonnet's *Queneau déchiffré* has a 'postambule' to balance the 'préambule' with which it began; Jean Queval ends his *Raymond Queneau* with a 'postface'; W. D. Redfern's analysis of *Zazie dans le métro* reaches a 'grand finale and con-clusion' and avoids 'trying to con-clude'.

Raymond Queneau's fiction: a select bibliography

Note. The most comprehensive and authoritative bibliography of Queneau's writings is that of Claude Rameil in *Les Amis de Valentin Brû*, no. 23 (1983), of which an earlier, abbreviated version appeared in *L'Herne*, no. 29 (1975), pp. 355–86. On secondary sources, see Wolfgang Hillen's very detailed *Raymond Queneau: Bibliographie des études sur l'homme et son œuvre* (Cologne: Édition Gemini, 1981), which includes unpublished theses and dissertations, and Vivian Kogan's more restricted, but usefully annotated 'Raymond Queneau', in *A Critical Bibliography of French Literature*, vol. VI: *The Twentieth Century, part 3*, edited by Douglas W. Alden and Richard A. Brooks (Syracuse: Syracuse University Press, 1980), pp. 1463–71. An indispensable source of information of all kinds on Queneau is the Centre de Documentation Raymond Queneau in Verviers.

CONTENTS

Note. Except where otherwise indicated, place of publication is Paris.

PART I QUENEAU'S WORKS

Only a fraction of Queneau's total output can be included. Translations, published extracts from completed works and, except in special cases, items of his art criticism have been omitted, and only a limited amount of his critical writing has been included. Within each section individual items are arranged chronologically.

1. FICTIONAL AND NARRATIVE WORKS

Le Chiendent (Gallimard, 1933)
> (see also *Le Chiendent: extraits avec des considérations sur la vie et l'œuvre de Raymond Queneau, une étude du 'Chiendent' et une bibliographie*, edited by Jean Queval with notes by Nicole Onfroy (Bordas, 1975))
Gueule de pierre (Gallimard, 1934)
Les Derniers Jours (Gallimard, 1936)
Chêne et chien (Denoël, 1937)
Odile (Gallimard, 1937)
Les Enfants du limon (Gallimard, 1938)
Un Rude Hiver (Gallimard, 1939)
Les Temps mêlés: Gueule de pierre II (Gallimard, 1941)
Pierrot mon ami (Gallimard, 1942)
Loin de Rueil (Gallimard, 1944)
A la limite de la forêt (Fontaine, 1947)
On est toujours trop bon avec les femmes (Éditions du Scorpion, 1947) published under the pseudonym Sally Mara
Une Trouille verte (Éditions de Minuit, 1947)
Le Cheval troyen (Georges Visat, 1948)
Saint Glinglin précédé d'une nouvelle version de 'Gueule de Pierre' et des 'Temps mêlés' (Gallimard, 1948)
Journal intime (Éditions du Scorpion, 1950) published under the pseudonym Sally Mara
Le Dimanche de la vie (Gallimard, 1952)
Zazie dans le métro (Gallimard, 1959)
Les Œuvres complètes de Sally Mara (Gallimard, 1962) contains *Journal intime, On est toujours trop bon avec les femmes* and 'Sally plus intime'
Les Fleurs bleues (Gallimard, 1965)
> (see also *Les Fleurs bleues*, edited by Barbara Wright (London: Methuen, 1971))
Le Vol d'Icare (Gallimard, 1968)
Contes et propos (Gallimard, 1981)

2. OTHER LITERARY WORKS

Les Ziaux, poèmes (Gallimard, 1943)
'En passant: Un plus un actes pour précéder un drame', *L'Arbalète* (Lyons), no. 8 (1944), pp. 123–48
L'Instant fatal, poèmes (Aux Nourritures Terrestres, 1946)
> (see also *L'Instant fatal, édition augmentée* (Gallimard, 1948) and *'L'Instant fatal' précédé de Les Ziaux* (Gallimard, Collection Poésie, 1966))
Bucoliques, poèmes (Gallimard, 1947)

Exercices de style (Gallimard, 1947)
Monuments, poèmes (Éditions de Moustié, 1948)
Petite cosmogonie portative, poèmes (Gallimard, 1950)
   (see also *'Chêne et chien' suivi de 'Petite cosmogonie portative' édition revue et augmentée et de 'Le Chant du styrène'* (Gallimard, 1969))
Si tu t'imagines, poèmes (Gallimard, 1952)
Le Chien à la mandoline, poèmes (Verviers: Temps Mêlés, 1958)
   (see also *Le Chien à la mandoline*, édition augmentée (Gallimard, 1965))
Sonnets (Éditions Hautefeuille, 1958)
Cent mille milliards de poèmes (Gallimard, 1961)
Courir les rues, poèmes (Gallimard, 1967)
Battre la campagne, poèmes (Gallimard, 1968)
Fendre les flots, poèmes (Gallimard, 1969) See also *Courir les rues, Battre la campagne, Fendre les flots* (Gallimard, Coll. Poésie, 1981)
Raymond Queneau en verve: propos, aphorismes, edited by Jacques Bens (Pierre Horay, 1970)
Morale élémentaire (Gallimard, 1975)

3. CRITICAL AND THEORETICAL WORKS

Bâtons, chiffres et lettres (Gallimard, 1950) (see also *Bâtons, chiffres et lettres*, édition revue et augmentée (Gallimard, Collection 'Idéas', 1965))
Bords: Mathématiciens, précurseurs, encyclopédistes (Hermann, 1963)
Une Histoire modèle (Gallimard, 1966)
De quelques langages animaux imaginaires et notamment du langage chien dans 'Sylvie et Bruno' (Éditions de l'Herne, 1971)
Le Voyage en Grèce (Gallimard, 1973)

4. ARTICLES AND PREFACES

This list does not include items which have been reprinted in Queneau's collections of critical and theoretical writings – *Bâtons, chiffres et lettres*, *Bords* and *Le Voyage en Grèce* – or in *Contes et propos*.
'Gueule de pierre (2ᵉ partie) (Fragments)', *Volontés*, no. 20 (1939), pp. 8–14
'Introduction à *Bouvard et Pécuchet*', *Fontaine* (Algiers), no. 31 (1943), pp. 42–7
'*Bouvard et Pécuchet*', *Action*, 26 avril 1946, pp. 12–13
'L'amour, la peinture', *Les Lettres Françaises*, 17 mai 1946, p. 4
'Le mythe du documentaire', *Labyrinthe*, no. 22–3 (1946), p. 28
'Note de l'éditeur' in Alexandre Kojève, *Introduction à la lecture de Hegel* (Gallimard, 1947), p. 8
'Sur quelques aspects relativement peu connus du verbe en français', *Le Surréalisme Révolutionnaire*, no. 1 (1948), p. 36
'Introduction' in *Les Écrivains célèbres*, tome 1 (Mazenod, 1951), pp. 7–10 (pagination of 1966 edition)
'Pétrone', *ibid.*, pp. 148, 151 (pagination of 1966 edition)

'Boileau 1636–1711' in *Les Écrivains célèbres*, tome II (Mazenod, 1952), pp. 224, 227

'Philosophes et voyous', *Les Temps Modernes*, no. 63 (1951), pp. 1193–1205

'Un nouveau genre littéraire: les science-fictions', *Critique*, no. 46 (1951), pp. 195–8

'Quelques maîtres du XXᵉ siècle', in *Les Écrivains célèbres*, tome III (Mazenod, 1952), pp. 434–9 (pagination of 1966 edition)

'Gertrude Stein', *ibid.*, pp. 470–2 (pagination of 1966 edition)

'Sagesse authentiquement féminine', *Le Figaro Littéraire*, 24 janv. 1953, p. 7

'La science-fiction vaincra', *Arts*, 29 oct. 1953, pp. 1, 4

'Portrait littéraire du Havre', *Richesses de France*, no. 19 (1954), pp. 39–40

'Le visionnaire', *Adam* (London), no. 250 (1955), pp. 23–4

'Français d'hier et français d'aujourd'hui d'après Rémy de Gourmont', *Les Lettres Françaises*, 14 juillet 1955, pp. 1, 8

'Bonjour Christophe!', *L'Express*, 17 nov. 1955, p. 6

'Préface', in *Histoire des littératures*, tome I: *Littératures anciennes, orientales et orales* (Gallimard, Encyclopédie de la Pléiade, 1956), pp. vii–xx

'Préface', in *Histoire des littératures*, tome II: *Littératures occidentales* (Gallimard, Encyclopédie de la Pléiade, 1956), pp. vii–xv

'Avant-propos' in *Pour une bibliothèque idéale* (Gallimard, 1956), pp. 7–11

'Introduction aux fous littéraires', *Bizarre*, no. 4 (1956), p. 2

'Préface' in *Histoire des littératures*, tome III: *Littératures françaises, connexes et marginales* (Gallimard, Encyclopédie de la Pléiade, 1959), pp. iii–ix

'Préface' in Gustave Flaubert, *Bouvard et Pécuchet* (Livre de Poche, 1959), pp. 7–11

'Zazie dans son plus jeune âge', *Les Lettres Nouvelles*, nouvelle série no. 2 (1959), pp. 5–7

'Zazie: Fragments d'une première version de *Zazie dans le métro*', *Biblio*, 28ᵉ année, no. 10 (déc. 1960), p. 7

'Une image de Queneau à travers le questionnaire Marcel Proust', *ibid.*, p. 8

'A world of fantasy', *Time and Tide* (London), vol. 42, no. 27 (6 July 1961), p. 1119

'Je suis dans une situation . . .', *Temps Mêlés* (Verviers), no. 50–2 (1961), pp. 9–12

'Paris qui bouge' in *Regards sur Paris* (Editions Sauret), pp. 229–51

'Promenade piétonne autour de Ionesco', *Cahiers de la Compagnie Renaud-Barrault*, no. 42 (1963), pp. 75–8

'Premières confrontations avec Hegel', *Critique*, no. 195–6 (1963), pp. 694–700

'L'analyse matricielle du langage', *Études de Linguistique Appliquée* (Besançon), no. 3 (1964), pp. 37–50

'Un lecteur de Duras', *Cahiers de la Compagnie Renaud-Barrault*, no. 52 (1965), pp. 3–5

'Modeste contribution à l'illustration de la langue française', *Subsidia Pataphysica*, no. 1 (1965), pp. 61–2

'Miroir double', *La Quinzaine Littéraire*, 1ᵉʳ oct. 1966, p. 27
'Erutarettil', *NRF*, no. 172 (1967), pp. 604–5
'Poésie et mathématiques', *Le Monde*, 18 mai 1967, p. iv
'Science and literature', *TLS* (London), 28 Sept. 1967, pp. 863–4
'Préface' in Pierre Mac Orlan, *Œuvres complètes* (Évreux: Cercle du Biblio-
 phile, 1969), pp. vii–xx
'La SPA', *Le Nouvel Observateur*, 4 mai 1970, p. 41
'Puérilia: "Aux enfers", "Roman fou", "Les Derniers Jours"', *L'Herne*,
 no. 29 (1975), pp. 15–30
'Alice en France', *ibid.*, pp. 51–4
'Pictogrammes', *Temps Mêlés Documents Queneau*, no. 150+8 (1980),
 pp. 21–37
'Le symbolisme du soleil', *Temps Mêlés Documents Queneau*, no. 150+10
 (1980), pp. 11–30
'Chêne et chien (inédit)', *Europe*, no. 650–1 (1983), pp. 7–14

PART 2 SECONDARY SOURCES

In Sections 1, 4 and 5 items are arranged alphabetically by author's name.
In cases where one author has written several items which are grouped in
the same section, these are listed in chronological order. In section 3
publications are arranged chronologically.

1. MONOGRAPHS DEALING WHOLLY OR MAINLY WITH QUENEAU'S FICTION

Bens, Jacques, *Queneau* (Gallimard, 1962)
Bergens, Andrée, *Raymond Queneau* (Geneva: Droz, 1963)
Canu, Emilio, *I Romanzi di Raymond Queneau* (Rome: Fema, 1972)
Cobb, Richard, *Raymond Queneau* (Oxford: Clarendon Press, 1976) The
 text of the Zaharoff Lecture for 1976
Duprez, Leif, *Clef pour 'Zazie dans le métro' par Raymond Queneau:
 vocabulaire, commentaires, questions, postface* (Stockholm: Almqvist and
 Wiksell, 1972)
Gayot, Paul, *Queneau* (Éditions Universitiares, 1967)
Guicharnaud, Jacques, *Raymond Queneau* (New York and London:
 Columbia University Press, 1965)
Kemmner, Ernst, *Sprachspiel und Stiltechnik in Raymond Queneaus
 Romanen* (Tübingen: Tübinger Beiträge zur Linguistik, 1972)
Kogan, Vivian, *The Flowers of Fiction: Time and Space in Raymond
 Queneau's 'Les Fleurs bleues'* (Lexington, Kentucky: French Forum,
 Publishers, 1982)
Langenbacher, Jutta, *Das 'Néo-français': Sprachkonzeption und kritische
 Auseinandersetzung Raymond Queneaus mit dem Französisch der
 Gegenwart* (Frankfurt, Bern: Lang, 1981)
Panaitescu, Valeriu, *Umorul lui Raymond Queneau* (Iasi: Junimea,
 1979)
Pauls, Jürgen, *'Les Fleurs bleues' von Raymond Queneau: Eine Analyse des*

Romans unter besonderer Berücksichtigung der Symbolik (Hamburg: Romanisches Seminar der Universität Hamburg, 1973)

Queval, Jean, *Essai sur Raymond Queneau* (Seghers, 1960)

Raymond Queneau (Seghers, 1971)

Raymond Queneau, portrait d'un poète (Henri Veyrier, 1984)

Redfern, W. D., *Queneau: 'Zazie dans le métro'* (London: Grant and Cutler, 1980)

Simonnet, Claude, *Queneau déchiffré (notes sur 'Le Chiendent')* (Julliard, 1962); (second edition published by Slatkine, 1981)

Siniscalchi, Maria, *Raymond Queneau o della sdramatizzazione del linguaggio* (Naples: Loffredo, 1981)

Starre, Evert van der, *Raymond Queneau en de geschiedenis* (Leyden, Universitaire Pers, 1977)

2. PERIODICALS DEVOTED TO QUENEAU

Les Amis de Valentin Brû (Levallois-Perret), first number 1977

Temps Mêlés Documents Queneau (Verviers), first number 1978 (this is a successor to *Temps Mêlés*, which always had a particular interest in Queneau)

3. SPECIAL NUMBERS OF PERIODICALS ETC.

Temps Mêlés (Verviers), no. 5–6 (1953)
  including
  Arnaud, Noël, 'Avènement d'un Queneau glorieux' (pp. 45–50)
  Blavier, André, 'Que Queneau marque . . .' (pp. 3–6)
  'Ceux qui y mordent . . . ceux qui y grincent' (pp. 32–3)
  H., A. v., 'Queneau, quenouille, quenelle' (pp. 41–4)
  Larue, Pierre, 'Qui bien se pèse bien se connaît/Qui bien se connaît bien se porte' (pp. 14–17)

Biblio, 28ᵉ année, no. 10 (déc. 1960) and *Livres de France*, 11ᵉ année, no. 10 (déc. 1960)
  including
  Clancier, Georges-Emmanuel, 'Raymond Queneau et le roman' (pp. 4–6)
  Salacrou, Armand, 'Raymond Queneau' (pp. 2–3)

Temps Mêlés (Verviers), no. 50–2 (1961): 'Raymond Queneau à la décade du Foyer culturel international de Cerisy-la-Salle (Manche) septembre 1960'
  including
  Bens, Jacques, 'Étude sur Queneau/Ch. IV: Les Hommes' (pp. 17–24)
  Blavier, André, 'De l'humour (?) à la sagesse' (pp. 36–52)
  Clancier, Georges-Emmanuel, 'Fragment d'une petite queneaulogie portative' (pp. 25–7)
  Lemoine, Antoine, 'En explorant Queneau' (pp. 32–5)

Versins, Pierre, 'Queneauctural' (pp. 28–9)

Il Caffè (Rome), anno IX, no. 6 (dic. 1961)

Cahiers du Collège de 'Pataphysique, dossier 20 (1962): 'Quelques études sur les œuvres du Transcendant Satrape Raymond Queneau, Grand-conservateur OGG'
including
Arnaud, Noël, 'Des goûts d'un Satrape en couleurs' (pp. 47–58)
Bens, Jacques, 'Le jardin zoologique du T. S. Raymond Queneau' (pp. 37–41)
David, Pierre-François, 'Consubstantialité et quintessence d'une fiction dérivée' (pp. 15–20)
Gayot, Paul, 'A travers le Paris de Zazie et de Valentin Brû' (pp. 27–32)
'Disparitions, escamotages et prestidigitations dans *Le Chiendent*' (pp. 21–6)
'Madagascar et Valentin Brû' (pp. 33–6)
'La Ville Natale – étude d'un milieu en crise' (pp. 5–13)
Kirmu, 'Lettre au Régent Tadjo' (pp. 43–6)

L'Arc (Aix-en-Provence), no. 28 (1966)
including
Belaval, Yvon, 'Les deux langages' (pp. 14–22)
Bens, Jacques, 'Littérature potentielle' (pp. 43–51)
Camproux, Charles, 'Du bleu' (pp. 23–8)
Caradec, François, 'Lectures d'une enfance' (pp. 29–32)
Clancier, Anne, 'Le manuel du parfait analysé' (pp. 33–40)
Clancier, Georges-Emmanuel, 'Le discours et ses méthodes' (pp. 69–74)
Faye, Jean-Pierre, 'Cidrolin sursautant' (pp. 11–13)
Micha, René, 'Le cinéma de Queneau' (pp. 59–68)
Pingaud, Bernard, 'Le parfait banlieusard' (pp. 7–10)

L'Événement, no. 27 (1968)
including
Grenier, Roger, 'Queneau et le chinook' (p. 26)

'Raymond Queneau en son dédale', a two-page supplement in *Le Monde* (des Livres), 26 oct. 1968
including
Gayot, Paul, 'Petite cosmogonie "quenienne"' (p. iv)
Limbour, Georges, 'Raymond mon ami' (p. iv)
Piatier, Jacqueline, '*Le Vol d'Icare*' (p. v)
Robbe-Grillet, Alain, 'Quelques enfants du limon' (p. iv)

Raymond Queneau (Le Havre: Bibliothèque Municipale, 1973)
including
Gayot, Paul, 'Le T. S. Raymond Queneau …' (unnumbered pages)
Klinkenberg, Jean-Marie, 'Queneau e(s)t le nouveau roman' (unnumbered pages)
Le Lionnais, François, 'Queneau à/et l'Oulipo' (unnumbered pages)

Magazine Littéraire, no. 94 (1974): 'L'Irrévérend Monsieur Queneau' including

Arnaud, Noël, 'Queneau, l'humour et la 'pataphysique' (pp. 24–6)
Bosquet, Alain, 'Le rire jaune et noir de Queneau' (pp. 20–2)
Juin, Hubert, 'Queneau le métaphorique' (pp. 11–13)
Venault, Philippe, 'Quand Queneau descend dans la rue' (pp. 14–16)
Wolfromm, Jean-Didier, 'Sally, ouisqui, Zazie et cie' (pp. 17–19)
Raymond Queneau (Brussels: Bibliothèque Royale Albert 1ᵉʳ, 1975)
L'Herne, no. 29 (1975)
    including
Belmont, Georges, 'Queneau' (pp. 233–40)
Bergens, Andrée, 'Apparences et réalités' (pp. 9–11)
    'Les personnages de Raymond Queneau' (pp. 88–97)
Bergeret, Claude, 'Une maladie existentielle, l'asthme' (pp. 254–6)
Blavier, André, 'A propos d'un Errata' (pp. 79–87)
Bordufour, Jean-Paul, 'La révolution langagière erratée' (pp. 183–91)
Borzic, Jean, 'Le pataphysicien' (pp. 296–301)
Boudot-Lamotte, Emmanuel, 'Quelques souvenirs d'un lecteur et ami . . .' (pp. 319–23)
Brenner, Jacques, 'Les amoureux du Havre' (pp. 178–82)
Calame, Alain, 'L'inversion géometrique' (pp. 263–71)
Caradec, François, 'Raymond Queneau 75012 Paris' (pp. 305–12)
Clancier, Anne, 'A la recherche d'une ascèse' (pp. 148–53)
Clancier, Georges-Emmanuel, 'Unité poétique et méthodique de l'œuvre de Raymond Queneau' (pp. 98–114)
Danan, Joseph, 'Étude d'un "mot poétique" dans *Le Chiendent*' (pp. 171–7)
Dobo, Frank, 'La petite histoire . . . du *Chiendent*' (pp. 324–7)
Fournel, Paul, 'Queneau et la Lipo' (pp. 257–62)
Grosjean, Jean, 'Raymond Queneau encyclopédiste' (pp. 302–4)
Harig, Ludwig, 'Sur le principe de la traduction des textes de Raymond Queneau' (pp. 347–9)
Helmle, Eugen, 'Raymond Queneau vu par la critique allemande' (pp. 350–3)
Jullian, Marcel, 'On n'est jamais assez infidèle aux bons auteurs' (pp. 313–16)
Krysinski, Wladimir, 'La voix des métaphores – la mise en scène du monde' (pp. 200–9)
Le Lionnais, François, 'Queneau à/et l'Oulipo' (pp. 231–2)
Morin, Violette, '*Le Vol d'Icare* ou l'art de la fugue' (pp. 125–38)
Panaitescu, Val., 'Le jeu des antinomies dans l'humour de Queneau' (pp. 139–47)
Picon, Gaëtan, 'Queneau plutôt à part' (pp. 69–73)
Pierre-Sylvestre, 'La fête quenienne: innocence et folie' (pp. 154–62)
Rameil, Claude, 'Bibliographie' (pp. 355–92)
Romano, Ruggiero, 'Un modèle pour l'histoire' (pp. 283–95)
Sareil, Jean, 'Sur le comique de Queneau' (pp. 115–24)
Simonnet, Claude, 'Note sur *Les Enfants du limon*' (pp. 192–4)

Smock, Ann Austin '. . . Le temps, le beau temps, le beau temps fixe' (pp. 163–70)

Wright, Barbara, 'Comment traduire Raymond Queneau' (pp. 343–6)

La Nouvelle Revue Française, no. 290 (1977) including

Blot, Jean, 'Si tu t'imagines . . .' (pp. 81–5)

Juin, Hubert, 'Le savoir et la banlieue' (pp. 86–90)

Le Lionnais, François, 'Raymond Queneau et l'amalgame des mathématiques et de la littérature' (pp. 71–9)

Queval, Jean, 'Queneau, discours et rêve' (pp. 64–71)

Thomas, Henri, 'Souriant et secret' (pp. 80–1)

Raymond Queneau plus intime (Bibliothèque Nationale, 1978)

Prospice (Portree, Isle of Skye), no. 8 (1978) including

Blavier, André, 'Anecdotes' (pp. 79–85)

Calame, Alain, 'Inclusion in *Les Fleurs bleues*' (pp. 72–4)

Camus, Albert, '*Pierrot mon ami* by Raymond Queneau' (pp. 36–7)

Hewitt, Nicholas, 'History in *Les Enfants du limon*: encyclopaedists and "flâneurs"' (pp. 22–35)

Queval, Jean, 'Queneau remembered' (pp. 86–8)

Rameil, Claude, 'Images of Queneau: an essay in filmography' (pp. 89–98)

Les Amis de Valentin Brû, no. 10–11 (1980) (published in collaboration with the *Cahiers de la Maison de la Culture André Malraux* (Rheims)): 'Raymond Queneau et le cinéma' including

David, Pierre, 'Raymond Queneau-ciné' (unnumbered pages)

Les Amis de Valentin Brû, no. 18 (1982): 'Queneau et après'

Europe, no. 650–1 (1983) including

Arnaud, Noël, 'Un Queneau honteux?' (pp. 122–30)

Aron, Thomas, 'Le roman comme représentation de langages ou Raymond Queneau à la lumière de Bakhtine' (pp. 46–58)

Bens, Jacques, 'A la limite d'un roman' (pp. 77–82)

Blavier, André, 'Chronologie de Raymond Queneau' (pp. 130–48)

Braffort, Paul, 'Queneau conique' (pp. 116–22)

Calame, Alain, '*Les Enfants du limon* et la constellation du chien' (pp. 65–76)

Caradec, François, 'Queneau éditeur de Sally Mara' (pp. 91–5)

Debon, Claude, 'Lire Queneau' (pp. 3–5)

'Les enjeux d'une narration' (pp. 15–16)

'Queneau horticulteur' (pp. 33–43)

Decaudin, Michel, 'Pourquoi des chaînes nom d'un chien?' (pp. 20–4)

Klinkenberg, Jean-Marie, 'Fenouil contre chiendent' (pp. 95–102)

Macherey, Pierre, 'Queneau scribe et lecteur de Kojève' (pp. 82–91)

Naudin, François, 'Un théorème botanique' (pp. 103–9)

Pestureau, Gilbert, 'Les techniques anglo-saxonnes et l'art roman-
esque de Raymond Queneau' (pp. 110–15)
Queval, Jean, 'Premières notes pour un portrait' (pp. 17–18)
'Une histoire modèle' (pp. 18–19)
Rameil, Claude, 'Livres et revues consacrés à Queneau' (pp. 148–
51)
Simonnet, Claude, 'Note sur la genèse du *Chiendent*' (pp. 44–6)
Vercier, Bruno, 'L'air du soupçon' (pp. 58–65)
Temps Mêlés Documents Queneau, no. 150 + 17–18–19 (1983): 'Ray-
mond Queneau romancier. Actes du 1er colloque international
Raymond Queneau, Verviers 27–30 août 1982, 1ere Partie'
including
Arnaud, Noël, 'Mais où est donc passé *Chêne et chien*?' (pp. 13–27)
Bens, Jacques, 'Douze remarques sur des personnages' (pp. 121–35)
Calame, Alain, '*Les Fleurs bleues*: rime et concordance' (pp. 77–92)
Caradec, François, 'Queneau témoin de son temps' (pp. 37–41)
Fertig, Stanley, 'Raymond Queneau et l'art de la défamiliarisation'
(pp. 43–54)
Klinkenberg, Jean-Marie, 'Queneau structuraliste¡' (pp. 103–20)
Morey, Philip, 'Les deux versions de *Gueule de pierre*' (pp. 57–64)
Panaitescu, Valeriu, 'Les personnages quéniens critiques de leur
statut' (pp. 137–50)
Pilcher, Ian, 'Aspects de la parodie dans les romans de Queneau'
(pp. 67–75)
Queval, Jean, 'Vrais romans et vrais romanciers'; 'De tout ce qu'il n'y a
pas dans les romans de Raymond Queneau' (pp. 29–36)
Sanders, Carol, 'Autour d'*Odile*' (pp. 97–101)
Temps Mêlés Documents Queneau, no. 150 + 20–21 (1983): 'Raymond
Queneau romancier. Actes du 1er colloque international Raymond
Queneau, Verviers 27–30 août 1982, 2e Partie'
including
Blavier, André, '"Orgueil et préjugés" et folie littéraire' (pp. 139–40)
Bordillon, Henri, '*Les Derniers Jours*. Biographie et roman'
(pp. 111–25)
Clancier, Anne, 'La question du père dans *Loin de Rueil*' (pp. 19–
29)
Debon, Claude, 'Récriture et identité dans *Le Vol d'Icare*' (pp. 31–45)
Decaudin, Michel, 'Ne passez pas *Un Rude Hiver*' (pp. 127–38)
Gayot, Paul, 'L'exotisme dans l'œuvre de Raymond Queneau'
(pp. 73–83)
Kogan, Vivian, 'Raymond Queneau, romancier modèle' (pp. 63–72)
McMurray, Line, 'Le même et l'autre dans *Les Œuvres complètes de
Sally Mara*' (pp. 9–17)
Shorley, Christopher, 'Queneau et l'(es) étranger(s)' (pp. 49–60)
Starre, E. van der, 'Sally Mara romancière' (pp. 85–107)
Cahiers de Recherches Interuniversitaires Néerlandaises (Groningen), no. 10
(1984)
including

Landheer, Ronald, 'Queneau et la rhétorique du sous-entendu' (pp. 74–104)

Luccioni, Jean-Michel, 'Joyce chez Sally' (pp. 22–34)

Mok, Q. I. M., 'L'art de faire des fautes' (pp. 57–73)

Schreurs, Bernadette, 'Notes sur l'ironie dans *Oettbalf*' (pp. 137–55)

Starre, Evert van der, 'Une histoire 'pataphysique' (pp. 105–36)

Topia, André, 'Sally Mara ou le sexe a-t-il une âme?' (pp. 1–21)

Zwanenburg, Wiecher, 'Aux frontières de la formation des mots' (pp. 35–56)

4. ARTICLES, ESSAYS, REVIEWS AND OTHER SIGNIFICANT REFERENCES

This list does not include items already enumerated in section 3 or featuring in the anthology section of Jacques Bens, *Queneau* (Gallimard, 1962) (pp. 9–25)

Angeli, Dina d', 'Incongruité et lyrisme du *Chiendent*', *Culture Française* (Bari), anno X, no. 3 (1963), pp. 139–42

Antoine, Gérald, 'Une inconnue: l'image chez Queneau', *Stanford French Review* (Saratoga) no. 1 (1977), pp. 153–65)

Astruc, Alexandre, 'Présentation de Raymond Queneau', *Action*, 26 avril 1946, pp. 12–13

Barthes, Roland, 'Zazie et la littérature', in *Essais critiques* (Seuil, 1964), pp. 125–31

Bataille, Georges, 'La méchanceté du langage', *Critique*, no. 31 (1948), pp. 1059–66

Belaval, Yvon, 'L'endroit et l'envers du lyrisme', in *Poèmes d'aujourd'hui: essais critiques* (Gallimard, 1964), pp. 132–54

'Préface', in Raymond Queneau, *Chêne et chien* (Gallimard, 1969), pp. 9–26

'Queneau l'oulimpien', *Critique*, no. 319 (1974), pp. 1061–74

Bell, William S., 'Andrée Bergens: *Raymond Queneau*', *Romanic Review* (New York), vol. 56, no. 4 (1965), pp. 316–17

Belmont, Georges, 'Cet étrange Monsieur Queneau', *Arts*, 3 mars 1965, pp. 4–5

Bens, Jacques, 'Le romancier et son secret', in Raymond Queneau, *Pierrot mon ami* (Culture, Arts, Loisirs, 1965), pp. 7–33

'Un réputé poseur de mines nous invite à deviner quelques énigmes', *La Quinzaine Littéraire*, 1er janv. 1976, pp. 5–6

Berry, André, 'De M. Queneau à Msieukeno', *Combat*, 12 mars 1959, p. 7

Bianciotti, Hector, 'Essai: Queneau contre l'humour', *Le Nouvel Observateur*, 30 avril 1973, p. 68

Billy, André, 'Queneau ou le français tel qu'on le parle', *Le Figaro*, 5 mars 1952, p. 11

Blanchot, Maurice, 'Chronique de la vie intellectuelle', *Journal des Débats Politiques et Littéraires*, 27 janv. 1942, p. 3, reprinted in *Faux-Pas* (Gallimard, 1975), pp. 224–31

'Chronique de la vie intellectuelle: de l'humour romanesque', *ibid.*, 2 sept. 1942, p. 3

'Le temps des encyclopédistes', *NRF*, no. 53 (1957), pp. 863–74

Blanzat, Jean, '*Saint Glinglin* de Raymond Queneau', *Le Figaro Littéraire*, 4 sept. 1948, p. 5

'*Zazie dans le métro* de Raymond Queneau', *ibid.*, 21 févr. 1959, p. 14

[Blavier, André], 'Deux sources de Queneau, l'une improbable, l'autre certaine', *Temps Mêlés* (Verviers), no. 59–60 (1962), p. 50

Blot, Jean, 'Raymond Queneau', *NRF*, no. 194 (1969), pp. 266–70

Bonnefoy, Claude, 'Un illustrateur et un maquettiste – exercices de style avec Raymond Queneau', *Arts*, 27 nov. 1963, p. 5

Bordillon, Henri, 'Lecture de Queneau lecteur', *Temps Mêlés Documents Queneau*, no. 150 + 9 (1980), pp. 33–7

Borie, Jean, 'Raymond Queneau: poésie et français parlé', *Romanic Review* (New York), vol. 57, no. 1 (1966), pp. 41–55

Bory, Jean-Louis, 'Raymond Queneau ou Enfin Quenherbe vint', in *Tout feu, tout flamme* (Juillard, 1966), pp. 127–32

Boyer, Régis, 'Mots et jeux de mots chez Prévert, Queneau, Boris Vian, Ionesco: Essai d'étude méthodique', *Studia Neophilologica* (Uppsala), vol. 40, no. 2 (1968), pp. 317–58

Brée, Germaine and Margaret Guiton, 'The Sunday of Life' in *An Age of Fiction. The French Novel from Gide to Camus* (New Brunswick, N.J.: Rutgers University Press, 1957), pp. 169–79

Brenner, Jacques, 'Les mystères de Queneau', *Le Nouvel Observateur*, 25 nov. 1968, pp. 35–7

'Queneau contre l'humour', *Le Figaro Littéraire*, 17 mars 1973, p. 16

Calame, Alain, 'Les Enfants du limon ou du bon usage des bâtards', *Les Lettres Nouvelles*, no. 5/71 (1971), pp. 174–80

'Queneau, poète et balayeur', *ibid.*, no. 5/72 (1972), pp. 150–5

'Échange de fleurs', *Temps Mêlés Documents Queneau*, no. 150 + 1 (1978), pp. 29–38

'De l'inclusion dans *Les Fleurs bleues*', *ibid.*, no. 150 + 2 (1978), pp. 72–4 (English version of the text published in *Prospice*, no. 8 (1978), pp. 72–4)

'Raymond Queneau, quadrateur', *Les Amis de Valentin Brû*, no. 15 (1981), pp. 33–40

Calvino, Italo, 'Qui est Raymond Queneau?', *ibid.*, pp. 5–22

Chessex, Jacques, 'Raymond Queneau, sage et savant', *NRF*, no. 152 (1965), pp. 475–9

Clancier, Georges-Emmanuel, 'Raymond Queneau' in *Les Écrivains contemporains* (Mazenod, 1965), pp. 44–5

Cobb, Richard, 'The writing game', in *TLS* (London), 1 June 1967, p. 487

'Queneau of Le Havre', *The Listener* (London), 28 Oct. 1976, pp. 533–4

'Queneau's itineraries', in *Promenades: A Historian's Appreciation of Modern French Literature* (Oxford: Oxford University Press, 1980), pp. 61–77

Criticus, *Le Style au microscope*: tome II: *Jeunes gloires* (Calmann-Lévy, 1951), pp. 177–94

'Criticus dissèque Queneau', *Aux Écoutes du Monde*, 17 avril 1959, p. 40

Cruickshank, John, 'Some aspects of French fiction, 1935–1960', in *The Novelist as Philosopher*, edited by Cruickshank (London: Oxford University Press, 1962), pp. 3–26

Danan, Joseph, 'La stratégie de la mygale', *Temps Mêlés Documents Queneau*, no. 150 + 11 (1981), pp. 15–21

Danoen, Emile, 'Les lettres: Raymond Queneau romancier', *Combat*, 17 déc. 1944, p. 2

Debon, Claude, 'Présence d'Apollinaire dans l'œuvre de Queneau', *Revue d'Histoire Littéraire de la France*, vol. 81 (1981), pp. 75–92

'Le moyen âge dans *Les Fleurs bleues* de Raymond Queneau', *La Licorne* (Poitiers), no. 6 (1982), pp. 285–98

Doppagne, Albert, 'Le néologisme chez Raymond Queneau', *Cahiers de l'Association Internationale des Études Françaises*, no. 25 (1973), pp. 91–107

Dumur, Guy, 'Les dimanches de Raymond Queneau', *Combat*, 28 févr. 1952, p. 7

Egen, Jean, 'L'insaisissable Raymond Queneau', *Lectures pour Tous*, no. 196 (1970), pp. 84–8

Esslin, Martin, 'Raymond Queneau, b. 1903', in *The Novelist as Philosopher*, edited by John Cruickshank (London: Oxford University Press, 1962), pp. 79–101

Fouchet, Max Pol, 'Un rire terrible', *Les Lettres Françaises*, 17 févr. 1945, p. 3

'Drôle de rire, drôle de drame', *Carrefour*, 5 mars 1952, p. 7

Fournel, Paul, 'Raymond Queneau: "Errata"', *Les Cahiers du Chemin*, no. 14 (1972), pp. 173–81

Galey, Mathieu, 'Un Meissonnier magique', *Arts*, 2 juin 1965, p. 8

Ganne, Gilbert, 'Raymond Queneau', *Réforme*, 10 mai 1952, p. 7

Gérin-Ricard, L. de, 'Les Derniers Beaux [sic] Jours', *Le Petit Marseillais* (Marseilles), 25 nov. 1936, p. 6

Gray, Stanley E., 'Beckett and Queneau as formalists', *James Joyce Quarterly* (Tulsa, Okla.), vol. 8, no. 4 (1971), pp. 392–404

Grenier, Roger, 'Farces et satrape', *Le Nouvel Observateur*, 3 juin 1965, p. 19

G[uérin], J[ean], 'Notes: divers', *NRF*, no. 107 (1961), p. 935

Guicharnaud, Jacques, 'Raymond Queneau's universe', *Yale French Studies* (New Haven, Conn.), no. 8 (1951), pp. 38–47

Gülich, Elisabeth, *Französische Literatur der Gegenwart* (Stuttgart: Alfred Kröner-Verlag, 1971), pp. 237–63

Hemmings, John, 'Alice in dropoutland', *The Listener* (London), 1 Aug. 1968, p. 152

Hoog, Armand, 'L'explosion du langage', *Carrefour*, 30 avril 1947, p. 7

Ionesco, Eugène, 'La littérature d'aujourd'hui', *Temps Mêlés Documents Queneau*, no. 150 + 1 (1978), pp. 18–19

Jansen, Conrad, 'Zazie et son critique', *Cahiers des Saisons*, no. 16 (1959), pp. 62–3

Johnston, Stuart L., 'Reflections on the philosophy of Raymond Queneau', *French Review* (New York), vol. 29, no. 1 (1955), pp. 21–7

Jones, Louisa E., 'Event and invention: History in Raymond Queneau's *Les Fleurs bleues*', *Symposium* (Syracuse, N.Y.), vol. 31, no. 4 (1977), pp. 323–36

Juin, Hubert, 'La lecture, pour quoi faire?', *Les Lettres Françaises*, 14 sept. 1961, pp. 4–5

'Aride Queneau', *ibid.*, 12 mai 1966, p. 6

Kanters, Robert, 'Exercices de critique', *L'Actualité Littéraire*, no. 56 (1959), pp. 18–19

'Queneau parle', *Le Figaro Littéraire*, 19 janv. 1963, p. 2

'Zazie mute', *ibid*, 3 juin 1965, p. 4

'Élémentaire, mon cher Watson', *Le Figaro*, 20 déc. 1975, p. 16

Kast, Pierre, 'Petite tyrannographie portative pour Raymond Queneau', *Les Cahiers du Cinéma*, no. 10 (1952), pp. 33–7

Klinkenberg, Jean-Marie, 'Jeu et profondeur chez Raymond Queneau', *Écritures* (Liège), 1967, pp. 45–52

'Français parlé et français écrit', *Cahiers* (Escuela de Frances, Universidad del Norte, Chile), no. 2 (1967), pp. 31–40

Kojève, Alexandre, 'Les romans de la sagesse', *Critique*, no. 60 (1952), pp. 387–97

'Legacies of a surrealist childhood', *TLS* (London), 22 June 1962, p. 464

Leiris, Michel, 'Préface' in Raymond Queneau, *Contes et propos* (Gallimard, 1981), pp. 3–8

L[emarchand], J[acques], 'Si tu t'imagines à la Gaîté-Montparnasse', *Le Figaro Littéraire*, 17 févr. 1966, p. 14

Léon, Pierre, 'Phonétisme, graphisme et zazisme', *Études de Linguistique Appliquée* (Besançon), no. 1 (1962), pp. 70–84

Leroy, Claude, 'Étude sur la perte d'information et la variation de sens dans les *Exercices de style* de Raymond Queneau', in Raymond Queneau, *Exercices de style* (Gallimard, 1963), pp. 99–114

Lescure, Pierre de, 'Le romancier', *Les Lettres Françaises*, 10 mars 1960, p. 4

Magny, Claude-Edmonde, *Histoire du roman français depuis 1919* (Seuil, 1971), pp. 55, 214–15

Littérature et critique (Payot, 1971), pp. 388–405

Magny, Olivier de, 'Un roman initiatique: *Zazie dans le métro* par Raymond Queneau', *Les Lettres Nouvelles*, nouvelle série no. 1 (1959), p. 16

'Préface', in Raymond Queneau, *Les Derniers Jours* (Lausanne: Éditions Rencontre, 1965), pp. 7–21

Marceau, Félicien, 'Queneau ou le triomphe de la grammaire', *La Table Ronde*, no. 53 (1952), pp. 137–41

Marcenac, Jean, 'La fonction queneauïque', *Les Lettres Françaises*, 30 nov. 1950, p. 3

Marguliès, Marc-Daniel, 'A propos des *Enfants du limon* de Raymond Queneau, essai d'interprétation arithmético-sémético-biblique', *Bulletin de Recherches de l'Université Aoyama-Gakuin de Tokyo* (Tokyo), no. 1 (1979–80), pp. 135–53

Mascolo, Dionys, 'Zazie ou la philosophie dans le métro', *France-Observateur*, 12 févr. 1959, p. 24

Mayne, Richard, 'The Queneau country', *Encounter* (London), vol. 24, no. 6 (1965), pp. 64, 66, 68–71

Mercier, Vivian, 'Raymond Queneau: the first new novelist?', *L'Esprit Créateur* (Minneapolis, Min.), vol. 7, no. 2 (1967), pp. 102–12

'Raymond Queneau: The Creator as Destroyer', in *The New Novel: from Queneau to Pinget* (New York: Farrar, Straus and Giroux, 1971), pp. 43–103

Miclau, P., 'Structure et information dans *Exercices de style* de Raymond Queneau', in *Le Réel dans la littérature et dans la langue: Actes du 10ᵉ congrès de la Fédération Internationale des Langues et Littératures Modernes* (Klincksieck, 1967), p. 221

Morey, Philip, 'The treatment of English words in Queneau', *The Modern Language Review* (Cambridge), vol. 76 (1981), pp. 823–38

Mouchard, Claude, 'Raymond Queneau: les consistances', *Critique*, no. 330 (1974), pp. 1022–30

'La littérature à l'ombre des sciences', *La Quinzaine Littéraire*, 16 janv. 1979, pp. 21–2

Nadeau, Maurice, 'Pelons l'oignon', *ibid.*, 1ᵉʳ déc 1968, p. 7

'A trente ans l'auteur du *Chiendent* marche déjà à contre-courant', *ibid.*, 16 nov. 1976, pp. 4–6

Noreiko, Stephen, '*Pierrot mon ami*: themes and an enigma', in *Mélanges de littérature française offerts à Garnet Rees* (Minard, 1980), pp. 241–50

Panaitescu, Valeriu, 'Ressources comiques du "troisième français" dans l'œuvre de Queneau', *Vie et Langage*, no. 273 (1974), pp. 702–6

'L'humoriste "Chêne et chien" et sa mythologie', *Temps Mêlés Documents Queneau*, no. 150 + 2 (1978), pp. 18–35

Petitjean, Armand, '*Gueule de pierre* par Raymond Queneau', *NRF*, no. 259 (1935), pp. 622–5

'*Chêne et chien* par Raymond Queneau', *ibid.*, no. 292 (1938), pp. 124–5

Petri, Horst, *Literatur und Musik. Form- und Strukturparallelen* (Göttingen: Sachse und Pohl, 1965), pp. 25–8

Pia, Pascal, 'Grands travaux de 'pataphysique', *Carrefour*, 18 févr. 1959, p. 13

'Quevalerie quenellisée', *ibid.*, 9 mars 1960, p. 20

'M. Queneau et la manière de s'en servir', *ibid.*, 14 mars 1962, p. 20

'Un "Goncourt" bien à part', *ibid.*, 9 juin 1965, pp. 20–1

'Les plaisirs de l'anachronisme', *ibid.*, 7 nov. 1968, pp. 18–19

Piatier, Jacqueline, 'Queneau mathématicien', *Le Monde*, 26 août 1963, p. 7

'Concert pour un déconcertant: relire Raymond Queneau', *Le Monde*, 13 août 1976, p. 7

Picon, Gaëtan, *Panorama de la nouvelle littérature française*, nouvelle édition (Gallimard, 1960), pp. 121–5

Piel, Jean, 'Nous sommes deux longs jumeaux', in *La Rencontre et la différence* (Fayard, 1982), pp. 61–82

Pilcher, Ian, 'Une source de la création littéraire: l'influence de la bande dessinée sur la composition des *Fleurs bleues*', *Temps Mêlés Documents Queneau*, no. 150 + 1 (1981), pp. 23–31

Poulet, Robert, 'Faux snobs de l'ordurier', *Carrefour*, 20 mai 1959, p. 22

Prince, Gerald, 'Noms équivoques dans l'œuvre romanesque de Queneau', *Romance Notes* (Chapel Hill, N.C.), vol. 11 no. 1 (1969), pp. 1–3

'Queneau et l'anti-roman', *Neophilologus* (Groningen), vol. 55, no. 1 (1971), pp. 33–40

Queval, Jean, 'Queneau chez Flaubert', *Mercure de France*, no. 1157 (1960), pp. 8–28

Ropars-Wuilleumier, Marie-Claire, *De la littérature au cinéma* (Armand Colin, 1970), pp. 178–9

Roudaut, Jean, *Michel Butor ou le livre futur* (Gallimard, 1964), pp. 230–4

Roy, Claude, *Descriptions critiques* (Gallimard, 1949), pp. 281–8

'Le Flaubert d'ailleurs et d'ici', *Les Lettres Françaises*, 1ᵉʳ juin 1950, p. 4

'Raymond Queneau', *La Gazette des Lettres*, nouvelle série no. 4 (1951), pp. 8–11

Saget, Justin, 'Billets doux: Raymond Queneau reconnaît les siens', *Combat*, 13 févr. 1948, p. 4

'Tequeneaulogie', *ibid.*, 9 nov. 1950, p. 4

Sainmont, J.-H., '*Les Enfants du limon* et le mystère de la rédemption: essai de 'pataphysique théologique', *Cahiers du Collège de 'Pataphysique*, no. 8–9 (1952), pp. 93–5

Sanders, Carol, 'Les fleurs bleues de Tarbes: Queneau et Paulhan', *Les Amis de Valentin Brû*, no. 20 (1982), pp. 34–8

Schmidt, Albert-Marie, 'Fantaisies du verbe et du moi', *Réforme*, 28 févr. 1959, p. 6

Shorley, Christopher, 'Raymond Queneau and the uses of non-verbal communication', *French Studies* (Oxford), vol. 34, no. 4 (1981), pp. 408–20

'L'auteur dans *Le Chiendent*, ou Chaussures et les mots sous les mots', *Les Amis de Valentin Brû*, no. 22 (1983), pp. 10–14

'Irish Mist', *Temps Mêlés Documents Queneau*, no. 150 + 22–23–24 (1984), pp. 50–4

Simonnet, Claude, 'Les livres: l'œuvre romanesque de Raymond Queneau', *Libertés*, 15 déc 1944, p. 4

'Raymond Queneau: la rhétorique', *Critique*, no. 13–14 (1947), pp. 16–23

'La parodie et le thème de *Hamlet* chez Raymond Queneau', *Les Lettres Nouvelles*, no. 34 (1959), pp. 12–17

'Time and weather: le temps chez Queneau', *ibid.*, nouvelle série no. 13 (1961), pp. 99–110

'The sky's the limit', *TLS* (London), 19 Dec. 1968, p. 1425

Smith, T. M. and W. L. Miner, *Transatlantic Migration. The Contemporary*

American Novel in France (Durham, N.C.: Duke University Press, 1955), pp. 66, 136

Sturrock, John, 'Free fall', *New Statesman* (London), 13 July 1973, p. 55

Targe, André, 'Un métro nommé Bonheur', *Poétique*, no. 29 (1977), pp. 61–76

'Poor Lehameau', *Silex* (Grenoble), no. 3 (1977), pp. 104–16

'To collect, classify and define ...', *TLS* (London), 13 July 1956, p. 422

Tyman, Dona Clare, 'Le thème de la fausse science dans *Saint Glinglin*. Étude théologico-historique de trois romans du Transcendant Satrape Raymond Queneau', *Les Lettres Nouvelles*, no. 2/73 (1973), pp. 117–27

'Queneau: chêne et chien', *Temps Mêlés Documents Queneau*, no. 150 + 2 (1978), pp. 39–47

Vanier, Jeannine, '*Pierrot mon ami* et la structure multiple', *Recherches et Travaux* (Grenoble), no. 13 (1976), pp. 53–73

Vercier, Bruno, 'Raymond Queneau', in J. Bersani, M. Autrand, J. Lecarme, B. Vercier, *La Littérature en France depuis 1945* (Bordas, 1970), pp. 385–401

'Voilà vingt ans que j'épluche le même oignon', *L'Union de Reims* (Rheims), 18 févr. 1962, p. 10

Warshow, Paul, 'An undiscovered master', *Commentary* (New York), vol. 45, no. 3 (1968), pp. 61–9

'The writing game', *TLS* (London), 25 May 1967, p. 438

Zeltner-Neukomm, Gerda, *La Grande Aventure du roman français au XXᵉ siècle* (Gonthier, 1967), pp. 77–85

5. INTERVIEWS WITH QUENEAU

This list does not include interviews published in *Bâtons, chiffres et lettres* and *Bords*.

Astier, Emmanuel d', 'De Zazie à Queneau', *L'Evénement*, no. 27 (1968), pp. 24–5

Aubarède, Gabriel d', 'Raymond Queneau, l'ami des fous et des mots', *Gavroche*, 18 avril 1946, p. 4

Berger, Pierre, 'Entretien avec Raymond Queneau, humoriste automatique', *La Gazette des Lettres*, nouvelle série no. 19 (1952), pp. 15–22

Bourdet, Denise, 'Raymond Queneau', in *Encre sympathique* (Grasset, 1966), pp. 250–8

Bourgeade, Pierre, 'Queneaulogie', *La Quinzaine Littéraire*, 15 mars 1967, p. 28

Chapelan, Maurice, 'Un basic français est-il souhaitable?', *Le Figaro Littéraire*, 5 janv. 1952, p. 4

Charbonnier, Georges, *Raymond Queneau: Entretiens avec Georges Charbonnier* (Gallimard, 1962)

Chonez, Claudine, 'Instantanés', *Les Nouvelles Littéraires*, 4 sept. 1947, p. 6

Danoen, Émile, 'Secrets de fabrication: Raymond Queneau remet souvent à la Saint-Glinglin la suite de ce qu'il vient d'écrire', *Les Lettres Françaises*, 29 juillet 1948, p. 3

Dubois, Jacques, 'Entretien avec Raymond Queneau', *Les Lettres Françaises*, 23 oct. 1952, p. 4

Duras, Marguerite, 'Uneuravek', *L'Express*, 22 janv. 1959, pp. 27–8 (English version in *Prospice* no. 8 (1978), pp. 51–5)

F., J., 'Cinq minutes avec Raymond Queneau', *Le Figaro*, 25 août 1942, p. 4

Ganne, Gilbert, 'Qu'as-tu fait de ta jeunesse?' *Arts*, 21 mars 1956, p. 8

Gillois, André, *Qui êtes-vous?* (Gallimard, 1953), pp. 303–9

Guth, Paul, '"Flemmard (qu'il dit) comme une couleuvre", Raymond Queneau, à quarante-huit ans, a enfanté déjà une vingtaine d'ouvrages', *Le Figaro Littéraire*, 17 mars 1951, p. 4

Jarlot, Gérard, 'Avec Raymond Queneau les abeilles et les planètes entrent à l'Académie Goncourt', *Les Lettres Françaises*, 15 mars 1951, p. 1

Joly, Pierre, 'Interview express: Raymond Queneau: "Ça m'est égal d'être le sabordeur de la littérature"', *Paris-Normandie*, 13 févr. 1959, p. 9

Keffer, Charles K., 'Rencontre avec Raymond Queneau', *Romance Notes* (Chapel Hill, N.C.), vol. 16 (1974–5), pp. 33–7

Knapp, Bettina, 'Raymond Queneau', in *French Novelists Speak Out* (Troy, N.Y.: Whitston Publication Company, 1976), pp. 41–7

Kréa, Henri, 'Un entretien avec Raymond Queneau. Propos d'un Normand', *Le Nouvel Observateur*, 11 févr. 1965, pp. 20–1

Montigny, Serge, 'A propos de la réforme de l'orthographe: Raymond Queneau: "Les Académiciens devraient prendre contact avec la langue du peuple"', *Combat*, 12 août 1952, p. 1

Rambures, Jean-Louis, 'Le cas étrange de l'académicien Queneau', *Réalités*, no. 216 (1964), pp. 74–8

Index